Popular Music, Power and Play

Popular Music, Power and Play

Reframing Creative Practice

Marshall Heiser

BLOOMSBURY ACADEMIC
NEW YORK • LONDON • OXFORD • NEW DELHI • SYDNEY

BLOOMSBURY ACADEMIC
Bloomsbury Publishing Inc
1385 Broadway, New York, NY 10018, USA
50 Bedford Square, London, WC1B 3DP, UK
29 Earlsfort Terrace, Dublin 2, Ireland

BLOOMSBURY, BLOOMSBURY ACADEMIC and the Diana logo are trademarks
of Bloomsbury Publishing Plc

First published in the United States of America 2022
This paperback edition published 2023

Copyright © Marshall Heiser, 2022

For legal purposes the Acknowledgements on p. viii constitute an extension of this copyright page.

Cover design: Louise Dugdale
Cover image © 3d electronic analog synthesizer/Frk/Shutterstock

All rights reserved. No part of this publication may be reproduced or transmitted in any form or by any means, electronic or mechanical, including photocopying, recording, or any information storage or retrieval system, without prior permission in writing from the publishers.

Bloomsbury Publishing Inc does not have any control over, or responsibility for, any third-party websites referred to or in this book. All internet addresses given in this book were correct at the time of going to press. The author and publisher regret any inconvenience caused if addresses have changed or sites have ceased to exist, but can accept no responsibility for any such changes.

Library of Congress Cataloging-in-Publication Data
Names: Heiser, Marshall, author.
Title: Popular music, power and play : reframing creative practice / Marshall Heiser.
Description: New York : Bloomsbury Academic, 2021. | Includes bibliographical references and index. |
Identifiers: LCCN 2021018245 (print) | LCCN 2021018246 (ebook) |
ISBN 9781501362743 (hardback) | ISBN 9781501362750 (epub) |
ISBN 9781501362767 (pdf) | ISBN 9781501362774
Subjects: LCSH: Popular music–Production and direction. | Sound recordings–Production and direction. | Creation (Literary, artistic, etc.) | Composition (Music)–Collaboration.
Classification: LCC ML3470 .H42 2021 (print) | LCC ML3470 (ebook) | DDC 781.64–dc23
LC record available at https://lccn.loc.gov/2021018245
LC ebook record available at https://lccn.loc.gov/2021018246

ISBN: HB: 978-1-5013-6274-3
PB: 978-1-5013-8542-1
ePDF: 978-1-5013-6276-7
eBook: 978-1-5013-6275-0

Typeset by Deanta Global Publishing Services, Chennai, India

To find out more about our authors and books visit www.bloomsbury.com and sign up for our newsletters.

Dedicated to the memory of Billy Wilder.

Contents

Acknowledgements	viii
Introduction	1
1 The frame	13
2 Power, play and creativity	25
3 Pushing Humpty	55
4 Playframing	67
5 Negotiations	97
Case study: *Remain in Light*	123
6 Beyond the frame	141
Case study: The struggle behind the *SMiLE*	159
Last thoughts	191
Appendix: Interview with Bill Bruford	198
References	208
Index	232

Acknowledgements

The book you are about to read is the fruit of two separate research projects. The first, culminating in my PhD dissertation, was narrow in scope, as is the nature of such beasts, and dealt primarily with the phenomenology of creativity within individuals. The second has been an attempt to contextualize these findings within the broader sociocultural discussion taking place today within popular-music and record-production studies. The initial phase of research, starting in July 2008, focused on the role played by humour in creative practice and was inspired by my own personal observations and experience confirmed by the studies of psychologist Avner Ziv. It was the writing of Rod A. Martin, however, that convinced me that it was, in fact, play theory that held the key to answering my deepest questions, since play forms the broader context in which instances of humour occur. Just as crucially, Martin's work introduced me to the phenomenological take on play adopted by Michael Apter, and as they say: 'The rest is history.' I would like to give a big thank you to Donna Weston for her guidance during this first stage, and for her invaluable feedback as I toyed with the idea of writing this monograph.

It was at the beginning of the second phase, starting in early 2018, that Albin Zak's advice and encouragement was crucial in inspiring confidence – both within myself and others – that a book of this sort was timely and had a potential audience: I am deeply grateful. I would also like to extend my gratitude to the interviewees – Joe Boyd, Bill Bruford, Kevin Godley and Jerry Harrison – for taking the time to so generously (and candidly) share their expertise, knowledge and experience, and for granting permission to reproduce their thoughts herein. Much appreciation also goes out to Katia Isakoff (along with everyone, past and present, at the *Journal on the Art of Record Production* (*JARP*)) for her encouragement and granting permission to include both the Bill Bruford interview (Heiser, forthcoming) and the first half of the *SMiLE* case study, which was originally published as *SMiLE: Brian Wilson's Musical Mosaic* (Heiser 2012) in *JARP* issue 7. Special thanks are in order for Leah Babb-Rosenfeld, Rachel Moore, Zoë Jellicoe, Sophie Campbell, Katherine De Chant, Amy Martin and everyone at Bloomsbury for the patience, guidance and professional respect they have extended to me at all times along the long and winding journey that spans basic proposal to finished manuscript. I'd also like to thank Joseph Gautham at Deanta Global for his support. Last, but not least, I am eternally indebted to my family: my wonderful wife Clara and darling daughter Rose; my dear mother Jillian and the fond memory of my father Ronald; my ever-supportive sister Jane and the goodwill of her family; also, to my cousin Bruce for his feedback and advice.

Introduction

I can remember the first time I set foot inside a recording studio. It was April 1983 and I was sixteen years old. I was so excited, I could hardly breathe. From the double doors, seemingly as thick and impenetrable as those in any bank vault, to the icy silence of the studio space with its parquetry floor, Steinway grand and occasional Persian rugs, it was a zone apart. The control room, dimly lit and boasting a large API mixing desk, was (but for its air-conditioning) a hermetically sealed bunker punctuated by softly glowing VU meters: a soundproofed shrine dedicated to imagination.

In those days, simply gaining access to the hallowed ground of a recording studio was a rare privilege. That the fruits of a recording novice's labours might not live up to expectations was not unusual, even for those possessing considerable musical talent (the difference between stagecraft and acting in cinema is an apt analogy here). Further experience taught that great records owed as much to the sensibilities and dedication of engineers and producers as they did to the songwriters and performers who fronted the affair. This goes some way to explaining famous long-term collaborations between the likes of Nick Cave and engineer-producer Tony Cohen or Neil Young and producer David Briggs. For most, however, such relationships were more tenuous and, quite often, less symbiotic.

Given the traditional demarcation of roles within studio practice – necessitated by the diversity of musical and technological skills involved – it shouldn't come as a surprise that conflicts of interest existed at times. Each group had not only their own respective subgoals and requirements but also zones with, most commonly, performers in the studio versus facilitators in the control room. For those artists who felt that the creative balance weighed too heavily in favour of the bottlers than the lightning, the dream was to, one day, build a modest studio to call their own.

Be careful what you wish for. Today, a 'democratization of technology' has brought powerful recording tools to the masses (Leyshon 2009) and, in doing so, broken down many of the barriers of the past. So much so, that the studio-as-instrument paradigm – notably exploited by artists such as 10cc, Queen and self-proclaimed non-musician Brian Eno – has today become something of a standard for musicians. The difference, however, is that a typical twenty-first-century recording studio exists largely (or even wholly) within a virtual space.

Although dependence upon the studios of old and their technological gatekeepers is a thing of the past, the new 'project studio' paradigm comes with problems of its own – not least, an ongoing glut of creative options to sift through and new multi-skilling challenges for practitioners to address. The latter include project management strategies and audio-technology-related skills necessary to carry out multifaceted projects and address sonic aesthetics. A deluge of free online music, together with ongoing changes in the structures of the music industry, complicates matters yet further. The effect of all this extra noise on musicians' ability to set and achieve goals should not be ignored, particularly when – as Albin Zak (2007) notes – practitioners today so often work on tracks from start to finish alone. The need to juggle so many (at times, conflicting) roles and responsibilities is a challenge that requires multidisciplinary theoretical frameworks capable of addressing the many creative-challenges-all-rolled-into-one that this new job description presents.

When Zak observes in his book *I Don't Sound Like Nobody*, 'Its power, in the end, was irresistible; it was time to embrace the machine as a musical partner' (2010a: 4), it might appear that he's referring to digital audio workstations (DAWs) such as Ableton Live, Logic Pro or even much earlier, but no less significant, stand-alone samplers like the Akai MPC-60. Instead, he's talking about a fundamental change in the way people have made popular music ever since recordings replaced live broadcast as the preferred content on radio in the United States during the late 1940s and early 1950s. Records – previously viewed by broadcasters of the 1930s as inferior to one-off live performances and derided as 'canned music' – were by the 1940s seen as the genuine article. Discs quickly flooded the marketplace in unprecedented numbers resulting in 'a cultural integration of the airwaves far more progressive than American society at large' (2010a: 34). It was a change that corresponded with the introduction of tape-based recording, meaning sounds could be more readily manipulated and performances edited, with recordings produced in small independent (often makeshift) studios responding to local rather than national tastes. The sound of these new records – so often 'unreal' performances in 'unreal' spaces – became as much a part of the music as the notes being played. These small-scale cultural producers, and the resulting musical pluralism they helped create, were not unlike those who today embrace the possibilities of the DAW and internet distribution revolution.

The shift, some seventy years ago, from syndicated live radio to the spinning of records by local disc jockeys, heralded a sea change in popular-music-making norms that continue to this day. Live performance, whether broadcast or in person, is no longer the primary mode of musical transmission. The record rules supreme! Moreover, such changes in post-war practice have made it possible for recordings to become more than mere audio facsimiles of live performance (Badman 2000: 256). According to producer Brian Eno, post-war recording methods constitute a plastic art instead of a temporal one (Sheppard 2009: 311). It is this plasticity that has arguably become the defining element of contemporary popular-music creative practice. Although tape-based recording has today been replaced by digital technology, popular-music makers still face the same fundamental challenges and concerns that first appeared early in the post-war period. In this way, Elvis's analogue slapback echo and the digital aesthetics of glitch can be seen to coexist within the same post-war continuum.

Despite the influence of technology being undeniable when it comes to popular-music making, it is important not to overstate it. After all, the pipeline flows both ways. Machines influence humans, but, equally so, humans influence machines. There is push and pull, give and take. Technological devices are designed, made, used and (importantly) misused by human beings. Innovations in creative thought can, at times, push technology to its limits, resulting in radical new ways of reframing creative practice that disrupt the intended usage of devices and, often unspoken, pecking orders inherent within small group dynamics. Such innovations might not only require new ways of approaching creative process but also necessitate new organizational structures and technologies.

In some rare cases, creative products might even transact with their musical culture (or subculture) in such a powerful way that the culture itself undergoes a metamorphosis of sorts. Decades before digital editing was commonplace, Brian Wilson, together with his band the Beach Boys, revolutionized record production with the jarring, jump-cut edits and non-linear working methods of 'Good Vibrations' (1966a), an approach he also adopted on their subsequent *SMiLE* project. And, long before Ableton Live made loops and DJ-style cuing/muting a bedrock of music production – allowing tracks to be playfully built up on the fly before song lyrics and melodies might be added later – Talking Heads and producer Brian Eno were doing just that on their album *Remain in Light* (1980b). Both records were made in analogue tape-based studios using the standard technology of the day. Nonetheless, analysis of their working methods, processes and innovations holds great relevancy for contemporary DAW-based creative practice. It is important to appreciate that the fundamental rules (and roles) of the games played by these artists fit today's digital-technology scenario more so than they ever did the analogue world. The power of these artists to innovate was not simply due to their access to technology but can also be attributed to their ability to playfully question the so-called givens of its use, as well as the creative-practice norms of their day.

The aim of this monograph is to present systematic new ways of understanding popular-music making, with an emphasis upon record production. In addition to making a contribution to knowledge and having obvious educational application, it is hoped that greater self-awareness (as opposed to self-consciousness) might empower practitioners, particularly those who, like so many of us at times, approach their craft in unconventional and playful ways. To them, the insights herein will come as something of a validation, if not vindication. There will be caveats, however, regarding when, where and how such behaviours might be either productive or counterproductive. As well as offering valuable insight for popular musicians wishing to understand themselves and their own creative process better, this book will also help make sense of the sometimes contradictory, flux-like behaviour of others, whether they be collaborators or an audience.

While much has been written over the past decade regarding creativity in a musical context (Cook 2018), there has yet to arise a book offering a methodical and fine-detailed exploration of the role that frame of mind plays within popular-music creative practice. This is not surprising, considering that in recent times one of the major trends in creativity research has been a resurgence of the sociocultural and historical approaches first popularized in the early twentieth century by Soviet psychologists Lev Vygotsky and Alexander Luria. For a time, individual psychology became passé for writers applying creativity theory to the arts. Nonetheless, researchers like R. Keith Sawyer (an advocate of Archer's (1995) emergentist 'analytic dualism' (Sawyer 2002, 2003)) are today acknowledging that individual psychology still has an important role to play in understanding creative endeavour (Csikszentmihalyi 1999; Sawyer and DeZutter 2009). Nowhere is this more the case than regarding the inner experience of practitioners, as well as how day-to-day interactions with collaborators, technology and the wider sociocultural environment affect motivation. Such concepts can be approached using multiple congruent frameworks, depending upon which (micro to macro) level of the overall personal, cultural and social creativity matrix is being navigated.

Some of the fine books that have addressed the concerns of popular-music creative practice and record production in the last ten years include Russ Hepworth-Sawyer and Craig Golding's *What Is Music Production?: A Producer's Guide: The Role, the People, the Process* (2010); *The Art of Record Production: An Introductory Reader for a New Academic Field*, edited by Simon Frith and Simon Zagorski-Thomas (2012), and its second volume *The Art of Record Production: Creative Practice in the Studio* (2019), edited by Zagorski-Thomas et al.; Zagorski-Thomas' *The Musicology of Record Production* (2014); and Robert Strachan's *Popular Music, Digital Culture and the Creative Process* (2018). Each book has its strengths and emphases. Hepworth-Sawyer and Golding's work is aimed at students and early-career practitioners, presenting a fine overview of the various tasks that music producers might encounter and related skills. The two *Art of Record Production* volumes are textbook primers aimed at undergraduate students. Each is organized into three parts according to the approaches adopted by contributors. These include case studies, along with historical and theoretical approaches, in volume one. Volume two gathers together technological and sociological appraisals, and theoretical analysis. Zagorski-Thomas's 2014 book maps out the overall territory and challenges to be faced by theorists and researchers exploring this nascent discipline, while Strachan's work focuses on recent changes to the popular-music landscape as evident within a subsection of the field (i.e. 'successful' pop, electronic dance music (EDM) and experimental forms). Most recently, Paul Thompson's *Creativity in the Recording Studio: Alternative Takes* (2019) is worthy of mention since it approaches its subject matter in a rigorous but easy-to-read fashion, applying Csikszentmihalyi's systems model of creativity to the task and grounding the theory in case studies. There are, however, areas within creative practice where, as Zagorski-Thomas (2014) points out, the systems model has blind spots. Such areas include the more nuanced personal and ('distributed') interpersonal aspects of creativity.

The monograph you are now reading fills a gap in popular-music and record-production scholarship. Employing an innovative new theoretical synthesis that is both elegant and cohesive, it will demonstrate how the phenomenology of individual creative practice relates to collaborative work and the wider sociocultural context in which both occur. Importantly, emphasis is placed upon usefulness in creative practice settings rather than theory for theory sake. Further, everyday language that anyone can understand is used wherever possible. Perspectives offered by three disciplines with considerable theoretical overlap (i.e. play studies, 'confluence' creativity theories and 'cultural psychology') are presented, as is a componential conceptualization of creative practice. This resulting synthesis, which views creativity as a constellation of discreet, interacting sets of elements within and without the individual, provides a means by which the process of popular-music making can be addressed in a thoroughly systematic fashion. This approach also considerably broadens the range of applicability and longevity of the findings presented by delineating between domain-specific factors (in this case, skills and knowledge specific to popular music and record production, like how to play an instrument, record a drum kit or mix a track in a particular style) and domain-transferrable ones.

Accordingly, creativity with a 'Big C' is not the primary concern here but, rather, components of creativity relating to cognitive style, personality characteristics, motivation and frame of mind (as well as how they might be distributed between collaborators). That isn't to deny the integral role that the remaining domain-specific aspects of creativity contribute within the popular-music sphere. It is, instead, an acknowledgement of the extant body of expert popular-music and record-production literature that has already extensively investigated such issues. The internet is similarly awash with how-to videos and candid contributions to online forums by producers and engineers of note.

It is assumed that the reader will bring their own unique skills, experience and tastes to the table. In my own (higher education) teaching experience, changes in musical taste and style occur so fast these days that, more often than not, students are more expert than educators when it comes to dealing with the minutiae of their preferred genres (at the very least in terms of recognizing what's appropriate where and what isn't). What this book offers, therefore, is the ways and means by which all music makers can better use the skills, knowledge and taste they already possess to move forward, along with the courage to accept themselves as bona fide practitioners of playfulness, and to challenge the forms and forces of the world that would appear to restrict them. It will also empower practitioners by providing a theoretical basis for restructuring their working environments or setting terms of task engagement to best suit their disposition, personal preferences and current abilities. Given that contemporary DAW-based music making requires not only musical but also extra-musical skills (such as technological and, even, interpersonal ones) the ability to negotiate the terms of tasks and projects in ways that set the skill-to-challenge bar at just the right level and harmonize the individual goals of collaborators is an invaluable skill in its own right.

Finally: to deal with the last few elephants in the room. The creative-practice examples provided in this book constitute a kind of popular-music *lingua franca* more so than any canon to be revered. As such, they form convenient points of reference and are ripe for reinterpretation through the lens of play-creativity theory. Moreover, it is the creative process informing these works that is being reappraised, rather than their cultural value, or the artists' individual or collective genius. One more caveat: these examples are not intended to be comprehensive or up to date but rather effective and transferrable. They are also broad ranging in terms of tasks that one might encounter in the overall record-production process. By focusing primarily on factors that transcend genre, considerations that are all too often drowned out by the specifics of genre and sub-genre (if not, sub-sub-genre) can surface. For example, dealing with the minutiae of nu skool breaks might not hold so much relevance for fans of grindcore, trap, K-pop or Tex-Mex.

The examples provided have been sourced primarily from a historical review of popular-music-related literature (not to be confused with the scholarly popular-music literature), including biographies, journal and magazine articles, film footage and the like. Rest assured, ad hoc examples of the intersection between play and popular-music making can be found in all corners of the post-war time frame (1945 to the present) and from a diverse range of music makers regardless of gender identification, ethnicity, skin colour or sexual orientation. These are featured throughout the book. Instances where practitioners have been documented as admitting to (or described as) using play, playfulness or humour as creative tools in a consciously competent manner, however (and on a more-or-less permanent or, at least, project-specific basis), are a statistical rarity. This is reflected in the choice of artists and projects presented as case studies. Another key rationale for selecting the case study examples relates to the granularity of information they offer. Some have broad and general application, while others are more detailed and context-specific. And, since it is the less-scrutinized aspects of creative action that are being examined – such as frame of mind and interpersonal dynamics – for a case study's subject to be considered appropriate, nothing less than reliable and detailed evidence from multiple sources is necessary so that clear patterns can emerge. If first-hand interviews are possible, all the better.

With fame comes attention; with attention comes documentation. With notoriety comes even more. Brian Wilson's aborted Beach Boys' project *SMiLE*

– the subject of this book's main case study – is arguably the best-documented music project of the last seventy years: on tape, in print and on film. This is in no small way the legacy of the 'Brian is a genius' media campaign, the brainchild of Beach Boys and Beatles publicist Derek Taylor. It is also a result of Wilson's inability (at the time, at least) to live up to the claim, creating a situation where over the coming decades bootleggers, influential musicians, industry insiders and fanzine writers continued to disseminate what they could piece together from the wreckage. This was despite the fact that Wilson himself had long since disowned the project as being too self-indulgent and not 'Beach Boys' music. Fortunately, *SMiLE* was also designed with the intention of using playful humour as a creative tool and pioneered a production method that predates the DAW by decades. Its influence shows no sign of waning soon and can be heard in contemporary music examples more so than ever before.

Other case studies explore the very well-documented creative processes of Elvis, Bob Dylan and the Beatles: artists who were afforded such opportunities in a disproportionate fashion compared to those available to women and people of colour by the music industry of the time. Nonetheless, each act used their privilege to playfully synthesize disparate genres and traditions, foregrounding each as an act of deep homage, as much as mere appropriation, in the headlights of mainstream popular culture. Their level of invention and influence makes them relevant to our discussion. No less important, however, are creative-practice examples transcending genre-specific concerns, regarding post-war artists as diverse as Daphne Oram, Booker T and the MGs, Syd Barrett and Pink Floyd, Parliament-Funkedelic, Keith Richards, Iggy Pop, Fela Kuti, David Bowie, Mike Rutherford, Miles Davis, Kevin Godley/10cc/Godley and Creme, Patti Smith, Richard Hell, Bootsy Collins, Kraftwerk, Devo, Andy Partridge, Kate Pierson and Cindy Wilson of the B-52's, King Crimson, the Police, Frankie Knuckles, Clive Langer, Laurie Anderson, Meredith Monk, Mimi Goese, Peter Gabriel, Sonic Youth, Tom Waits, De La Soul, Daniel Lanois, Laetitia Sadier and Tim Gane of Stereolab, RZA, DJ Shadow, Shirley Manson, Gorillaz, Karen O, Danger Mouse, Mitski, Anna Meredith and more.

There can be no doubt that in terms of cultural impact and influence, there were none more powerful (or indeed, at times, more playful) than Elvis, Dylan and the Beatles. These artists were the 'big three' who did more to *publically* negate the musical conventions of the pre-war period and, by the dawn of the 1970s, codify the basic rules of the record-production game that we still play by today. Although they may not have been the originators, there can be no doubt that they were, by-and-large, the disseminators. It was the colour of their skin that allowed them to sneak the innovations of their African-American influences past the gatekeepers of popular culture at the time. And it was this same state of play that, all too often, confounded the best efforts of Elvis and Dylan's early mentor-mediators to promote the talents of a more diverse group of artists to the same extent.

Even if Sam Phillips had never met Elvis, he would still be remembered today for his earlier work with African-American artists including Jackie Brenston, Howlin' Wolf, Junior Parker, James Cotton, Rufus Thomas and the Prisonaires. Only after years of failing to make any 'real money' did Phillips's integrity give way to pragmatism, as he turned his attention exclusively to 'white boys' like Elvis who could sing like the Black artists he had previously worked with (ironically, Phillips made the bulk of his fortune later, investing in the Holiday Inn chain). That isn't to suggest that Elvis was a carbon copy. If you need convincing, compare Presley's early (Sun) records with the originals he reinterpreted. Such fiscal considerations never sullied the judgement of music lover and Vanderbilt heir John Hammond. This is reflected in the fact that not only did he discover and produce Bob Dylan, but he also (famously) signed and/or discovered Billie Holiday, Aretha Franklin, Babatunde Olatunji, Asha Puthli, Count Basie, George Benson and Charlie Christian, among others. Sociocultural factors skyrocketed Dylan into a whole other level of influence that went far beyond mere music, much to Dylan's chagrin. The fact that artists such as Elvis, the Beatles and the Rolling Stones were considerably younger than many of their influences also, in part, accounts for why it was their images that adorned middle-class, white teenager's walls instead of, say, Arthur 'Big Boy' Crudup's or Howlin' Wolf's.

The issue of skin colour may have mattered to American TV producers and concert promoters of the 1940s and 1950s, but the sonic medium of independent radio provided a vibrant, virtual world where such considerations had far less influence. Young musicians lapped up the diversity of sounds. Consider that the A-side of Elvis's first record ('That's All Right', 1954c) was originally an Arthur Crudup 'race' record, while the B-side was composed by bluegrass artist Bill Monroe. For each Motown cover featured on their early albums, there was more than a little Carl Perkins twang in the Beatles' sound. The Little Richard and Elvis records played on radio were key influences upon the young Bob Dylan, long before he ever heard of folk singer Woody Guthrie. And, in the case of the Beach Boys, each and every Chuck Berry guitar riff was augmented by a Disney-esque Four Freshmen-style vocal harmonization. Similarly, the Talking Heads were a white punk band that loved funk and disco. To this day, articles continue to emerge both praising their 1980 album *Remain in Light* (the subject of the remaining case study) and discussing its debt to Afrobeat music and Fela Kuti. Interestingly, Beninese singer-songwriter Angélique Kidjo only recently released her own interpretation of the album in full (2018), and in doing so, has taken its West African roots full circle, as several media commentators have observed.

The book you are reading is organized roughly into three basic sections: theory, ad hoc creative-practice examples (including three small case studies) and discreet project-length case studies. Since the theory is derived from multiple disciplines – which may, at first, seem curious to those used to reading music-making and record-production texts focused solely on domain skills and knowledge – the information presented is, at first, more generalized, allowing readers adequate space to orientate themselves to new disciplinary perspectives before progressively filling in the gaps as the book progresses.

The first three chapters introduce the reader to the various theoretical frameworks employed throughout the book, each derived from separate but interrelated disciplines – play theory (Chapter 1), cultural psychology (Chapter 2) and creativity theory (Chapter 3) – with the common link between each being play and playfulness. Each chapter presents the basic principles, rhetorics and assumptions of their perspectives respectively, and demonstrates their relevancy to popular-music creative practice. In the case of Chapter 1, individual, psychological and sociocultural understandings of play and creativity are reconciled using Brian Sutton-Smith's theory of play-as-performance (1979), one which proffers – in common with the phenomenological interpretations of adult play proffered by Csikszentmihalyi (1979) and Apter (1991) – the idea that individuals (and small groups) have the power to transform the 'reality' they experience by discriminating what information is allowed into awareness at any given point in time, as well as how that information will be processed. In Chapter 2, play scholar Sophie Alcock's (2006) adoption of 'cultural-historical activity theory' (CHAT) – part of a larger contemporary Vygotskian research movement known as 'cultural psychology' that emphasizes the 'mutually constituting' nature of the social, cultural, psychological (Barrett 2011) and historical – helps broaden the discussion of play's role in popular-music creative practice.

Chapter 3 picks up where Chapter 2 leaves off, likewise acknowledging that for creativity to occur, a confluence of interdependent components must first converge, both within and without the individual. In the past, many creativity theories have mistaken these smaller component parts for the whole. In this chapter, a variety of such approaches to creativity adopted in the twentieth century are briefly compared and contrasted before presenting two confluence theories that inform part of the theoretical synthesis offered by this book: Teresa Amabile's social psychology of creativity (1996) and Mihalyi Csikszentmihalyi's systems model of creativity (1999). Amabile's theory, in particular, eloquently explains how adopting the playful frame of mind acts to mitigate the salience of external constraints detrimental to creative action. Its componential approach prises apart the noise of domain-relevant skills and knowledge from the remaining transferrable components of creativity upon which playfulness acts, having the benefit of considerably broadening the range of applicability and longevity of findings presented. Also discussed is the topic of 'combinatorial play', an essential component of creative process whereby aspects of extant ideas (or works) can be broken down, playfully reshuffled and recontextualized in order to see what new artefacts might emerge.

Chapters 4, 5 and 6 focus upon the application of theoretical insights explored in the first three chapters within a variety of popular-music-making scenarios. Sutton-Smith's concept of playframing is presented in Chapter 4 as a creative-practice tool that promotes cognitive flexibility, creative-risk taking and spontaneity. Importantly, it will be demonstrated how creative practitioners can use playframing to break complex, multifaceted music projects down into manageable chunks, filter out the unwanted noise of stimuli or information not relevant to individual tasks and set the stage so that current skills are matched to challenge (in order to promote optimal experience). The relevance of intrinsic motivation and its relationship to self-imposed and extrinsic constraints is also given due consideration.

In Chapter 5, the topic of playframing is further explored with an emphasis placed upon its use as a negotiation tool. Also discussed is collaboration as 'configuration', the influence of technology (and how to disrupt or channel it) and the interdependence of individuals and their sociocultural milieu. Chapter 6 explores how the playful frame of mind might be successfully integrated into the larger scheme of creative action: a world where present action does indeed have consequences, and where the reality of external demands, constraints and 'briefs' impose themselves upon practitioners. In particular, topics addressed include the iterative nature of creative action, oscillations in and out of the serious and playful frame of mind, fringe consciousness and cognitive incubation. Also discussed, is how reframing creative products as 'artefacts of play' can benefit practitioners and how, at times, adopting the playful frame can do as much harm as good.

The first case study – Talking Heads' *Remain in Light* album (1980b) – explores a project that exemplifies the playful approach to record production and contextualizes many of the theoretical concepts presented in this book including: heuristic (as opposed to algorithmic) approaches to idea generation in situations of uncertainty; reframing sociocultural 'givens' in new playful ways; the creative benefits of self-imposed constraints and acting 'as if'; creative-risk taking; and the power of small groups of creative individuals to bring about change within their cultural domain. The second, larger, case study extensively explores Brian Wilson and the Beach Boys' abandoned (but very well documented) 1966–7 *SMiLE* project, a work that is at once rebellious and risky. And, since *SMiLE* was decidedly non-linear in its 'cut and paste' approach to record production and composition, it will be of great interest to contemporary practitioners using DAW-based project studios. In order to further contextualize the theoretical material presented, a first-hand interview with author and progressive-rock pioneer Bill Bruford (King Crimson, Yes, Genesis) is located in the appendix.

By the time you have finished reading this book, it will be possible to look at popular-music making with new eyes. For practitioners, hopefully, this means you will be able to see your own shortcomings and quirks as creative variables that can be used to your advantage (rather than blocks to progress), reconcile your need for conformity and nonconformity, exert greater influence upon your immediate environment, and in instances where doing so isn't possible, reframe extrinsic restrictions as a fun challenge. Practitioners will also learn about creativity-relevant skills and how they can be applied to any popular-music genre, production process or creative setting. This will be achieved by understanding the influence that frame of mind exerts upon cognition, task motivation and personality in creative practice, and how individual psychological perspectives reconcile with sociocultural understandings of popular-music making. Lastly, and perhaps most importantly, you will learn how to negotiate the terms of creative tasks in a manner that inspires confidence, imagination and spontaneity instead of apprehension, anxiety or impulsiveness. Good Luck.

1

The frame

Two young men stand in a small laneway, peering through a display window at caged birds. The one on the right lights up a cigarette, turning to survey nondescript wording on two plain white columns straddling the pet shop entrance. Peering from behind sunglasses – despite the weather being overcast – the smoker tucks a matchbox into the right breast pocket of his suede jacket as he focuses on reading the signs' text out aloud verbatim. Brandishing a gun-like raised left hand, he starts to play a game, his gaze alternating between each column as he hesitantly reshuffles select words into nonsense prose. With each new recombination, his confidence increases until, soon enough, he is gesturing emphatically, swinging his arms around and stamping his feet. Finally, grinning, laughing and swinging his body, he almost shouts out his (now fluid) improvisation, finishing off with a triumphant, mock 'left hook'.

This example, featured in Martin Scorsese's film *No Direction Home: Bob Dylan, Part 2* (2005), reveals a young Bob Dylan playfully manipulating a mundane aspect of his immediate surroundings as might a bored child. This he does to provide stimulation lacking in his direct environment, as evidenced by his behaviour: his spontaneous, emphatic movements; the tone of his voice; his smile and laughter; his manifest joy. Dylan's wordplay here – using limited, arbitrary material – provides valuable insight into the workings of his creative process at the time (mid-1960s). It is evidence that, had it been gathered in a more auspicious setting, might easily have been drowned out by the noise of extraneous detail.

Watching the clip, it is easy to imagine how Dylan might have approached shaping a lyric like 'Tombstone Blues' (1965e) some months earlier, invoking legendary figures from the biblical to the Jazz Age: only to then wring them through some sort of sardonic, blues kaleidoscope. Moreover, there is no reason why such spontaneous (combinatorial) play might not be applied to any musical or technological facet of record production imaginable. Indeed, self-confessed playful practitioners like Brian Eno and 10cc's Godley and Creme have applied similar principles to any number of music-making scenarios, ranging from lifting the mood of group recording sessions to the disruption of predictable patterns inherent in music-technology design and clichéd popular-music tropes.

Play as a frame of mind

Play scholar Brian Sutton-Smith states that 'to "play with something" means conceptually to frame it in another way' (1979: 305). The playful reframing of experience is an 'act of reversal, an exercise in autonomy' (1979: 316) in which activity itself becomes a reward in its own right. It also challenges the usual contingencies of power, logically negating (or rather suspending) the usual framing classes and relations, allowing the expression of feelings and ideas that everyday frames might otherwise inhibit. Sutton-Smith's ideas regarding play and reframing experience arose as an attempt to reconcile collective and individualistic understandings of play. Whether or not play occurs in a solitary or group context, he argues, it can be best understood as a performance: a quadralogue. That is, a communicational frame between a real or imagined (i) director(s) and (ii) spectator(s) is first set up, within which dramatic content (i.e. 'the manipulation of excitement arousal through contrastive elements' (1979: 300–1)) is supplied by actual or imagined (iii) actor(s) and (iv) co-actor(s). Although characteristics of the playframe must first be negotiated before any dramatic content can occur, it should be emphasized that both are intrinsic to play, with players oscillating in and out of the contrastive action and subsequent renegotiations of the terms of the frame.

The playful frame of mind has been linked by seminal studies to instances of improved creativity (notable examples include: Amabile 1996; Getzels and Csikszentmihalyi 1976; Getzels and Jackson 1962; Lieberman 1965, 1977; Tegano 1990; Torrance 1961; Truhon 1983; Wallach and Kogan 1965). It is described as a psychological 'world apart' wherein action is intrinsically motivated and an end-in-itself. Within such a zone, the concerns of the real world and one's usual mundane values are somewhat distanced. Sutton-Smith goes on to note that in play, frames 'not grounded in the usual material of natural and social life' (1979: 317) still possess a coherent logic of their own and depend upon rules that are totally binding, albeit only temporarily so. Avner Ziv describes such frames as possessing a 'local logic':

Creative people have the ability to look beyond the obvious, to see relationships in unusual and new ways, and to be open and flexible. They are not prisoners of habitual ways of thinking. They can use novel approaches, and 'local logic' is quite acceptable to them in the appropriate frame of reference. Therefore, their intellectual processes are open to humor. (1984: 134)

Sutton-Smith's concept of playframing has many possible applications within the sphere of creative practice in the arts. In this context, playframes can be defined as explicitly negotiated, proscriptive-in-origin frames, in which a playful (i.e. present-moment-orientated) attitude is encouraged within their temporary boundaries. The accompanying benefits for practitioners are cognitive, conative (motivational), affective (emotional) and social. In terms of cognition, play encourages divergent thinking so that logical alternatives are generated, even though doing so may not be strictly necessary (1979). Adopting a playful frame of mind results in a present-moment orientation (Apter 1982) whereby the motivation for instigating and sustaining creative action arises from genuine interest rather than external pressures or rewards (Amabile 1983). Physicist and Nobel Laureate Richard P. Feynman once commented that his best work stemmed unwittingly from playing with ideas without consideration for how they might find practical application: a process he described as effortless (Feynman, Leighton and Hutchings 1985).

While the affective quality of play is not exclusively positive, playfulness – an observable behaviour that may be present in instances of play – facilitates 'psychological distancing' (Hutt 1971; Lieberman 1977) and tolerance of ambiguity (Tegano 1990). Many highly creative individuals have acknowledged the importance of the playful frame of mind and cognitive spontaneity in their own work. Albert Einstein famously described his creative process as one of combinatorial play (Hadamard 1945). Arthur Koestler, similarly, likened creativity to an act of playful recombinations when he observed, 'The creative act is not an act of creation in the sense of the Old Testament. It does not create something out of nothing; it uncovers, selects, re-shuffles, combines, synthesizes already existing facts, ideas, faculties, skills. The more familiar the parts the more striking the new whole' (1964: 120). In a longitudinal study of artist students, Getzels and Csikszentmihalyi (1976) asked students to choose from a set of objects and to make a still life drawing of those elements chosen. The students who showed a more playful orientation towards the task, who started out with a less concrete idea of what to do, allowing the composition to emerge from their toying with the various compositional elements, and who were willing to change direction or alter the work as it progressed were independently judged as producing work that was more novel and aesthetically pleasing.

Play empowers practitioners by offering the means by which they might challenge the status quo of their respective sociocultural milieu. As Sophie Alcock asserts, 'The potentially subversive nature of both humour and playfulness invites their use as strategies for resistance' (2006: 23). It can also help practitioners exert greater influence within their peer group. Simon Zagorski-Thomas, in his book *The Musicology of Record Production* (2014: 161), cites Goffman's work on 'dramaturgy' as a useful framework for interpreting how team members might more effectively 'play along' with each other. Even in a solo context, play can be used to reframe situations in a manner that encourages the challenging of assumptions and limiting the noise of non-task-relevant information. Playframe negotiations can even be said to take place between humans and machines or instruments since – as Zagorski-Thomas (2014) and Zak (2010a) both point out – technological devices must be considered active partners in modern creative process, influencing how practitioners go about their work, and empowering and constraining action in equal measure.

Playframing by adults in a creative-practice context also promotes creative-risk taking and spontaneity, makes the delegation of roles and tasks a more transparent, less adversarial process and (where possible) matches current skill level to challenge so as to promote optimal experience. As will be demonstrated in Chapters 4 and 5, such playframes can take on the form of simple terms of engagement; constitute procedural, physical or software systems; or, be expressed as temporal or spatial zones, each with their own unique sets of totally binding rules, limitations and phenomenological flavour.

Opening the floodgates: Duchamp's 'Fountain'

Play is not the only form of expressive behaviour that relies upon novel frame making as a 'fundamentally creative response to life' (Sutton-Smith 1979: 319). The reframing of experience is also a key feature of art. Musician Frank Zappa has the following to say:

> The most important thing in art is **The Frame**. For painting: literally; for other arts: figuratively – because, without this humble appliance, you can't **know** where The Art stops and The Real World begins. . . . Anything **can** be music, but it doesn't **become music** until someone **wills** it to be music, and the audience

listening to it decides to **perceive it as music**. (1997: 196, bold emphasis in original)

The frame that art offers applies equally well to both product and process. In the latter case, it can be understood as a protective one. Just as in play, art provides a psychological buffer from the consequences of one's actions and, in doing so, encourages cognitive flexibility and risk tasking. Music producer Brian Eno once reflected, '"Art is a net",... "Art is safe".... You're creating a false world where you can afford to make mistakes' (Tamm 1995: 21).

Play is not just about frame making; it is just as much about frame breaking (Sutton-Smith 1979). It is now just a hair over 100 years since Marcel Duchamp's infamous piss-take on the art establishment the 'readymade' sculpture 'Fountain' (1917/1964) was first exhibited: in a manner. This seminal, playful work was a simple, but radical, reframing of an everyday object (a men's porcelain urinal), reorientated on its side and elevated on a pedestal for consideration, if not reverence. As modern-art champion and photographer Alfred Stieglitz pointed out at the time, when viewed through eyes detached from notions of functionality or the Western art canon, it could be interpreted as a most aesthetically pleasing object. Not everybody in the modern-art world of the time agreed, however. Rather than contravene their charter by rejecting the work outright, the exhibition organizers who received it simply hid it behind a partition and hoped the problem would go away. Needless to say, it didn't. If anything, Duchamp's audacious offering not only challenged contemporary conceptions of what constitutes art, but it opened the floodgates (pardon the pun) for Surrealism, Pop art, Fluxus and Conceptual art: movements that took on the old art establishment with a sense of humour.

If 'Fountain' can be considered the Big Bang of twentieth-century art, then several aftershocks are also worthy of mention. While not as iconoclastic – if only by virtue of their chronology – three works from the fields of painting, music and dance/theatre (let's call it *kabarett*) share with 'Fountain' the notion that a work of art or performance need only provide a physical or conceptual frame, with the content left to someone (or something) else. Robert Rauschenberg's 'White Painting' (1951), John Cage's '4'33"' (1952) and Valeska Gert's 'Pause' (*c*. 1920s) each present frames ranging from the physical to the temporal and corporeal. 'White Painting' is a collection of canvases painted white, with each of the five (single and multiple-panel) works designed as 'receptive surfaces'. It was a concept not lost on composer John Cage, who described the paintings as 'airports for lights, shadows and particles' (San Francisco Museum of Modern

Art 2020). In fact, so impressed was Cage that, soon after, he published '4'33'", a three-movement composition with a score directing the performer(s) to simply sit silently at their instrument(s) for its duration. 'Pause', which pre-dates both works by some thirty years, involved Gert striking a pose, arms stretched overhead, and holding it, motionless. Performed as an *entr'acte* in front of Berlin cinema-goers while the movie reels were changed, it was a shocking display even for those accustomed to Gert's lively 'grotesque burlesques' that lampooned bourgeois society and celebrated 'the ones who fell through the cracks' through dance and mimicry (Gert 1931). Also a film actor of note, Gert later influenced punk rockers such as Nina Hagen in the 1970s. And yet, her work today remains relatively obscure, at least when compared to Rauschenberg and Cage's oft-celebrated efforts. This may be due to her having been a woman (Goldwyn 2011). It may also stem from the fact that her performances occurred outside of a high-art context. Whatever the reason, she is deserving of greater recognition than she has thus far received for her contribution to the arts.

No discrimination, no information

Many of the mechanisms informing the playful reframing of experience can be explained using phenomenological interpretations of adult play, such as those proffered by Csikszentmihalyi (1979) and Apter (1991). Csikszentmihalyi explains: 'Since what we experience is reality, as far as we are concerned, we can transform reality to the extent that we influence what happens in consciousness and thus free ourselves from the threats and blandishments of the outside world' (1990: 20). This insight echoes Guilfords' assertion, 'No discrimination, no information' (1975: 38). The ability to momentarily filter out the noise of information not congruent with immediate goals optimizes efficiency of mental effort. At best, a pleasurable state of mind emerges from such a process that is symptomatic of a particularly high sense of order in consciousness. Csikszentmihalyi calls this state 'flow' (1979, 1990) and notes that 'play [is] the experience of flow in a particular situation where it's voluntary . . . and has no implications for real life' (1979: 284).

Similarly, Apter comments that any given situation can be experienced in very different ways depending upon one's frame of mind. He emphasizes that while traditional trait psychology views people something akin to statues (i.e. consistent, unchanging) we are, in fact, more like dancers. He continues, describing the relationship between motivation, frame of mind and personality: 'there is an ever-changing internal context to our actions as well as external environmental forces. We want different things at different times and, partly as a consequence, we see things differently. In this respect our personalities are shifting and unconstant' (2003: 474). Apter argues that motivation influences the framing of experience so much so that arousal can be experienced in opposite ways depending on the particular needs and desires of the moment. In the present-moment-orientated playful frame of mind, future implications of one's thoughts and actions are pushed aside. As a result, incongruities, ambiguity, paradox and even confrontation and conflict – along with the high arousal they produce – are experienced as enjoyable and exciting.

Apter defines the playful state of mind as 'paratelic' since 'the activity comes first and the goal is secondary and chosen in relation to the activity' (1991: 16). In the serious ('telic') frame of mind the situation is simply reversed, with action in the present motivated primarily by its future consequences. In the telic state, high arousal results in feelings of anxiety. Henricks concurs: 'play directed to concerns beyond the event turns into work' (2008: 177). This is not to say that the playful frame of mind only provides a psychological retreat or a denial of life's tribulations. Play can be described as 'biomimetic' in that it imitates the struggles inherent in life (Elitzur 1990b). A playful phenomenological zone provides challenges, just as in real life, albeit of a different type. In play, challenges have been consciously chosen and (at best) optimally matched to one's current skill level (as in the flow state).

Phenomenological understandings of play need not be restricted to individual psychology. They can also help explain playful behaviour in groups. For example, the concept of play-as-flow can be applied to interaction between individuals where their goals are in harmony. Moreover, when a playful frame of mind is adopted by one member of a group, it is not uncommon for it to affect the mood of the others. Alcock (2006, 2009) explains how playfulness can be distributed between group members, mediated by artefacts both personal (including cues such as smiles, winks and laughter) and other signs, symbols and tools. While Csikszentmihalyi and Apter each emphasize the dynamic, temporal aspects of play and playfulness, Alcock, in addition, states that the dynamics of activity as a whole should, likewise, be stressed: 'activity [should be] understood as interconnecting, always changing, activity systems with multiple overlapping relationships between and across the elements of the activity. Elements include the rules, roles, community and artefacts that mediate activity' (2009: 20).

R&D: Risk and disruption

Whether used in a solo or group context, or as a means of dealing with technology, playframing in a creative-practice context is a form of power management. To playfully reframe experience is to remind oneself (and others) that there is more than one valid way of interpreting any given creative situation, and in doing so, assert oneself more fully within the greater social, cultural and interpersonal system of creativity. As Sutton-Smith once observed, 'ridiculing the world of letters, numbers, dates and alphabets is what they deserve, given the way the world pressures us into accepting them. Making nonsense is making belief that we count for as much as the sense from which it temporarily delivers us' (1979: 319). Adopting the playful frame of mind makes rebelliousness – which Apter defines as 'wanting or feeling compelled to do something contrary to that required by some external agency' (1982: 198) – thrilling, rather than a potential source of anxiety, since the future implications of one's thoughts and actions are pushed aside.

There are, however, limits to the appropriateness and usefulness of 'proactive negativism', which might include (as well as rule-breaking) elements of danger and gratuitous risk-taking (Apter 1991; McDermott 1991). Rebelliousness and risk-taking are the currency of many aspects of the popular-music experience, but without knowing the where, when, how and whys of their relationship to creativity – and, in particular, which specific components of creativity they influence – dysfunction might result. This is why these topics will be discussed in some detail throughout the book.

Proscription versus prescription

Playframing is a proscriptive approach to creative practice since the frame suspends the usual ways of organizing behaviours, relationships, and thinking in favour of 'flexible dallying and rearrangement' (Sutton-Smith 1979: 315) of experienced phenomena. To negotiate the terms of a playframe is to actively challenge 'what is' and, for a limited time, replace it by 'what if' or to act 'as if'. That is, any perspective adopted need only be 'psychologically valid' rather than logically so (Oring 2003). The selective rejection of the concerns of both the sociocultural past and creative-product future in favour of present-moment pleasure turns the creative person into a gatekeeper of sorts in their own right, picking and choosing elements from their domain as they please. As Elitzur explains, play 'requires a narrowing of awareness' (1990a: 20). Such a narrowing is the function of the frame itself, whose boundaries must first be negotiated.

Whereas well-meaning peers and educators might encourage thinking 'outside the box', the playframing approach instead requires thinking *inside* the box. It is just that the figurative box in question is one of the practitioners' own design and a rejection of the usual ones on offer. It is a 'channeling of attention to a limited set of goals and means [which] allows effortless action within self-created boundaries' (Csikszentmihalyi 1990: 81). A key purpose of playframing in a creative-practice context is therefore to make the necessary negotiations explicit, consensual and understood to have potential for a positive and immediate impact upon creativity, regardless of domain skills. In this manner, practitioners can make more out of the domain skills and knowledge that they already possess.

Several writers and composers of note state that their approach to creativity is essentially a negative one. However, in such cases, the use of constraints is adopted as a means to an end rather than an end-in-itself. Record producer and generative-music pioneer Brian Eno admits to embracing a 'reductive' approach to creative practice in order to bring a sense of focus to his work, recalling that in 'the early 70s, when recording had just gone from four to 24 tracks in a very few years. Rock became grandiose and muddy, like a bad cook who puts every spice and herb on the shelf in the soup' (Zwerin 1983: 7). King Crimson guitarist Robert Fripp, on the other hand, likens his proscriptive approach to group work as defining a sports field on which he and his bandmates can play together: 'initiating a situation so that you can concentrate energy' (Fricke 1982: 25). Sutton-Smith concurs:

> as anyone who has had to react to balls thrown and kicked by other persons, and who has been confined by the rules of a game, can attest. These phenomena do show that much of the pleasure of playing lies in the fact that the game plays you; that your reactions are often more reflexive or involuntary than voluntary; that the game takes you out of yourself. It frees you from one self by binding you to another. (2001: 183)

The proscriptive approach is facilitative rather than autocratic since the negotiated 'rules of the game' afford collaborators a level of creative autonomy while keeping their individual goals in harmony. In contrast, prescriptive approaches constitute hierarchical systems with the composer/arranger wielding most of the power. Frank Zappa is a good example of such a bandleader who, by the late 1960s, wrote out Western stave music notation parts for his players, demanding that they perform them faithfully (Lewis 2010). Such an approach is typical of early- to mid-twentieth-century art music composers such as Stravinsky and Xenakis, both of whom Zappa so admired. Admittedly, Xenakis – an architect and engineer, as well as a composer – at times, utilized what he called 'stochastic' processes, including randomly determined elements informed by statistics, in the generation of his scores. But scores they remain. The reading of scores is a process that holds limited relevance to our particular discussion, since it informs a mode of collaboration that resembles more closely the pre-war, hierarchical, music-production model. This is not to say that such ways of working, once so central to hit-record making, are not part of modern-day practice – the *SMiLE* case study being a case in point – nonetheless, the DIY ethos that underpins so much of the post-war popular-music experience (whether expressed as rockabilly, skiffle, punk, techno-electronica or, not least, the studio-as-instrument paradigm that emerged in the 1970s) has pushed the demarcation of composer/arranger/session-player/star-performer roles further and further towards the periphery. Even in circumstances where such clear-cut roles remain, traditional scores have more often than not been replaced by 'charts': simplified arrangement sketches mapping out only such basics as form, chord changes, key melodies and riffs. Keeping notation limited to such fundamentals affords a far greater degree of input from 'hired guns' employed not just to play by rote but because of their ability to contribute ideas and provide feedback when required. Neil Young recently commented that artists like the Memphis Horns contributed key hooks in the spur of the moment during sessions for artists like Same and Dave, elements seemingly so integral to the finished record that listeners might be forgiven for mistaking them as being part of the songwriter's original idea (*Neil Young Reveals the Secrets to Hit Records* 2019).

The final word in this chapter will go to self-confessed polymath and playful popular-music maker Kevin Godley:

> I think the playful thing doesn't necessarily mean everything has to be joyful or funny. It's how you come at something. It's how you come up with a tune. It can be working on a very a sad song or something that's a disturbing song. You can still be playful in the way you work it and the way you develop it. It's about not being precious about it somehow. The best songs, you know, are the ones that write themselves. Where you get a certain distance into a song and you

come up with something that has told you in essence where this thing has to go, and you follow it. Those are the best songs. Where the song writes you. That does actually happen sometimes. So, you have to be open to that all the time. And not just in songs, in anything. It can tell you what the next cut is if you're putting a film of some description together. You always have to be open to the unexpected, and you have to enjoy the process. If you've got something in your head that you need to get out to become something, you have to create a working environment and a process that allows the thing to blossom and allows you to enjoy the process. It can be frustrating sometimes. You do have to enforce some discipline sometimes, because you live in the real world. But you have to enjoy doing it. That's the thing. When you've finished it, you have to either look at it or listen to it and you go, 'Fuck me! That's not half bad!' That's a very big part of it. (Personal communication, 28 June 2018)

The topics of power, play and creativity will be discussed in the next chapter, using sociocultural interpretations of play as a basis. In particular, the ways in which individuals and groups are not only shaped by their environments but can shape them in return will be emphasized. A reinterpretation of the contributions of three seminal, and very powerful, post-war popular-music acts – Elvis, Dylan and the Beatles – is presented, with emphasis placed upon the roles played by their early record producers – men who mediated each act's power and encouraged their playful rebelliousness. Also explored, is the crucial role of underground music and art scenes in nurturing young talent along with the implications of recent changes to the music industry – as a result of the advent of the project studio and internet distribution – for theoretical interpretations of contemporary creative practice.

2

Power, play and creativity

In 1966, Barry Miles and John 'Hoppy' Hopkins spearheaded the formation of the counterculture newspaper *IT* (*International Times*). The publication quickly became the focal point for a fledgling London underground arts scene. Not so much an organized movement as a loose constellation of young avant-garde artists, musicians, filmmakers and poets, the scene was a collective awakening of sorts that pitted the vigour of youth against an entrenched British establishment. There would be no storming of the Houses of Parliament, however. This was more a playful, sociocultural phenomenon and largely apolitical. The editorial from *IT*'s first issue offered the following advice for readers:

> if you decide you want to change things at base, you are taking on governments, you are deciding to be your own government.
>
> This doesn't mean that you're going to go out and do a Guy Fawkes, or even get as far as knocking a policeman's hat off. But it does lead to more direct, albeit sometimes devious, methods of social action. Examples: you know there is a housing problem so you start moving people in on all the disused warehouses and offices in town; the city is ugly so you start to paint it bright new colours; people are tense so you start a live-on-the-dole – don't rush to work – only work at what you enjoy – movement: governments are a drag so.
>
> Change begins with you. ('Editorial: YOU' 1966: 8)

From the outset, art and pop culture made good bedfellows. This shouldn't be surprising given that Pop art had its origins, at least in part, in the ideas and seminal works of UK Independent Group artists such as Eduardo Paolozzi and Richard Hamilton. Visiting American Beats including the poets Allen Ginsberg, Gregory Corso and writer William S. Burroughs were also instrumental in helping set the tone for the nascent scene, as was New York-based Fluxus artist Yoko Ono. Beatle Paul McCartney was an early supporter and advocate, indirectly helping raise revenue for *IT* and helping out at Miles' earlier venture, the Indica bookshop-gallery, co-founded with artist John Dunbar and pop singer Peter Asher, and where Ono had her first UK exhibition. Two key cultural events associated with *IT* included its launch at the Roundhouse in October 1966 and, some six months later, the '14 Hour Technicolour Dream' benefit held at Alexandra Palace. Both shows featured an up-and-coming psychedelic act, the Pink Floyd, regulars at Hopkins and Joe Boyd's UFO Club, Powis Square Free School benefits and Steve Stollman's (invitation only) Spontaneous Underground events where they could 'stretch out' and play extended (at times, atonal) instrumental jams for audiences open-minded enough to appreciate their sonic experiments (Personal communication with Joe Boyd, 11 January 2019).

Other notable acts involved in the scene included the proto-progressive rock outfit Soft Machine, co-founded by Australian Beat poet and guitarist Daevid Allen, and AMM, a free improvisation group produced by Boyd and Hopkins for Elektra Records (Chapman 2010; Miles 1998, 2006). When I asked Boyd how crucial UFO, Indica and the Spontaneous Underground were in bringing like-minded people together, he replied, 'I think very. The first few weeks at UFO everyone was looking at everyone else wide-eyed, having never before realized how many other "freaks" there were in London' (Personal communication, 11 January 2019).

As the nearly ten-minutes-long free-rock track 'Interstellar Overdrive' (1967b) clearly demonstrates, Pink Floyd were influenced by approaches to group improvisation not unlike that heard in Ornette Coleman's double-quartet album *Free Jazz: A Collective Improvisation* (1961). On the track, lead singer, songwriter and guitarist Syd Barrett can be heard adopting some of the unorthodox ways of extracting sounds from his instrument that he'd heard Allen and AMM's Keith Rowe use firsthand at underground events. As things turned out, Pink Floyd would be pop stars by July 1967, appearing on BBC TV to promote their hit 'See Emily Play' (1967c). Despite being a fairly typical pop ditty for the time, running at less than three minutes and with a refrain not unlike a children's song, the track features glimpses of the more experimental sounds that the band was known for unleashing live, albeit safely cordoned off within two bridge sections. The first, a comically sped-up four-second Mozart-esque solo keyboard, is introduced via a climatic rush of sound, a *musique concrète*-style jumpcut edit piece that wouldn't be out of place in an EDM track. The second takes the form of what would have most certainly been an extended modal improvisation if the confines of AM radio and the seven-inch single format could have permitted. Instead, its distorted and echoey high-pitched slide-guitar squawks and meandering organ line are compressed into a mere half-minute. Just a few years later, the rise of FM radio and the long-playing (LP) album format liberated the band from such restrictions, but not before Barrett had become a casualty of stardom.

For Syd, being in a band was merely an interesting diversion from his true passion of painting. Joe Boyd, producer of Pink Floyd's first single 'Arnold Lane' (1967a), says that Syd was only ever interested in 'trying to write what he liked . . . he wasn't trying to write hit songs', and that the fact that he couldn't care less about other people's expectations had a positive impact on his writing (Personal communication, 11 January 2019). However, since Pink Floyd had been suddenly catapulted into the competitive, conformist limelight of the pop mainstream, in-the-moment spontaneity and freedom of creative expression were no longer the order of the day. The rest of the band, the record company and new producer Norman Smith all had continued chart success as their primary objective. Understandably, they were all leaning on Syd to come up with the goods since he'd previously been a prolific writer of catchy tunes, many of which adopted the same humorous Pop-art-inspired spontaneity found in his paintings (Chapman 2010: 40–3). Often, his lyrics simply reflected what was happening in his immediate environment at the time of writing (Chapman 2010: 92–3).

The second half of 1967 saw the pressure for more hits only increase, with most of Barrett's increasingly obscure efforts deemed unsuitable for release. This was in addition to a strenuous and inefficient regime of national and international touring imposed upon the band. Close friend David Gale remembers Syd hadn't foreseen that being a pop star would involve so much mundane, repetitive and exhausting work (Chapman 2010: 173). Fuelled by habitual hallucinogenic drug use, the charming young artist's behaviour became increasingly unpredictable and obtuse, the glint in his eye giving way to a vacant stare. Complicating matters further was the fact that he had always been a nonconformist trickster of sorts, making any reliable diagnosis of his condition difficult. By early 1968, a remnant of his former self, Syd was deemed a professional liability and dropped by the band. Pink Floyd went on to spend the next five years trying to shake off their 'summer of love' image, redefine themselves artistically and emerge as songwriters in their own right. One is left to wonder how Syd and the band together might have fared if they'd had more time to mature creatively within the nurturing confines of the underground scene. Some years later in New York City, a small group of young local bands – very much out of step with the popular-music trends of the day – got the chance to do just that. Their cultural impact endures to this day.

Playground

Once a small club in the New York City's Bowery district, CBGBs has since become synonymous with the emergent 1970s punk music scene (later renamed 'new wave' by CBGBs stalwart and record-label boss Seymour Stein, in an effort to get his acts played on radio). Club owner Hilly Kristal had originally envisaged starting a country, bluegrass and blues bar but was forward thinking and flexible enough to give the somewhat radical artists, poets and musicians who turned up a shot. He was also generous enough to give the bands a fair share of the profits. Early acts included Television, Patti Smith and, later, the Ramones, Blondie, Talking Heads and (Television co-founder Richard Hell's new band) Richard Hell and the Voidoids. Hell's way of dressing later inspired the *de rigueur* spikey-haired and safety-pinned, torn-clothing look adopted by British punks via the Situationist-inspired, ex-New York Dolls manager Malcolm McClaren. Several writers, including Talking Heads' David Byrne (2012), have commented on the fact that the socio-economic situation in New York at the time was conducive to the evolution of such a vibrant and, ultimately influential, group of bands. Kristal, in particular, has been singled out for praise, having provided an optimal, nurturing environment for young artists. So much so that when Talking Heads were inducted in the Rock and Roll Hall of Fame, they insisted that Kristal join them onstage for the presentation. I asked Jerry Harrison of Talking Heads if he thought the state of New York City at the time and the emergence of clubs like CBGBs, the Mudd Club and, to a lesser extent, Max's Kansas City (which Harrison noted had been reopened by Micky Ruskin and remodelled along the CBGBs line) were as crucial to the development of this legendary scene as has been stated. He replied:

> No. I don't think it is overstated at all. I would say that two really wonderful things happened. The first being, because there was a lot of building in the late 60s/early 70s that there was this access to inexpensive places to live, and that helped create a scene where artists lived near each other and there was a sense of interaction and collaboration. I would also say that the bands that thrived coming into CBGBs were, for at least a year if not longer, ignored by the record companies. Record companies at that time were signing a lot of acts that were very similar to prog rock. And so, this group of bands such as The Ramones, Blondie, the Talking Heads, or Television were really far away from what they actually thought people wanted to hear and that gave all of us, first of all, a sense that we were probably more supportive of each other than is often the case, often

there's a great deal of competition between bands who are playing in the same club or in the same area [laughs], and also, the fact Hilly Kristal would allow the bands to make most of what came in through the door that bands could really survive on what they made at CBGBs and a few other gigs and not have to have us all have other jobs. It meant that people could really concentrate on their craft. And also, if you played there you got in for free, so therefore, it was your chosen place to go out to 'cos you got in free. It was also designed in a way that if there were forty people to see you that they would fill up the front, and if the band that was playing at ten o'clock wasn't really your cup of tea then you might be at the back of the bar or go outside, and then you'd come forward when what you wanted to see was playing. So it was sort of an ideal situation for bands to feel like they had an attentive audience and for there to be a place to hang out for hours because they would have shows where they would sometimes have four bands play through the entire evening. (Personal communication, 21 February 2019)

The chicken and the egg

Groos (1898) famously suggested that play has the function of preparing participants for real life. However, as noted in Chapter 1, play is as much about frame breaking as it is frame making (Sutton-Smith 1979). It can function equally well to provide cognitive alternatives with which to challenge the status quo as much as socialize. Although play provides clear benefits that are conative (motivational) and affective (emotional), as well as cognitive and social, the immediate environment and larger sociocultural milieu directly influence the extent to which these benefits might have any impact. Play merely potentiates successful adaptation. Cosaro and Eder observe:

> Social structure and culture are not merely static niches or environments, they are public and collective processes of negotiation and interpretative apprehension. . . . From this interpretive perspective, socialization is not only a matter of adaptation and internalization, but also a process of appropriation, reinvention, and reproduction. Central to this view of socialization is the appreciation of the importance of communal activity. (1990: 217)

The process of shaping and being shaped is ongoing and unremitting, much like the proverbial chicken and the egg. Play and playfulness researcher Sophie Alcock cites Cosaro's (1997, 2012) use of the term 'interpretive reproduction' to describe the way in which pre-school children construct their own unique peer cultures by appropriating and reimagining aspects of the adult world. Peer cultures should not to be confused with peer groups, and are defined as autonomous and creative social systems: 'stable set[s] of activities or routines, artifacts, values, and concerns that children produce and share in interaction with peers' (Cosaro and Eder 1990: 197). In this way, peers are understood to be active agents, creating and breaking rules as a form of resistance that 'motivates activity [so that] cultural practices are re-created anew' (Alcock 2006: 25). Alcock goes on to emphasize the collective nature of such agency and the role of 'proxy agents':

> since the exercise of power involves relationships, and is always situated historically, culturally, and socially, agency does extend beyond individuals. Wertsch (1998) uses the concept of the 'agent-acting-with-mediational-means' (p. 24) to emphasise the artifacts that mediate and connect individuals with each other and the physical environment. Artifacts can include other people, who may also act as proxy agents. (Alcock 2006: 24)

Adults too, form peer cultures (and subcultures) as a way of dealing with concerns specific to their particular cohorts. One of the ways subcultures resist the dominant culture is by adopting and recontextualizing its signs (i.e. semiotic artefacts). Culture jamming, also, is a form of cultural resistance and re-creation. While subcultures merely offer respite in self-contained alternative structures (Gelder 2007), culture jammers attempt to transform society by fostering cultural production that undermines the 'social and political hegemony' of popular culture (Sandlin and Milam 2008: 343).

Recording artists have, in the past, depended upon proxy agents such as record producers, engineers and 'artist and repertoire' (A&R) representatives to mediate their creativity. Certain prominent post-war performers have been lucky enough to attract the attention of mediators who saw the value of their playful rebelliousness: Elvis Presley had Sam Phillips; Bob Dylan had John Hammond; and the Beatles had George Martin. Each producer encouraged his respective act to express their subversiveness through their recordings. Rebellion against the previous generation's values was, after all, a key part of the emerging 1960s youth *zeitgeist*. But it was more a playful mockery of society's sacred cows than any fully fledged iconoclasm. Joe Boyd provides some context:

> There was probably more consciousness of history in those days than there is now, including the [then] recent history of the Beatniks, which felt very

inspirational. It seemed obvious to my friends that the straight '50s middle-class world should be overturned or at least shaken up. . . . It was exciting and fun and stimulating. There was a feeling of optimism. (Personal communication, 11 January 2019)

One can only guess how much less Elvis's cultural impact might have been if Sam Phillips hadn't encouraged him to integrate his crooning into a mix of styles that harnessed his extensive knowledge of rhythm and blues (R&B) and country. Or what might have become of Dylan – referred to at the time as 'Hammond's folly' – had that Columbia A&R man not staked his reputation on securing a second album for the witty, young Woody Guthrie fan. Similarly, the Beatles' origins were less-than-stellar. Having been turned down by every record company in England, they were eventually signed by Martin, a producer of comedy records who, like Hammond with Dylan, saw in the band not great musicianship but wit and charisma. Martin resolved to record and market the Beatles in a raw and unadulterated fashion, instead of following the pop music conventions of the time. It was a risky move, but no less so than the risks he had taken when making comedy records for the likes of the Goons, Peter Sellers, and *Beyond the Fringe* (1961). The vision, tenacity and personal power of Phillips, Hammond and Martin can be seen to have had an undeniable, though indirect, impact upon popular-music culture. Importantly, it was not just their artists that transformed the face of the musical mainstream but also the influences (musical and subcultural) that each act snuck past the pop-culture gatekeepers of the time. Presley, Dylan and the Beatles each provided a convenient focal point for young people's dalliance with alternatives to the mainstream culture. Beatle John Lennon once described his band as a 'Trojan horse' (Badman 2001). He was alluding to the fact that they were pumping the counterculture back to the public through the conduit of the mainstream media.

The spirit of playful rebellion that benefited Elvis, Dylan and the Beatles creatively also provided a means by which they could deal more effectively with the rigours and tedium of public life. By taking themselves less seriously and refusing to buy into the hype that they themselves helped manufacture, they could fulfil their many obligations while maintaining a higher level of cognitive flexibility, mental health and creative flow. When attention from fans and the media – whether in the form of adulation or anger – became as much of a hindrance as a help, each act simply played with the norms of the media circus. As the Beatles became increasingly engulfed by interview obligations in their early days, they kept sane by playing a game to see who could get the biggest lie printed (Miles 1998). Dylan, likewise, concocted numerous conflicting stories about his past. And when audiences began to protest his use of electric instruments onstage, he would softly babble into the microphone (an old carnival sideshow trick) to distract hecklers and make them strain to listen (Blake 2005). Elvis once bet his band he could get a particularly rowdy audience to scream in adulation if he belched loudly into the microphone: they did. During his first two-week-long engagement in Las Vegas, Presley simulated copulation with a band member in front of an audience full of disapproving sophisticates and celebrities (Guralnick 1994).

Elvis and Dylan both found fame harder to deal with as the years progressed. While Dylan suffered from without, Presley eventually came unstuck from within, succumbing to what Lennon described as the 'king [being] killed by his courtiers ... overfed, overdrugged, overindulged, anything to keep the king tied to his throne' (Graustark and Garbarini 1988: 22). Lennon was referring not only to Presley but rock stars in general. Despite intense, increasing pressure over the years, the Beatles flourished, attributing their resilience to having four members, each with the same shared experience and distinctly 'Scouse' sense of humour (Du Noyer 1995; *The Beatles Anthology* 1995). Theirs was a 'hermetic Liverpool bubble ... a secret language of wisecracks and references, gestures and behaviour [that provided] an impregnable protective wall' (Miles 1998: 71). The Beatles' group glee provided a far greater phenomenological buffer than any solo act could muster.

The rhetoric of power

In his book *The Ambiguity of Play* (1997), Sutton-Smith maps out the scholarly play landscape in terms of the most common theoretical vantage points assumed by writers. One such perspective he calls the 'rhetoric of power'. Seen from this perspective, play is interpreted as a battle or contest between individuals, groups or nations, with each struggling to advance their own status. The concept of play as an expression of clashing forces is famously explored in Johan Huizinga's *Homo Ludens* (1949), a landmark text in the literature that interprets culture as having emerged in the spirit of play. Huizinga explains that despite the fact that the primordial 'play-element' recedes as each society matures, it may erupt again at any time in full force. Beatlemania is but one example that comes to mind: a historically significant cultural marker of the explosion of Western youth power in the 1960s. Mihai Spariosu (1989) frames both the civilizing and uncivilized aspects of play historically, stating that the view of play in the West oscillates back and forth between play as an idealized, rule-governed expression of power (e.g. Plato and, later, Schiller) and the violent clash of irrational forces (e.g. Heraclitus and, later, Nietzsche). Thomas Henricks expands upon the concept of play as a manifestation of Nietzsche's 'will to power':

> People feel the rush of the world inside themselves. Attuned to those conditions, play attempts not just to control and contemplate but also to experience vitality and movement. For such reasons, play often seems semi-chaotic, compulsive, excessive, and socially unfair. People play to claim a position – and to indulge their feelings – in the ever-changing circumstances of the moment. (2008: 168)

Just as competitive behaviour and aggressive urges need to be factored into any balanced discussion of play and culture, the same is true for creativity. In instances of collaborative creative action, the act of offering speculative propositions puts participants in a vulnerable position. In such situations, feedback from peers can easily be perceived as threatening. In order to reassert a sense of personal power and bolster self-esteem, get-even action might result later on, even if it is at the expense of the group's efforts (Prince 1975). Amabile (1996) cites two of her own studies where win-lose competition between peers had a negative impact upon creative action (dependent upon some individual-difference variables). She is careful to point out, however, that the same is not true of competition with outside groups, which may actually have a positive effect on a work teams' efforts. In instances where power can be shared, the peer group as a whole will reap the benefits of increased problem solving, idea production and group satisfaction. Conversely, individuals pitching ideas can benefit by making their speculative propositions seem less final and unalterable. In this way, an idea can be shared and appreciated in the same non-threatening manner that one might a joke: 'more akin to an expression of taste than . . . a fact' (Prince 1975: 261). They should also attempt to consciously detach their sense of self-worth from the perceived effect of their peers' critical evaluations.

In order to navigate the minutiae of collaborative creativity and play, Alcock (2009) uses – in addition to individualistic phrases like cognition and subjectivity – collective terms such as 'distributed cognition', 'distributed imagination', 'intersubjectivity' and 'group glee' (the latter term coined by Sherman 1975) to connote the ways that thoughts, perspectives and moods might be passed between individuals participating in shared activities. Alcock adopts Luria's (1928) term 'artefact mediation' to describe the 'processes by which words, gestures, gaze, and other signs, symbols, and tools [mediate] children's shared and distributed playfulness' (Alcock 2009: 20). Sawyer and DeZutter have, similarly, applied the concept of distributed cognition to the topic of group creativity, coining the term 'distributed creativity' to express how creative artefacts that emerge from collaborative contexts cannot be adequately explained with regard to the intentions, or actions, of any one individual: an 'empirical focus on the moment-to-moment interactional process of the group' is required instead (2009: 81). They are careful to point out, however, that any full understanding of distributed creativity requires a synthesis of methodologies capable of traditional individual psychological study, as well as analysis of the interactions between participants.

Although applied specifically to the context of playfulness in groups of pre-school children, Alcock's (2006) ideas are transferrable to adults since, as Guitard, Ferland and Dutil (2005) explain, the components of adult playfulness (i.e. spontaneity, pleasure, sense of humour, curiosity and creativity) are the same as for children. The difference, however, is that adults tend to use their imagination to fuel creativity, whereas young children – lacking the domain skills necessary to express themselves fluently – usually channel their imagination into fantasy. Sense of humour is also mentioned as being much more sophisticated in adults, with (conversely) the pursuit of pleasure coming less easily to most grown-ups as it does for children.[1]

Further complicating matters is the fact that, as McIntyre (2008) observes, creative practitioners don't usually act from positions of equal power. He frames the distribution of creative power in the record-production world between musicians, producers, record companies and technicians in terms of 'cultural production' (after Pierre Bourdieu). Bourdieu's 'field' is an 'arena of social contestation' that equates roughly with play-creativity theorist Mihalyi Csikszentmihlayi's entire creative system model. Bourdieu's is a Marxist interpretation of cultural power relations involving various forms of capital, any

---

[1] Since sense of humour is a key component of playfulness, as Guitard, Ferland and Dutil (2005) and Lieberman (1977) assert, it is worth noting how stages of cognitive, social and emotional development might affect it. For example, pre-school children tend to find humour in playful incongruity for its own sake but are unable to comprehend sophisticated forms of incongruity-resolution humour that involve abstract concepts such as double meanings. Martin observes that most humour in childhood 'arises from spontaneous verbal and nonverbal behaviors during playful social interactions' (2007: 245). McGhee (1979) notes that the topics most likely to elicit laughter from children are ones associated with the tensions, conflicts and anxieties specific to the child's particular stage of development (e.g. potty humour when going through toilet training). Alcock states that, irrespective of age, 'both humour and playfulness involve degrees of openness, flexibility, and adaptability' (2006: 21).

of which can be used by individuals or groups to aid their struggle and exert greater influence. These include economic, social (i.e. personal connections and networks), cultural (such as domain-relevant skills) and symbolic capital (i.e. in the context of popular music: celebrity status). Like Huizinga, McIntyre asserts that social contestation is not necessarily a negative phenomenon. Rather, it constitutes 'a productive network which permeates sociocultural systems' (after Foucault) and may have a '"transformative capacity" . . . that can be used by agents to enact change either in things or the actions of other people' (McIntyre 2008). When interpreted through the lens of play theory, negative or positive value judgements might be understood as a matter of perspective. Bourdieu's field may appear to constitute an epic battle from the individual's standpoint, but when viewed from the greater systemic perspective (i.e. from the 'outside in') might seem more like a grand, creative spectacle.

The greater creative system isn't just impacted by sociocultural forces but also by technological influence. So much so, that it is not always clear who the gatekeepers, tastemakers and power brokers of the popular-music world are at any given time. Strachan (2018) observes that access to the popular-music market (at least in such a way so as to produce any large-scale impact) is still controlled by major music companies. What *has* changed is that in recent years, their considerable institutional clout has been redirected away from traditional manufacturing and distribution roles towards online marketing and promotion. He adds (after Hesmondhalgh) that the impact of the internet has resulted in a series of 'disturbances' by 'small-scale cultural producers' (i.e. independent artists) rather than any utopian overturning of the huge concentrations of power within the industry. Nonetheless, the wheel is still in spin.

Today's online scenario bears striking similarities with the decentralization of radio programming and advent of tape recording in the United States in the years immediately following the Second World War. These changes in broadcasting and record production resulted in small-scale cultural production disturbances by 'small start-up record companies specializing in regional or ethnic styles', eager to supply music to local radio stations who were now able to respond to local audiences' requests (Zak 2010a: 10). Now that the corporate entertainment heavyweights had all turned their attention to the latest-and-greatest medium of television, the radio inmates had taken over the asylum. The resulting diversity freed listeners 'from the social constraints associated with live music making' (Zak 2010a: 11), allowing them to sample exotic musical styles they might otherwise never have heard.

Over the following decade, unprecedented and unexpected stylistic cross-pollenizations occurred in makeshift studios that slowly revolutionized popular-music culture 'one record at a time' (Zak 2010a: 7). The music made by Elvis Presley and the Blue Moon Boys at Sun Records is but one such example. He may have conquered America in 1956 as an act recording for RCA (the recording arm of a major US electric company) but Elvis's radical new and echoey mix of crooning, R&B and country was developed slowly, empirically and playfully at Sun, a small owner-operated label operating out of Memphis.

That an artist as unpolished as the young Elvis could emerge from such humble beginnings and then go on to dominate the pop-music charts seems obvious enough with the benefit of hindsight. It was, however, anything but obvious to an unsuspecting corporate music world of the early 1950s. As we shall see, a sense of playfulness was a key element of Elvis's ability to channel what was, until then, the unchannelable into the consciousness of white-middle-class America via the conduit of radio, television and, later, film. Sutton-Smith was well aware of this insurgent potential of play when he remarked, 'Play is the fool that might become King' (1979: 320).

The Memphis boy who would be (The) King

Atlantic Records co-founder Ahmet Ertegun sums up the status quo of the US music industry in the late 1940s/early 1950s as follows:

> The people in the music business did not understand where the real American taste was. They were making songs for a bourgeois society that they imagined existed in this country. The people at RCA Victor, they didn't know shit from Shinola. And they didn't know that 'I wanna rock you baby' meant more than 'I'm putting on my Top Hat, polishing my nails' and had no particular appeal to a longshoreman in Seattle or a cotton-picker in Alabama. (*The Atlantic Records Story* 1994)

That the major labels – most of which were recording divisions of national broadcasting networks – were so out of touch with popular taste at the time provided an opportunity for small-scale independents like Atlantic to promote untapped talent (ignored, so often, because of the colour of the artists' skin) and have fun in the process. Atlantic's in-house engineer Tom Dowd remembers:

What we were doing was having a good time. We'd lived through a helluva time. We'd survived the war and every other fool thing and here we were finally playing. But we were 25 and 30 year olds playing! And we were having a good old time making records and telling stories and communicating with people who were not the spoon-fed people that you were accustomed to hearing by the major record companies. (*The Atlantic Records Story* 1994)

Atlantic Records started off in the late 1940s as a small operation running out of a cramped office in Manhattan. To save money, the office doubled as a recording space, with desks and chairs moved out of the way to make room for the performers and microphones at night. Despite such challenges, Atlantic was responsible for releasing a wealth of key R&B records in the early 1950s, including sides by Ray Charles, Ruth Brown, Big Joe Turner, the Clovers, the Drifters and LaVern Baker. Ertegun and his older brother Nesuhi (later, a partner in the venture) were sons of the Turkish ambassador to the United States. Having moved to Washington in their teens, both were avid music lovers. Being something of outsiders themselves, they sympathized with the plight of African Americans and took every chance to immerse themselves in – and later promote – live jazz music. When their father passed away in 1944, the rest of the family moved back to Turkey while the brothers stayed on in America to further document and promote the music they so loved.

Atlantic's early sound owed much to the fact that Ahmet encouraged his acts to perform in a style that was appealing to their peers, rather than try to emulate the schmaltzy records marketed to mainstream audiences at the time. He was also one of the first label owners to appreciate the records being made by Elvis Presley and the Blue Moon Boys, an act recorded by an even smaller independent label running out of Memphis: Sun Records (*The Atlantic Records Story* 1994). So strong was his belief in the young Presley that Ahmet bid $25,000 for his contract when it came up for grabs in 1955. At that time, Elvis had yet to gain national recognition or even appear on television. His new manager 'Colonel' Thom Parker instead signed him to RCA Victor for the unprecedented sum of $45,000 (*The Atlantic Records Story* 1994), and although RCA gave Elvis the promotional clout and distribution he so needed to make it to the top, they had no idea how to nurture his talent.

Having released ten consecutive sides sounding as vital today as when they were recorded, producer Sam Phillips was doing something right with Presley at Sun: something that RCA just didn't get. 'Specialty singles' man Steve Sholes was, ostensibly, the producer for Elvis's early RCA Records but, according to

Phillips, couldn't fathom Presley's creative process in the studio: so Elvis just supervised his sessions himself (Guralnick 1994: 247). The new label was so out of touch with Elvis's muse that they had grave misgivings about releasing the song 'Heartbreak Hotel' (1956), one of his most revered tracks (Guralnick 1994: 239). By the end of 1957, Presley's original, raucous blend of hillbilly country, R&B and crooning gave way to the formulaic. No longer did he sound mischievous, dangerous or unpredictable. One is left to wonder what might have been if he'd signed to a label run by lovers of music and fun, like Atlantic, instead of a corporate behemoth.

In the early 1950s, Sun Records, like Atlantic, excelled at recording African-American artists. Before becoming a fully fledged label, it was a studio known simply as the Memphis Recording Service. There, Phillips produced tracks on behalf of labels like Chess in Chicago and RPM in Los Angeles. B. B. King, Howlin' Wolf, Rufus Thomas, Jackie Brenston's Rhythm Cats, the Prisonaires, Little Junior Parker and James Cotton were all recorded by Phillips at 706 Union Avenue during that time. Sam had great respect for these performers and was passionate about capturing their unique styles with as little interference as possible. However, he was well aware that a segregated American society (and segregated music charts) severely limited the potential market for his product. Financial pressures eventually forced him to scout for a white singer who could take the R&B sound to a broader audience.

Although Presley had paid to make a one-off acetate recording at Sun in 1953, he wasn't considered as a candidate for Sam's plan, since he adopted a crooning, balladeer style at the time. A year later, at secretary Marion Keisker's insistence, Sam teamed the young amateur up with guitarist Scotty Moore and bassist Bill Black (the Blue Moon Boys). Sam didn't think like typical white producers of the time who crafted sedate remakes of African-American R&B and doo-wop records by white performers (*The Atlantic Records Story* 1994). Instead, he had a much less polished sound in mind and wasn't satisfied until Presley, Scotty and Bill had produced something 'raw and ragged' and unlike anything they'd heard before (Cajiao 1991: 19).

Elvis wasn't a songwriter, but he possessed an encyclopaedic knowledge of songs spanning R&B, blues, country, gospel, country and pop. Sam exploited this talent by letting him run through any song he knew until something eventually moved the both of them. He also patiently encouraged Elvis to find his own sound when covering other artists' songs, often over many days of recording sessions that produced nothing to live up to his goal of 'that damn row that hadn't been plowed' (Guralnick 1994: 131). Though Elvis famously mixed country and R&B elements together during his time at Sun Records, he was influenced equally by the crooning singing style popularized during the early 1930s. Bing Crosby biographer Gary Giddins claims a direct 'lineage of influence' spanning from Crosby to Frank Sinatra and, later, Elvis. Each artist shared Crosby's 'way with a microphone [and] the canny informality of his phrasing' (1981: 16). In fact, the first track Elvis recorded with Scotty and Bill was Bing Crosby's 1950 hit 'Habor Lights'.

It was Dean Martin, however, who was Elvis's true idol. For his second single, Elvis covered 'I Don't Care If the Sun Don't Shine' (Presley, Moore and Black 1954a), a song Martin performed in the comedy film *Scared Stiff* (1953). In particular, it was Martin's sense of mischievousness in his delivery that appealed to Elvis and unified his style of song interpretation while at Sun. Though shy, Presley is described at the time as being impish – even 'wild' – loving pranks and practical jokes (Guralnick 1994: 141). Irrespective of what genre a song may have originated from, Elvis's records sound like he and the Blue Moon Boys are jamming just to amuse themselves. Each track embodies a 'kind of playfulness and adventurous of spirit that Sam was looking for, [a] fresh, almost "impudent" attitude that he was seeking to unlock' (Guralnick 1994: 132), with the listener feeling privy to a private moment. One track, the aptly named 'Milk Cow Blues Boogie' (1954b) – a jumped-up version of Kokomo Arnold's 'Milk Cow Blues' (1934) – gives the appearance of just that, seemingly placing the listener as a fly on the wall at a recording session. The record opens with a *faux* false start, as if the band is tentatively noodling its way through Johnny Lee Wills and His Boys' (1941) Western-swing version of the song. For the first twelve seconds, Elvis lampoons the crooner vocal style until, suddenly, the music gives way to an exclamation: Elvis says he's not feeling it and urges his mates to goose it up. The music restarts at a much faster tempo and off they go. It is, of course, an illusion but one based on fact. What the track doesn't let the listener in on is that each and every inspired recording the group made was preceded by days of uninspired trial and error, and musical dead ends.

On 5 July 1954, Sam's foresight, patience and tenacity paid off: suddenly and unexpectedly. Elvis, Scotty and Bill had attempted recording numerous frustrating takes of a country ballad that night, but it clearly wasn't working. During a break, Elvis started fooling around with a 1947 Arthur Crudup blues number. Guitarist Scotty Moore recounts:

we were taking a break, having a coke or coffee. . . . Elvis, with nervous energy, he just jumped up and started beatin' the fire out of his guitar and he started singin' 'That's All Right' – more or less acting the fool, y'know just kibitzing around. Bill grabbed up his bass, started just slammin' it and slappin' it, just carryin' on . . . and then I just tried to find out what key they were in and joined in. Sam hit the door open from the control room, came out and said, 'What are y'all doin?' We said, 'Just goofin' around'. He said, 'Well goof around a little bit more, that's got a pretty good beat to it' . . . we ran through it probably two or three times, and that was it. (Cajiao 1991: 18)

'That's All Right' (1954c) became the benchmark for all subsequent Presley recordings to be released by Sun. The only problem was that no one involved was quite sure what made the track work or if it was just a fluke (Guralnick 1994: 97). The team tried again, in vain, for another week to record a suitable B-side. This time it was Bill Black who stumbled onto a song and approach that worked. Again, letting off steam during a session break, Bill started joking around with Bill Monroe's country waltz 'Blue Moon of Kentucky' (1947), mocking the singer's vocal delivery in a high falsetto (Cajiao 1991: 18–19) and speeding it up as a 4/4 boogie. Both tracks had come about as mistakes, and both tracks emerged during downtime after many frustrating days of searching for 'that sound'. Another key element of this second track's sonic impact was Phillips' enhancement of Elvis's deep full vocal tone, using heavy Les Paul-style tape delay. Elvis made good musical use of the tape echo, later putting it to almost comical effect in his version of Arthur Gunter's 'Baby, Let's Play House' (Presley, Moore and Black 1955), adding his 'Bay-Beh, Bay-Beh, Bay-Beh' hook, not featured in the original (Gunter 1954). If you listen carefully, he can be heard laughing in the last refrain.

Both records somehow work by mixing together all the wrong ingredients. Even after getting their first record pressed and released, the team were still unsure about what they actually did right. Just as frustrating perhaps was the struggle Phillips faced to find appropriate distribution channels for the single across the South, despite Memphis radio listeners clambering to buy it (Guralnick 1994). It wasn't country or hillbilly music; neither, was it blues, R&B or pop. It was something unprecedented: music without a category. Scotty Moore recollects that he and Black had been country-music performers with the Starlite Wranglers prior to the first sessions with Presley, and had only intended to temporarily work in a trio format while developing Presley's sound. Once Elvis's first record was played on radio, however, the rest of the Wranglers became surplus to requirements since it was more of an R&B audience turning up at shows. Country audiences weren't exactly enamoured with the blend anyway. The trio's first and only performance at country-music institution 'The Grand Ole Opry' in September 1954 went down less-than-spectacularly since the audience didn't appreciate the band's irreverent take on 'Blue Moon of Kentucky' (Cajiao 1991: 19).

The core principal informing Phillips' approach to the Presley sessions was that they had to be fun (Guralnick 1994: 133). He had specific techniques for pushing the musicians out of their comfort zones, encouraging them to playfully isolate and manipulate the individual musical components of each song. 'He would insist that they play nothing but rhythm, he would have them change keys, just when they finally got used to the one they were in, he called for tempos [sic] so slow sometimes that everyone was ready to scream' (1994: 133). Sam also encouraged the players to simplify their parts wherever possible and focus on their interactions with each other. He knew when to be silent and – without drawing undue attention to the technical aspects of recording process – gave the artists room to find themselves. He was also acutely aware how the studio context and/or criticism from an outsider could negatively impact the delicate sensibilities of (often insecure) performers.

Playfulness and a sense of humour were similarly evident at Presley and the Blue Moon Boys' live performances. In the early days, Bill Black's stage antics helped get audiences into a frame of mind positive enough to accept Presley's odd appearance, bodily gestures and vocal mannerisms (not to mention his occasional vulgarity and bad jokes). Watching the band's appearance on the 3 April edition of *The Milton Berle Show* (1956) from the deck of the USS Hancock, Bill Black can be seen acting the fool at the end of their rendition of Carl Perkin's 'Blue Suede Shoes'. He flaps his arms like an eagle, double bass wedged between his legs, all the while managing to slap its strings. Finally, he raises his arms exuberantly in triumph, whooping and hollering without missing a beat. The crowd goes crazy, as they always did. Unfortunately for both Black and Moore, new manager Thom Parker vowed that no one would ever steal the limelight away from Elvis again. This was no rural hoedown. The stakes were so much higher now.

After signing Elvis to RCA Records, Parker set about progressively isolating him from the creative team, setting up a system that kept all collaborators a few handshakes away from his young cash cow. Neither Scotty, Bill or songwriters Jerry Leiber and Mike Stoller were allowed to fraternize with Presley in their spare time. When caught playing pool with the star at his hotel in Hollywood,

Stoller was ordered to leave, despite being a key part of Elvis's production team (Guralnick 1994: 417). Leiber and Stoller were even forbidden from presenting new songs to Elvis when they were producing his sessions. All new material had to be submitted formally to publisher Jean Aberbach, who then gave it to a third party to play for Presley. Moore, Black, and Leiber and Stoller all felt so stifled, unrewarded and, eventually, simply uninterested that by September 1957 they'd each quit.

King Crimson drummer Bill Bruford (2009) explains that separation is a tool commonly used by record companies and managers to keep control over all aspects of a recording artist's creative and business affairs. In a worse-case scenario, once a formula has been developed, everyone – apart from the singer – becomes expendable. Eventually, even the singer becomes no more than a brand: a mere shadow of a once-creative former self. And so the story was with Elvis. He was never to reach the creative heights of his formative years again. The final word should go to Scotty Moore:

> I'd seen such changes in [Elvis] during the non-touring period, during all the dumpy movies, 'cause he hated them, he hated the songs. . . . The Colonel made the deals and he'd just do it. He tried to do the best he could, but he really hated the stuff. They could have . . . you get back to the politics and publishing and cliques and all this stuff. They'd put out scripts to different writers tellin' 'em a song was needed for a certain scene and hundreds of songs would come in. And they didn't want to take the time to go through 'em, they just stuck with their own guys . . . I mean there could have been real good top-notch songs in every slot in every movie he made. But they sold anyway because of him. (Cajiao 1991: 26–7)

Dylan and his diabolical weapon

Sam Phillips' contribution to the art of record production was not lost on a young folk singer signed to Columbia Records in 1961 by the name of Bob Dylan: 'I'd always thought that Sun Records and Sam Phillips himself had created the most crucial, uplifting and powerful records ever made. Next to Sam's records, all the rest sounded fruity' (Dylan 2004: 216). Like Elvis before him, Dylan's talent was nurtured by a producer with great foresight. Talent scout and producer John Hammond Sr had already discovered Billie Holiday, Benny Goodman, Count Basie, Big Joe Turner, Peter Seeger and Aretha Franklin before meeting Dylan.

It was not his musicianship or vocal skill that impressed Hammond but rather 'a point of view, and . . . a great wit' (*Discovering the genius of Bob Dylan* 1978). Hammond's role in championing Dylan throughout the early stages of his recording career was critical. Not only did he provide the right kind of patient, open-minded support that Dylan needed for his potential to be realized, but even put his job on the line (threatening to quit) when Columbia Records attempted to drop the young singer after his debut disc sold poorly. Label executives at the time referred to Dylan as 'Hammond's Folly' (*Discovering the genius of Bob Dylan* 1978) with Hammond himself admitting, 'They all thought I was crazy. Dylan thought I was crazy. He had been turned down by Folkways and every other label there was at the time. But I thought he had something' (Blake 2005: 28).

A second album, *The Freewheelin' Bob Dylan* (1963d), featured the anti-war anthem 'Blowin' in the Wind' (1963b) and, with it, Hammond was vindicated. The LP includes many of Dylan's most famous and enduring songs, showcasing a diverse set of approaches and moods that would be further developed throughout his career. Four out of the thirteen tracks are humorous in tone, with the overall mood being buoyant, if not jubilant. Murray writes, 'As the title implies, it's bursting with energy and exuberance and idealism and the sheer sensual pleasure of making music' (2005: 21). Written at the time of the Cuban Missile Crisis, the album comes across as a defiant affirmation of life in the face of death, a case in point being the song 'A Hard Rain's A-Gonna Fall' (1963a). A similarly apocalyptic track, 'Talking World War III Blues' (1963c), attempts to see the funny side of love during a nuclear winter. Polizzoti states that gallows humour and the ability to 'blend comedy and fear' are key traits of Dylan's lyric writing style (2006: 143). Dylan explains that he was inspired by artist Red Grooms' use of humour in his paintings and wondered if he could do something similar in his songs: 'There was a connection in Red's work to a lot of the folk songs I sang. . . . He incorporated every living thing into something and made it scream – everything side by side created equal . . . everything hilarious but not jokey' (2004: 269). He goes on to describe Grooms' use of humour as a 'diabolical weapon' (2004: 270).

In time, Dylan began to apply the same sense of humour to other aspects of his professional life, questioning many of the mundane conventions of popular music at the time and turning them to his own creative end. Press conferences were dealt with in a detached, laconic, mocking manner. Boring, closed questions were often met by answers not so much illogical, as having their own quixotic 'local logic'. Journalists either saw the funny side and laughed or were at a loss as to what to ask next (*Press Conference: Bob Dylan* 1965). Collaborator Levon Helm confirmed that the modus operandi when playing with Dylan was that work should be fun or they wouldn't work at all (Harris 2005). It was standard practice in the early to mid-1960s for album sleeves to feature liner notes written by some expert, publicist or critic. These were replaced on Dylan's albums by his own, often-irreverent, stream-of-consciousness musings and poetry.

Even Dylan's image was transformed by humour as the years passed. His clothes morphed from leftist, workman-like dungarees and drab, earthy colours in the early 1960s, to the bold polka-dot shirt, sunglasses and electric guitar he wielded at the 1965 Newport Folk Festival. Dylan had long since stopped modelling his public personae on Woody Guthrie and now had more in common with Beat writer Jack Kerouac's semi-fictional character, 'holy goof' Dean Moriarty (Polizzoti 2006: 40). Dylan saw in the Beat poets a rebelliousness similar to the rock 'n' roll of Elvis, Chuck Berry and Little Richard that he'd embraced as a teen. The Beats, however, were more focused, he noticed. They were rebels *with* a cause: 'To the Beats, the devil was bourgeois conventionality, social artificiality and the man in the gray flannel suit' (Dylan 2004: 247).

More than a few tracks on *Highway 61 Revisited* (1965c) exemplify Dylan's playfulness with words and his taste for the absurd. The title track 'Highway 61 Revisited' (1965d), 'Ballad of a Thin Man' (1965a) and 'Desolation Row' (1965b) are all strong examples. In the song 'Tombstone Blues' (1965e), Dylan's wordplay pushes Gypsy Davey – one of folk music's most notorious archetypal characters – into Pop-art-collage territory. The character, who steals away bored housewives to a life of rambling, is known by other names, like Black Jack Davey, and possesses many similarities with the daemon lover featured in the traditional ballad 'The House Carpenter'. Although taken to the extreme in this track, a cheeky irreverence for the characters, themes, materials and conventions of the folk songwriting tradition were nothing new to Dylan. It was something that informed his creative practice since he was first discovered.

When Leeds Music first signed Dylan to a publishing contract, at Hammond's request in 1961, the young performer had few original songs. Company head Lou Levy asked Dylan to make some demo recordings in his office. In order to make up the shortfall, he simply improvised some new ones in real time:

> I was making up some compositions on the spot, rearranging verses to old blues ballads, adding an original line here and there, anything that came into my mind – slapping a title on it. . . . Nothing would have convinced me I was a real

songwriter and I wasn't, not in the conventional sense of the word . . . I could slip in verses or lines from old spirituals or blues. That was okay; others did it all the time. There was little head work involved. What I did was start out with something, some kind of line written in stone and then turn it with another line – make it add up to something else than it originally did. (Dylan 2004: 227–8)

Even Dylan's 2004 autobiography borrows freely from other writers' texts without giving credit. The words of Mark Twain and Marcel Proust – even old copies of *Time* magazine – have been plundered and freely woven among his own (Warmuth 2010).

It was a similarly playful irreverence and spontaneity that informed the poetry, prose and humorous wordplay of Beatle John Lennon's first book, *In His Own Write* (1964). It wasn't until 1966, however, that Lennon saw the possibility of letting this kind of freedom inform his song lyrics, which until that time centred around love and relationships. Lennon later attributed his change in approach to following Dylan's example (Cott 2009). The influence didn't only flow in one direction though. The Beatles and Dylan impressed each other equally. As early as January 1964, the Beatles had been carefully scrutinizing *The Freewheelin' Bob Dylan* album (1963d) and singing its praises. Dylan, likewise, saw the Beatles' 'I Wanna Hold Your Hand' (1963) as the start of a bold new phase in popular music: 'In my head, The Beatles were it. It seemed to me a definite line had been drawn' (Lowe 2005: 46).

Whereas the Beatles flourished despite the mounting pressure of stardom, Dylan progressively found both the press and public's insatiable appetite stifling to the point of all but killing his creativity as a songwriter-performer. By 1967, he'd started a family and no longer identified with youth culture or radical causes. Some fans even picketed his house, denouncing his refusal to comment on issues like the Vietnam War (Gilmore 2013). According to Dylan, his fans felt he was 'shirking [his] responsibilities as the conscience of a generation' (2004: 118). He goes on to say:

> Art is unimportant next to life, and you have no choice. I had no hunger for it anymore anyway. Creativity has much to do with experience, observation and imagination, and if any one of those key elements is missing, it doesn't work. It was impossible now for me to observe anything without being observed. Even if I walked to the corner store someone would spot me and sneak away to find the phone. (2004: 121)

His response, in 1970, was to release a double album so lacklustre and uncharacteristic that he hoped his fans would simply move on (Gilmore 2013).

Much of Dylan's creative output since then has been patchy. It is almost as if he fears a return to the days when he could do or say no wrong. Despite the consensus among fans and critics that the albums *Blood on the Tracks* (1975), *Oh Mercy!* (1989) and *Time Out of Mind* (1997) are among his best, several collaborators have accused Dylan of being impatient, difficult to work with and guilty of sabotaging recording sessions with his eccentric behaviour. Although this might be attributed, in part, to a love of immediacy and a disdain for overdubbing and wearing headphones, less easy to explain is why he is so often accused of omitting the best tracks from his albums (Jones and Love 2014).

Dylan is reputed to have always preferred process over product (Polizzoti 2006), but there is, perhaps, a better explanation for his recalcitrance. As Elitzur points out, the direct fulfilment of a goal resembles death more than life: 'Life ... abhors short circuits' (1990b: 168). That is, a certain degree of distress and frustration provided by obstacles and challenges is necessary for humour, play and art to unleash their power. If Dylan ever feared being killed by the kindness of his courtiers, then being difficult and unpredictable are most effective ways of generating the dynamic tension necessary to keep the creative ball rolling.

The Fab Four and their comedic mentor

In 1962, the Beatles were signed to EMI Records' comedy imprint Parlophone Records by staff producer George Martin (Emerick and Massey 2006). Although Martin's 'stock-in-trade' at the time was making comedy records, he was also a classically trained musician wanting to branch out into producing rock 'n' roll records. Martin described himself as being at the time a 'maverick ... very much the joker in the music-business pack' (Martin and Hornsby 1994). By the time the Beatles first auditioned for him, every major record label in Britain, including EMI's popular-music division, had already rejected them. Despite being unimpressed by their ability as performers or songwriters, Martin signed the group anyway. What he saw in the Beatles was something they had in common with the comedic talent he'd previously worked with: charisma. He liked being with them and thought the public would feel the same way (*George Martin Interviews* 2007):

> [The Beatles] had a zany sense of humor. ... Without that sense of humor, the Beatles wouldn't have existed, and certainly we wouldn't have hit it off as well

as we did. Even after the Beatles, I did covers of certain songs with [comedian] Peter Sellers . . . so it's a kind of tradition. I don't think there's much difference between a performer in music and a performer in spoken word or humor. (Larry the O 2009)

At first, not sure how to market the band, Martin resolved to let their natural team dynamic shine through rather than adopt the usual trend of singling out one member as the star and casting the rest in his shadow. And although he was nervous about bucking the usual trend, he reminded himself that he'd taken many such risks with his comedy records, so why not do the same in the music field? (Martin and Hornsby 1994: 124). Any fears Martin may have had regarding the Beatles' commercial viability were soon to be proven unfounded. The band increased their fan-base and record sales with each subsequent release throughout 1963, eventually attracting a record-breaking 73 million viewers on their first Ed Sullivan show appearance in the United States in February 1964 (Smeaton and Wonfor 1995; Kelly, Foster and Kelly 2010).

The Beatles' early success in Britain was a product of the economic, sociopolitical and cultural context of the time. After more than a decade of postwar austerity, a new-found affluence was being experienced. This, along with the abolition of compulsory National Service army training and Elvis Presley's continuing influence, was fuelling a decidedly rebellious youth. Rock 'n' roll, R&B, modern jazz and Beat poetry were all highly regarded by young people, as was the comedy of *The Goon Show* and satire of *Beyond the Fringe*, both of which were produced for record by George Martin. The Beatles' early influences included Little Richard, Larry Williams, the Shirelles, the Drifters, Chuck Berry, Motown artists such as Smokey Robinson and the Miracles, Buddy Holly and the Crickets, Ben E. King, Carl Perkins, the Four Seasons and Phil Spector (Gillett 2009). To this list can be added Elvis Presley and, later, Bob Dylan and the Beach Boys (*The Beatles Anthology* 1995).

Contemporary accounts of the Beatles' initial impact attest to their embodiment of the element of surprise. Everything about them seemed fresh and unexpected (Evans 2009: 345). Fox argues that the band's appeal largely stemmed from their personification of ambiguity (Apter 1982). They were a living, breathing paradox, simultaneously coming across as male/female (e.g. their long hair), adults/children, good boys/bad boys (Fox suggests they were good boys posing as bad ones; it was, of course, quite the opposite) and sophisticated-yet-homespun, clad in Pierre Cardin suits but giving rough performances (at least by the standards of the day, Apter 1982: 147). The same sense of ambiguity informed the Beatles' approach to musical style, with a protean quality broadening the band's appeal to that of a multi-generational one, or at least softening the blow for anxious parents.

From the start, the Beatles flitted around from genre to genre without alienating fans or fearing any crisis of musical identity. They were able to continually adapt and grow, and kept up with rapid changes in popular taste: Paul McCartney, himself, once noted the importance of 'being up-to-date and including something for everybody' (Badman 2000: 222). Both McCartney and drummer Ringo Starr claimed that the Beatles' ability to musically shapeshift began as a coping mechanism when playing long sets in Hamburg's Reeperbahn club district during 1960 to 1962. McCartney recounts:

> We've always been a rock 'n' roll group. It's just that we're not just completely rock 'n' roll. . . . When we played in Hamburg, we didn't just play rock 'n' roll all evening, because we had these fat old businessmen coming in, and thin old businessmen as well, coming in and saying, 'Play us a mambo or a rhumba', or something. So we had to get into this kind of stuff. We just haven't got one bag you know, in The Beatles. (Badman 2000: 394)

Ringo follows:

> Hamburg is really where we got our stuff together . . . our two groups [The Beatles and, Ringo's band at the time, Rory Storme & The Hurricanes] played twelve hours a day between us. You can't play 'Johnny B. Goode' for six hours a night, so we had to stretch and play anything we could think of – experiment and try new things: throw in waltzes and all kinds of madness. (Garbarini 1988c: 41)

The Beatles never saw their many obligations as recording artists, performers and celebrities as work. When asked about his ability to keep working so hard at music, McCartney spoke about the difference between work and play, explaining that he doesn't work, he makes his living by doing what children do: play (Hutcheon 2011). He also commented that despite being under unrelenting pressure to continually come up with new material during their years with the Beatles, he and songwriting partner John Lennon only ever felt that writing was fun. He likens the process of songwriting to a magician pulling rabbits out of a hat, admitting that he was usually as surprised as the next person to see what kind of songs they could conjure out of thin air (Miles 1998: 163). Neither did the Beatles take any aspect of their professional lives too seriously. Guitarist George Harrison attributed the band's ability to withstand the pressures of public life directly to their Liverpudlian sense of humour. He went on to say that he'd 'heard of people cracking up and having nervous breakdowns without even a fraction of what [they] went through' (DuNoyer 1995: 124). McCartney claims that humour helped the Beatles affect change outside themselves, as well as within. 'Our whole gig was to shake down the temple with our native wit and our blunt remarks. Blunt northern humour' (Miles 1998: 159). Guitarist and singer John Lennon has been singled out often as having possessed a 'weapons-grade' wit that owed much to the tradition of British humour (Williams 2009). Collectively, the Beatles' sense of humour was most clearly evident at their press conferences (Badman 2001: 424). Fluxus artist Yoko Ono was surprised when she first met the group to see that they weren't serious like the other composers she'd known. Instead, she was impressed that they had a sense of humour and that their creative process had a 'fun element to it' ('Beatles Reunion' 2007).

Humour and playfulness helped the Beatles in ways that not only kept them functioning; it also provided a means by which they could transcend the limits of their own creative-practice habits. In doing so, they also helped change the norms of record production in general. By 1966, the group had clearly outgrown their roots. In August of that year, having decided to no longer tour, one major problem – that of not being able to perform any of the songs from their latest album *Revolver* (1966b) onstage – was solved. At the time, the band's influences were expanding at such a rate and in such a manner that, even on record, the Beatles' brand couldn't possibly incorporate everything they wanted to add to the mix. They'd pushed the envelope as far as they could as lovable 'moptops'. The song 'Tomorrow Never Knows' (1966c) – inspired by Lennon's reading of *The Psychedelic Experience* (Leary, Metzner and Alpert 1964) at the Indica bookshop and including the line 'Whenever in doubt, turn off your mind, relax, float downstream' (Leary, Metzner and Alpert 1964: 5) – signalled that there could now be no turning back. Complete with sitar drone, backwards distorted guitar and multiple *musique concrète* tape loops, the track was the sonic equivalent of an ego-destroying acid trip. McCartney, in particular, wrestled with the fact that the musical vehicle that had brought them thus far wasn't able to take them places that, for instance, Brian Wilson had taken the Beach Boys to with *Pet Sounds* (1966b). McCartney's solution to the problem was both ingenious and playful: The Beatles were dead. Long live The Beatles! He elaborates:

> It was my idea to say to the guys, 'Hey, how about disguising ourselves and getting an alter ego [Sgt Pepper's Lonely Hearts Club Band], because we're the Beatles and we're fed up? Every time you approach a song, John, you gotta sing it like John would. Every time I approach a ballad, it's gotta be like Paul would.' And it freed us. It was a very liberating thing to do. (Aldridge 2009: 166)

Recorded over a period of months between late 1966 and April 1967, the album *Sgt Pepper's Lonely Hearts Club Band* (1967a) was approached in a manner that gave the band much-needed psychological distance from their creative process (Garbarini 1988b): McCartney remembers, 'it gave us a laugh. It was to get some light relief in the middle of this real big career we were forging' (Miles 1998: 276). Each and every component of the recorded text being produced could be freed up by adopting an 'as if' approach to music making: the type of material written; the choice of instrumentation; arrangements; vocal and instrumental timbre; and the sonic 'soundstage' itself could be manipulated beyond the limits of normal Beatle fare, if not the physical laws of acoustics. Martin has since commented that the band didn't quite know what they wanted when making the album and that, slowly over time, it 'grew of its own accord' (Badman 2000: 258). He likened the process to that of a painter, adding something here and there, followed by periods of inaction and reflection: just standing back and gazing, before moving onwards.

Along with recording engineer Geoff Emerick, it was Martin's job to translate the Beatles' hazy ideas into practical tasks. Despite having a 'slight niggle of worry' that the album might be too pretentious for Beatles fans (Badman 2000: 268–9), he encouraged the band to try out any new idea they fancied, even using some of the sound effects and tape-collage techniques he'd previously tried out on comedy records (Miles 1998: 318). Emerick states that the band kept asking him and Martin for 'fantastic things, which just seemed impossible at the time' (Badman 2000: 268–9). Martin adds that the crazy demands actually spurred them all on to do better things, with one of the most important lessons he learnt from the Beatles being, 'Never accept the obvious . . . and always to look beyond what's there' (Massey 2000: 77).

Harrison recalls that the Beatles continued to use the 'as if' approach to music making long after the *Sgt Pepper's Lonely Hearts Club Band* (1967a) album was finished. The arrangement for the track 'Sun King' (1969b) from the album *Abbey Road* (1969a) is a case in point, with the band imagining they were Fleetwood Mac playing 'Albatross' (1968), an instrumental hit of the era featuring a slow tempo, laconic feel and copious amounts of reverb (Forte 1987). Harrison says they did so simply to keep things interesting in the studio, adding that the atmosphere at EMI's Abbey Road studios was quite drab and dirty at the time. In order to cope with less-than-optimal conditions, the band used their imagination to create their own sense of atmosphere (Badman 2000: 258).

Whatever happened to the gatekeepers?

Comedian Dana Carvey does a stand-up routine where he presents an imaginary exchange between the 2016 Paul McCartney and the ghost of his former creative partner John Lennon. Having died in 1980, Lennon can't quite get his head around modern-day phenomena such as Kim Kardashian's cultural contributions, mobile phones and Facebook (*Dana Carvey* 2016). If we were to eavesdrop in on the entire conversation, we might hear McCartney go on to explain how the popular-music domain has changed since the late 1970s. He might mention how large commercial recording studios had all but vanished, superseded by home computers and DAWs operated by multiskilled, independent musician-cum-producers; that record companies, as we once knew them, have merged themselves seemingly into oblivion; and how he himself had signed a record deal with a coffee-shop chain! He might also recall how vinyl records had long since given way to (supposedly) superior CDs, which in turn were superseded by digital streaming via the internet, only to be complimented by the return of vinyl as a hi-fi analogue alternative; and that social media and YouTube had transformed the way people access and promote music and video. He might then finish off by explaining how high-profile bands like De La Soul could win a Grammy with an album financed by their investor fans, using something called 'crowdfunding'. Given this sea change in the way popular music is made and distributed today, Lennon might well wonder if proxy agents like Ahmet Ertegun, Sam Phillips, John Hammond, George Martin and Seymour Stein, once so crucial in mediating the power of creative practitioners, have been made redundant? Well, yes and no.

To use Bourdieu's terminology, those men brought their own considerable cultural and social capital to the table when working with their respective acts. They also provided access to economic capital and, by association, lent them their symbolic capital (status). Music makers toady still require these same forms of power, but the arena of social contestation within which they operate has changed so that (multinational record companies aside) the power is no longer concentrated within the hands of the few. In order to map out the changes in the arena methodically, a framework such as Csikszentmihalyi's systems model of creativity, as McIntyre (2008) recommends, can be applied with good effect.

Csikszentmihalyi (1999) states that creativity doesn't occur in a vacuum, it emerges from the flow between three necessary and interdependent components of a huge dynamic system: 'domain', 'person' and 'field'. Tropes, traditions, tools and rules from a domain (a cultural field of works) can be said to mediate the power and creative efforts of individuals or groups. That is, practitioners take elements from the domain, make novel variations to them and then attempt to pass their innovations back out into the cultural sphere. In order to complete the loop successfully, however, they must first get their efforts past the gatekeepers of the domain, who Csikszentmihalyi refers to as the 'field'. This third part of the creative system triangle – described by Sawyer as 'a complex network of experts with varying expertise, status, and power' (2006: 124) – includes individuals with the ability to either champion the work of practitioners or ignore them, effectively blocking their efforts. Sounds simple enough – especially, when applied to the music industry of the 1950s, 1960s and 1970s. However, the domain has since evolved so much so that key tools (such as recording devices) and global distribution channels once accessible only to the 'few' are now in the hands of the 'many'.

That the popular-music domain has been so successful in mediating the power of the creative practitioner doesn't mean that the field's power to discern who will and who won't be heard has been compromised. Rather, it is the *composition* of the field, and how it functions, that has changed. But this is nothing new. Some thirty years ago, the field underwent a change arguably every bit as dramatic as that brought about by digital streaming. Multiple Grammy award-winning producer and engineer George Massenburg provides some background:

> [Today] there are no 'gatekeepers' that recognize great recordings (that is, great tunes, great performances, and/or great innovations) and introduce them to a broader audience. Now it's many-to-many, with what seems to be at once a hugely democratic opportunity and a denial of the requirement for uniquely individual, idiosyncratic *talent* . . . the music business has gone through overwhelming

upheaval . . . what once were big labels have simply come apart . . . everything started going into the toilet around 1989 to 1991 – not coincidentally, the dawn of the leveraged buyout. More specifically, I remember when we started taking direction from accounts rather than the 'gatekeepers' we had grown up with . . . Music men – people like Mo Austin, Lenny Waronker, and Bob Krasnow, among others – were ousted to be replaced by accountants. . . . Among those axioms brushed aside were the importance of building an artist's long-term career and the expectation that no more than one out of 20 recordings would turn a profit. . . . Projects were directed by numbers alone; gone were the men and women who made decisions from their instincts, quick brains, sincere heart, and guts. (Massey 2009: ix, italics in original)

The concept of a field as a filter still holds credence, but the filtering out today takes place *within* the dominant distribution channel (i.e. the internet) rather than prior to it, as was once the case. And what is being filtered out is not necessarily the bad from the good. In their article, *A Systems View of Creativity in a YouTube World*, Danah Henriksen and Megan Hoelting of the Deep Play Research Group suggest that Csikszentmihalyi's systems model needs to be fine-tuned in order to accommodate the ways in which twenty-first-century technology has impacted the 'globalization and diversification of knowledge, [along with] the sharing of idea, art, culture, and other forms of content' (2016: 102). In particular, they point out that the ability to disseminate one's work via the internet is not controlled by experts in the traditional sense. Nonetheless, since simply gaining access to the internet doesn't guarantee reaching a sizeable audience, the growing importance of influencers within the field should be emphasized: expert and non-expert alike (2016: 105). Winning a Grammy is a good example of how the popular-music field influences the domain today, since winning leads to greater prestige and potential sales, as well as heightened profile and increased professional opportunities for those already-established acts that win. But who is it that up-and-coming artists need to impress in order to reach a wider audience?

The field today can be said, at least to some degree, to include the many as well as the few. When a recording artist's online work receives a spike in views corresponding to social-media referrals rather than one-off searches, then access back into the cultural domain can be said to have been mediated by an influencer. The more expert or, at least, the better connected the influencer, the greater the impact. In the former case, they have lent both their cultural and symbolic capital; in the latter instance, access to social capital has been provided. Even a single 'like' is an example of the influencer at work. While such examples may not have quite the same impact as the stroke of a gold pen by a music-industry heavyweight, they remain forms of mediation by proxy agents all the same. And since there are so many more independent cultural producers operating today than ever before – each with unrestricted access to the means of digital distribution – practitioners need all the help they can get to rise above the fray.

In the next chapter, Csikszentmihalyi's systems model of creativity (1999) will be discussed in more detail, along with another prominent 'confluence' approach to understanding creativity presented by theorist Teresa Amabile (1996). Together, these models further compliment the frameworks already discussed and provide a systematic method with which to navigate the arena of contemporary popular-music making and break down the (multifaceted) artform into manageable theoretical chunks. Again, emphasis is placed on the importance of playfulness in creative action, along with how individuals, small groups and their environments influence each other.

3

Pushing Humpty

The artist Henry Matisse once confessed, 'Naivete is the chief cause of every artist's suffering. It is also the source of anything good that he [*sic*] may do' (Eliot 1972: 104). When discussing the findings of their longitudinal study of several hundred young artists (painters and sculptors), Getzels and Csikszentmihalyi further commented, 'Only naive persons risk questioning phenomena that everyone else takes for granted, or dare impose their own interpretations on percepts that have established meaning' (1976: 44). They also emphasized that although the creative process for artists is still very much a goal-directed activity, just as it is for non-artists, the manner in which the goal is formulated differs considerably. Artists – good ones, at least – are not so much problem solvers as 'problem finders', they observed. That is, undefined (though deeply felt) goals that lay 'beneath the threshold of awareness' (1976: 251) may emerge during play rather than in response to external pressures. In such cases, 'sensitivity [particularly to one's inner states], intuition and holistic evaluation' are the necessary required skills (1976: 155) rather than analytical ability or objective reasoning. It shouldn't be surprising, then, that for those with an artistic bent (perhaps yourself), the thought of analysing creativity might seem like a futile exercise in reductionism and a real 'mojo' killer: something akin to pushing Humpty Dumpty off the wall to see what makes him tick. And yet, in doing just that, creativity researchers of yesteryear – armed with their various analytical and methodological tools – provided the foundations for a more holistic vision of creativity to eventually emerge. It has, however, been a long and winding road to putting Humpty back together again.

150 years of creativity research

Over the last 150 years, creativity research has been forthcoming primarily from the discipline of psychology. Early systematic approaches were inspired by Sir Francis Galton's (1869) exploration of genius (defined as 'recognised achievement'), together with Caesare Lombroso's (1891) psychopathological research in the late-nineteenth century. At various junctures, researchers have sought to identify the personality traits of eminent creators, dissect thinking in ordinary individuals (i.e. isolating the various 'operations, contents and products' at play (Guilford 1959)), develop rubrics for assessing creative products or view creativity as arising 'through a system of interrelated forces operating at multiple levels' (Hennessy and Amabile 2010: 571). Although sociologists have by-and-large made little attempt to explicitly theorize creativity until recently (Chan 2011) – the term 'innovation' instead having been the preferred rubric (Burns, Machado and Corte 2015) – psychologists are today acknowledging that an interdisciplinary approach to conceptualizing creativity 'as a product not only of individuals, but also societies, cultures and historical periods' (Chan 2013: 25) is necessary to fully explain the phenomenon. Less numerous perhaps, but no less important, have been contributions made by researchers working within the arenas of 'communication and cultural studies as well as literary theory, education and philosophy' (McIntyre 2013: 84).

Despite all this multidisciplinary activity, wide agreement regarding what creativity actually is has thus far eluded scholars. Furthermore, the parts of creativity have all too often been mistaken for the whole. This state of affairs can be attributed in no small part to the unidimensional focus of many seminal creativity studies and a 'parochial isolation' of findings originating from different disciplines. Wehner, Csikszentmihalyi and Magyari-Beck liken the situation to the proverbial blindmen [*sic*] and the elephant, with each believing they understand the whole based solely upon which part of the beast they are holding (1991: 270). Even within the same discipline, rigid organizational structures can lead to a fragmentation of knowledge and theoretical blind spots. Sternberg and Lubart note:

> In many psychology departments, cognitive and social psychologists seek to maintain their separate identities because of resource considerations (e.g. funding and faculty positions). Furthermore, apart from the two journals specializing in creativity research, most of the prominent journals are unidisciplinary in approach. Cognitive psychology journals take cognitive work and social psychology journals take research with social-personality variables. (1999: 9)

At other times, the 'extreme simplification' of how creativity had been conceptualized was intentional, a price willingly paid in order to 'operationalize variables and gain experimental control over them' (Feldman 1999: 169). A famous case in point was J. P. Guilford's Structure of Intellect (SI) model (1959). Guilford saw his psychometric approach in terms of a larger multidimensional matrix, emphasizing as he did in his landmark 1950 address to the American Psychological Association (APA) the need to explore creativity as a phenomenon involving not only cognitive but social processes (in addition to the well-established study of the role of personality traits). Similarly, theorist Mel Rhodes reminded scholars in his oft-quoted paper 'An Analysis of Creativity' that 'creativity cannot be explained alone in terms of . . . [any] single component, no matter how vital that component may be' (1961: 306). Rhodes organized the plethora of creativity definitions up to that time into overlapping, intertwining approaches forming four basic strands of enquiry: his famous 'four Ps of creativity' (i.e. 'person', 'process', 'product' and 'press' (i.e. the climate)). He was, however, careful to point out that although each represented a discreet academic identity, all four were necessary to describe creativity as a functioning whole.

Psychological approaches to understanding creativity

The fact that creativity theory and studies from the mid- to late-twentieth century may be limited in scope when compared with more recent conceptualizations does not necessarily make them redundant: often, they are merely incomplete. As Montuori and Purser observe, 'One can only hope that . . . creativity research will not fall prey to a tendency to dismiss earlier creativity research and reinvent the proverbial wheel' (1995: 105). Even research based on the positivist assumption that creativity is an attribute residing solely within the individual can nonetheless shed light on components that operate at that level. It should not be forgotten, however, that such elements emerge from, and are embedded within, a larger dynamic system: a 'complex multidimensional set of related components or areas interacting' (Taylor 1975b: 297). As Sawyer notes, neither cognitive processes (micro-level phenomena) nor 'the social dimension of creative fields' are immune from the effects of the other (2012: 10). Therefore, an understanding of both is necessary.

There are many possible ways of categorizing pervading trends in creativity research. The following list focuses on key perspectives having emerged from within psychology over the last 100 years. It is by no means a conclusive survey, and there is, at times, considerable overlap between certain categories. The primary rationale informing the given groupings is their rhetorical position. That is, how creativity is viewed from the perspective of a broader value system, along with the inherent assumptions that unavoidably colour how creativity is understood. Sociological approaches have not been included. This is since the formulation of comprehensive creativity theories by sociologists have only recently been forthcoming (e.g. Sawyer 2012) and consensus is yet to be reached regarding what a true sociology of creativity might look like (Chan 2011). Moreover, many of their concerns have already been addressed by social psychologists (in particular, psychological 'systems' approaches, according to Burns, Machado and Corte (2015)). Non-systematic perspectives such as the mystical or pragmatic have likewise been omitted, as have psychological trends where, thus far, creativity has received little attention.

Two caveats: each approach listed represents a sufficiently complex area of study for the danger of misrepresentation to be present in so brief a summary. Similarly, there exists (to varying degrees) some disagreement among key proponents of each approach over how creativity actually works. For erudite (though succinct) discussions of the areas concerned please refer to Getzels (1975), Sternberg and Lubart (1999) and Taylor (1975a). The psychological approaches to theorizing and researching creativity over the last 100 years that will help the reader understand key concepts discussed within this monograph, along with the assumptions upon which they depend, are as follows:

1. **Psychoanalytical approaches** suggest that creativity is a means of tension/stimulus *reduction* via sublimation: that is, an overt and culturally appropriate manifestation of un- or pre-conscious psychopathological (i.e. 'primary') processes (e.g. Freud ([1908] 1990); Kris 1952; Kubie 1958).
2. **Humanistic approaches** interpret creativity as a tension/stimulus-*seeking* activity symptomatic of a healthy openness to the world and a means to reach one's fullest potentialities (e.g. Fromm 1959; Maslow 1954, 1959; Rogers 1963; Schachtel 1959).
3. **Associationistic approaches** define creativity as the forming of mutually remote, associative elements into new useful combinations (e.g. Koestler 1964; Mednick 1962; Ribot 1900a, 1900b).

4. **Cognitive approaches** explore the mental representations/processes that inform creative thought (e.g. Boden 1992, 1994; Finke, Ward and Smith 1992; Johnson-Laird 1988; Weisberg 1986).
5. **Behavioural approaches** (e.g. Epstein 1996; Goetz 1989; Wells 1986; Winston and Baker 1985) view creativity as 'the result of an interconnection or integration of previously established behaviors' (Epstein and Laptosky 1999: 183).
6. **Psychometric approaches** assess creative potential using objectively scorable, paper and pencil tests based on models developed via factor analysis (e.g. Getzels and Jackson 1962; Guilford 1959; Torrance 1974).
7. **Product assessment** is an attempt to understand creativity in part by studying its artefacts (concrete or symbolic) in terms of sets of agreed-upon sociocultural criteria (e.g. Bessemer and Treffinger 1981; Brogden and Sprecher 1964; Jackson and Messick 1965; Rhodes 1961; Taylor and Sandler 1972).
8. **Social-personality approaches** take into account the influence of personality and motivational variables, as well as the sociocultural context within which creativity may occur (e.g. Amabile 1983, 1996; Barron 1968, 1969; Eysenck 1990).
9. **Confluence approaches** emphasize the need for multiple components, both within and without the individual, to converge in order for creativity to occur (e.g. Amabile 1983, 1996; Csikszentmihalyi 1999; Gruber and Davis 1988; Sternberg and Lubart 1991, 1992, 1995, 1996).

Break it down: Two complimentary confluence theories

Teresa Amabile's social psychology of creativity (1996) and Mihalyi Csikszentmihalyi's systems model of creativity (1999) are two theories that explain the greater creativity matrix as a confluence of interacting components. They precede from opposing vantage points, however, making each an effective compliment for the other. While neither can claim to be truly comprehensive, when used in tandem, they systematically map out the whole creative terrain (as it is generally understood within the contemporary (multidisciplinary) creativity literature) from the micro up to the macro level. Moreover, if used in conjunction with play theory and cultural psychology (both discussed in previous chapters) a cohesive interdisciplinary framework results: one that emphasizes not only the importance of musical, technological and cognitive skills in creative action but also the centrality of motivation and personality states (as opposed to traits). It is a framework that indicates precisely where in the overall personal, sociocultural and historical creative matrix these latter often-overlooked components reside, along with how they help initiate and sustain task engagement.

Whereas Amabile's discussion predominantly explores the psychology of the individual as affected by the social environment, Csikszentmihalyi's model – as outlined in Chapter 2 – takes more of a 'bird's-eye view', emphasizing equally the three components which he argues make up the overall creativity system (i.e. person, field and domain). He explains:

> while the mind has quite a lot to do with genius and creativity, it is not the place where these phenomena can be found. The location of genius is not in any particular individual's mind, but in a virtual space, or system, where an individual interacts with a cultural domain and with a social field. It is only in the relation of these three separate entities that creativity, or the work of genius, manifests itself. In popular usage, 'genius' is sometimes used as a noun that stands by itself, yet in reality it appears always with a modifier: musical genius, mathematical genius, scientific genius, and so forth. Genius cannot show itself except when garbed in a concrete symbolic form. (2014: 99)

A key tenet of the systems model is 'circular causation'. That is, person, field and domain are equally important components of creativity (McIntyre 2008), and it is only through the interaction of all three that creativity emerges: a phenomenon with properties not displayed by any one component in isolation. As Sawyer states, there are 'two level of analysis, a componential level and an emergent higher level' (2003: 217). For this reason, the systems model is an appropriate theoretical tool for dealing with such macro-level interactions, as well as what emerges as a consequence. Amabile's theory, likewise, breaks creativity down into three discreet components, but instead of delineating between the individual, the cultural and the social, she describes her components simply as 'sets of elements that control, determine, and enter into processes' (1996: 81). They are:

1. **Domain-relevant skills:** pre-existing skills and knowledge that may be brought to the specific task at hand: the larger the set, the greater the number of alternatives available for creating something new.
2. **Creativity-relevant skills and processes**, consisting of cognitive style; knowledge of 'heuristics' (i.e. ways of dealing with problems that have no

obvious path to solution or where a clearly identified goal has yet to be generated); and personality characteristics conducive to creativity.
3. **Task motivation:** one's basic attitude towards a given task, along with the *perception* of one's reasons for initiating and sustaining task engagement, either in response to inherent qualities of the task (i.e. 'intrinsic') or as introduced by the environment (i.e. 'extrinsic').

The concurrent use of Csikszentmihalyi's and Amabile's theories is a pragmatic choice but one justified by the fact that micro- and macro-levels of the overall creativity matrix require theoretical tools appropriate to their particular level of focus. For example, while Csikszentmihalyi's theory adequately explores issues relating to the individual, along with the roles that personality and motivation play at that level, it is executed in a relatively ad hoc manner when compared with Amabile's micro-level componentialization. Amabile's approach also provides an effective and rigorous means by which the relationship of play and playfulness can be unpacked with regard to creativity-relevant skills and processes, and motivation alone (i.e. creative action theoretically divorced from its domain). This last point is important, since it is exclusively within non-domain areas where playfulness and creativity intersect. The ability to make such a distinction makes insights regarding the relationship of playfulness and creativity largely domain-transferrable. It does not, however, make creative-practice examples or case studies redundant. Much of this monograph stands as a testament to that fact.

Amabile's theory is not to be misunderstood as an exercise in reductionism, but rather a sizeable step towards developing a truly methodical approach to understanding creativity as a whole. She admits as much, openly acknowledging the limitations of her work and stressing that theorists such as Csikszentmihalyi, who consider 'the influence of domains, fields, social forces, and historical forces on the creative productivity of entire cultures and subcultures' have much to contribute towards the development of a 'truly comprehensive theoretical model of creativity' (1996: 274). Amabile is, nonetheless, critical of such theorists' lack of specificity regarding the precise mechanisms by which social factors influence creativity (1996: 126), concluding:

> Whatever resemblance a comprehensive theory of creativity will ultimately bear to the componential framework that I have presented, such a theory must include a set of distinct components of abilities, characteristics, and conditions that can each independently influence creativity but can also interact. (1996: 269)

Creativity-relevant skills/processes, motivation and play

The attention capacity of human beings is limited (Amabile 1996: 111). Therefore, directing attention away from task-irrelevant issues (such as expected external evaluation, reward and extrinsically imposed constraints) in favour of matters intrinsic to task engagement has been shown to have a positive impact upon creativity (Amabile 1996). When intrinsic motivation is high, individuals are more likely to explore options and play with possibilities at length. The process has become its own reward: work has become play. The reframing of experience as play (which suspends the usual mundane framing classes, and effects what Csikszentmihlalyi describes as 'a contraction of the perceptual field' (Amabile 1996: 110)) can mitigate the salience of social influences deemed detrimental to creative action by allowing individuals (and groups) to 'temporarily "step away"' (Amabile 1996: 110) from perceived extrinsic pressures and enjoy task engagement as an end-in-itself. Amabile asserts that improving motivation by making extrinsic constraints 'seem distant and unimportant' (1987: 251) has the additional benefit of providing a potentially instantaneous improvement in creative flow. Increasing creativity- or domain-relevant skills (the obvious alternate strategy) requires much more time and effort.

Although manipulation of motivation is a temporary fix, a sustained high level of intrinsic motivation can, over time, bolster a larger repertoire of (domain-transferrable) creativity skills as cognitive risk-taking and set-breaking become more commonplace (Amabile 1996). Amabile states that a cognitive style conducive to creativity includes the following playful abilities: breaking perceptual set; breaking cognitive set; breaking out of 'performance scripts'; using wide categories; suspending judgement; and keeping response options open as long as possible (1983: 364–5). Similarly, Getzels and Jackson point to their study where students displaying high levels of 'creativity' were differentiated against those merely displaying high IQ by the following abilities: to '"make the given problematic", "to express the ridiculous"' and display '"playfulness" with "givens," with "conventions," and with "predetermined categories"' (1962: 54). Csikszentmihalyi also emphasizes two playful characteristics of creative individuals that he deems most salient: firstly, 'a constant curiosity, an ever renewed interest in whatever happens around them ... part of the "childishness" attributed to creative individuals' (1999: 330) and, secondly, the malleability of their personality dimensions. He continues:

> One view I have developed on the basis of my studies is that creative persons are characterized not so much by single traits, as by their ability to operate the entire spectrum of the personality dimensions. So they are not just introverted, but can be both extroverted and introverted depending on the phase of the process they happen to be involved in at the moment . . . sensitive and aloof, dominant and humble, masculine and feminine, as the occasion demands. (1999: 331)

Emphasizing play's relationship to such domain-transferrable factors does not belie the importance of domain-relevant skills but rather highlights how they might be exploited more efficiently, effectively and with greater flexibility. According to Amabile (1983), domain-relevant skills form the basis upon which creativity-relevant skills and processes must act. That is, the more skills, experience and knowledge individuals possess specific to a given domain, the more elements there are to play with. She adds that if domain skills and knowledge are to be used in the service of creativity they must be organized in such a manner that they are easily accessed according to general principles rather than narrow ('by rote') contextual applications. In this way, existing domain skills and knowledge mediate creative expression rather than force it into ruts. To illustrate, Amabile states, 'it is possible to have too many algorithms, it is not possible to have too much knowledge' (1983: 364).

Mix it up: Combinatorial play

In 1977, Josefa Nina Lieberman suggested in her seminal work *Playfulness: Its Relationship to Imagination and Creativity* that adults who wish to enjoy the creative benefits of playfulness need a strong ego. This is due to the fact that playfulness is rarely deemed acceptable behaviour in adults as it is for children. Certain components of playfulness (with Lieberman's particular conceptualization referred to as '[PF]') are more taboo for grown-ups than others. Physical and cognitive spontaneity are most heavily frowned upon, while manifest joy and sense of humour fare a little better at times. For arts practitioners, this is an important observation since cognitive spontaneity is inextricably linked with 'combinatorial play', a process where pre-existing knowledge or compositional elements are shuffled and recombined to form surprising new products (1977: 84). Combinatorial play is only as good as the domain-relevant knowledge/skills and task motivation the individual has to work with, however. Social factors, too, help determine 'how much knowledge the [adult] individual acquires and how comfortable the person is moving around his [*sic*] storehouse of facts' (1977: 58).

Lieberman likens combinatorial play and cognitive spontaneity to a figurative kaleidoscope: 'The bits and pieces of glass are the givens or familiar facts. The twist of the hand produces ever-different pictures with the same components into unique and original patterns' (1977: 83). She also goes to some length to differentiate between spontaneity (think helpful) and impulsivity (think counterproductive), stating that the two behaviours are indicative of very different motivational states. Spontaneity results from a sense of competence, confidence and joy, whereas impulsive behaviour stems from a lack of control and feelings of anxiety. Moreover, spontaneity is intrinsically motivated and occurs in familiar settings.

Since artists must not only collect facts, figures and ideas but also play with them, it is fair to say that a sense of irreverence and rebelliousness are required skills. Lieberman goes as far as to call artists the 'practitioner[s] of playfulness' (1977: 10). The result of all this playfulness, at times, might be creative products deemed controversial or, even, shocking by those who see facts and social 'givens' as sacrosanct. Nonetheless, even the most radical of creative concepts and products can eventually be reabsorbed into the cultural mainstream. As Getzels and Jackson note, 'today's fact was yesterday's fancy and today's fancy may very well turn out to be tomorrow's fact' (1962: 127). In terms of the macro-level system of creativity as described by Csikszentmihalyi, one can say that when any given domain begins to stagnate, or the social field that guards it gets too smug and complacent, then the time is ripe for the next generation of artists to come along and 'fuck shit up' again.

Batteries not included: The elusiveness of playfulness

Simply engaging in activities usually associated with play does not guarantee that playful behaviour or thinking – along with all their creative benefits – will ensue. Play and playfulness are not one and the same. Lieberman (1977) describes playfulness as an observable behaviour that might – or might not – emerge in specific instances of play. Although playful behaviour and thinking is precisely what can be observed growing steadily in Dylan's wordplay game discussed in Chapter 1, playfulness in adults, as Sutton-Smith (1979) notes, is actually quite rare. Nonetheless, 'when people are engaged in novel frame construction, playfulness often bubbles momentarily to the surface as if the voluntary engagement allows such greater looseness of spirit and thought' (1979: 318).

While it may be unreasonable to expect playfulness to emerge from instances of play in any reliable manner, simply valuing playfulness can help. It is even possible (as one writer put it when discussing a perceived spirit of 'wonder and openness' in the work of polymath Meredith Monk) to be 'conscientiously playful', adding that Monk 'literally tells herself "Remember to be playful" when she is making music' (Reyes 2020). Playfulness may even emerge spontaneously outside of instances of play, as the following observation by Guitard, Ferland and Dutil emphasizes:

> Playfulness allows adults to approach activities with the same openness of mind which the child approaches play. . . . With playfulness, difficult situations are perceived as challenges to be raised, occasions to learn, and possibilities to increase one's competence and skills. Furthermore, mistakes are no longer considered failure but rather a possibility to learn and grow. In adulthood, playfulness crosses the boundaries of play and extends to all life situations. (2005: 19)

In the following chapters (4, 5 and 6), it will be demonstrated how the concept of playframing can be used to help better understand the process of popular-music making. Together with the help of real-world examples, characteristics of play will be unpacked that relate to either the formulation of musical creative problems or the generation of novel responses to them. In Chapter 4, the concept of play being a 'zone apart' with its own inherent logic, power relations and skill-to-challenge correlations will be examined. The finer points of playframing negotiation will be explored in its own dedicated chapter (Chapter 5). And, since there is both a time and place for spontaneity and reflection within creativity, the interdependent relationship of play and playfulness to serious, critical frames of mind will be presented in Chapter 6.

4

Playframing

Bateson once observed that a picture frame embodies 'a message intended to order and organize the perception of the viewer' and which 'tells the viewer that he [*sic*] is not to use the same sort of thinking in interpreting the picture that he might use in interpreting the wallpaper outside the frame' (1972: 187–8). This meta-communication (i.e. communication about communication) is what occurs when people give each other cues to indicate, 'This is play.' Although composer John Cage has argued that the dividing line between art and real life has long since been made redundant, his own experimental approach to music still depended upon the meta-communication of the frame, admitting, 'I've thought about music as a means of changing the mind' (Kostelanetz 2000). It would seem that art and frames continue to go hand in hand if only in conceptual, rather than physical form. Stereolab co-founder Laetitia Sadier reflects on the power of music to 'change the mind':

> Somehow the world around me made more sense when music – preferably the stuff that I liked – was being played. Everything would liven up; take on a more significant and consequential countenance. So I've always experienced music as something transformational, a true alchemic force that has worked as an intangible bridge from which there is a view to transforming myself and the world. (Blau 2012)

Blocking out the noise

Taking an avid interest in music and music making can often be motivated by a desire to experience a psychological protective frame, one that, as Apter (1991: 14) points out, transforms and sterilizes the threats of the real world. Regardless of whether or not the creative context is one of work or play, the *experience* can be playful (Csikszentmihalyi 1975). This is possible since focusing on the moment-to-moment intrinsic concerns of creative tasks effectively blocks out task-irrelevant information, creating a phenomenological zone apart that temporarily becomes 'our entire world' (Elitzur 1990a: 20). When asked about what first inspired him to get into music, house-music and remix pioneer Frankie Knuckles (an artist who referred to his interaction with sounds as 'play') once recalled:

> I think it saved my life in some kind of way. It gave me a focus away from something that could possibly have taken me under. When you grow up in the inner city, like New York when things are as tough as they are . . . if you've got some kind of focus that will take your mind away from that . . . then that's the thing that saves your life. (Mao 2011)

Although playframes are essentially phenomenological in nature, their characteristics can be embodied in many ways: as cues and prompts; spatial and/or temporal zones; or physical systems that favour certain types of interaction over others. Even terms of engagement, software/hardware set-ups or procedural systems can serve to mark out a 'field' of play. It is even possible for the protective frame of play to be distributed across a network of like-minded creative individuals and appreciative audiences. Punk-rock progenitor Richard Hell recalls how, in early 1974, he and his school friend Tom Verlaine (both of the band Television) helped transform a fledgling country, bluegrass and blues club into a haven for free-thinking poets and musicians:

> Part of the purpose of what we were doing was to suggest other ways of doing things. . . . And we wanted to find an audience for that. At CBGB's, we imagined our own world into being, because we didn't feel comfortable in the existing one. It was a place you could go to every night and feel like you belonged. And that's because it flowered out of our own brains. (Hasted 2005)

Singer-songwriter and poet Patti Smith elaborates:

> It fulfilled a need. There wasn't any place for people to try new ideas and new things, to go out on a limb and make mistakes. . . . What makes it is the people and their collective energy. . . . The sense of self and new energy was instantaneous. The confidence it inspired was strong, and the sense of community was immediate. William S. Burroughs lived down the street. He came all the time. We gave him a little table and a chair, and he'd sit there. All of our friends came – Robert Mapplethorpe, Jim Carroll. CBGB was the neighborhood – the artists and poets and musicians – and we all inspired each other. CBGB validated our mission. (Fricke 2006)

Eliminating the '"noise" of irrelevant information' is an essential aspect of not only play but 'any form of perception or communication' for that matter (Elitzur 1990a: 18). Artists and musicians may even find that (supposedly) relevant information, when there is too much of it, limits spontaneity. In the current era of the project studio, with its plethora of affordable DAWs, software applications ('apps') and sample-based music-creation platforms, vast arrays of creative possibilities are continually on offer. This can present quite a problem for music makers, whether they know it or not. Limiting the flow of information and options deemed surplus to the requirements of a given task can free up a great deal of time and energy for practitioners, when done in an autonomous fashion. Stereolab co-founder Tim Gane confessed in a recent interview that rather than having a clear idea of the sounds he wants to make before engaging creative tasks, he tended to proceed in a reductive, 'playful' manner: 'I tend to have a clearer idea of what I don't want than what I do want. It's more about deciding some guidelines, some rules you want to stick by so you don't have every choice in the world' (Awbi 2016).

Gane is renowned for preferring vintage gear from the 1960s and 1970s – and not much of it – to MIDI systems. Producer Brian Eno has some thoughts regarding why such an approach might be beneficial to creative action:

> with modern technology, one of the biggest difficulties is cutting out options. So, actually that's the problem with digital technology, because options keep proliferating... you very quickly can understand what you can do with an electric guitar, or a violin, or a set of drums, and you stop looking for more options, and you start grappling with it. You say, 'OK, this is what it does. So what do I do?' The problem with software-based work is that you never know what it does, you can never exhaust what it does, basically. So you can always cover the fact that you haven't got an idea by trying another option in the tools. So, if you have a lot of options, you don't usually have a lot of rapport with the instrument. If you have a few options, your rapport keeps increasing, because you understand the options better and better. And this is why people still make good music with crude instruments, simple instruments. Because they understand them better than us software people understand our instruments. . . . When I'm working with other people, one of the things I spend quite a lot of time doing is banning options. (Warren 2013)

Eno raises an interesting point regarding how familiarity with a certain tool negates the need for exploration (i.e. asking 'what does it do?'), turning attention, rather, to ask (as one does in play), 'What can *I* do with this thing?' or 'How can I use this tool for a purpose other than what it was designed for?'

Reducing options and encouraging spontaneity can even be achieved in an arbitrary fashion. Guitarist Robert Fripp notes that irrespective of whether any given decision is judged to be right or not, arguably, matters less than how removing choice(s) frees up energy for engaging tasks as they arise:

> I wish to have, from one point of view, absolutely no choice, so what is obvious presents itself to me. In the sense having committed myself... I don't really have to worry too much about what I'm doing. Obviously, the details will be filled in... from a practical point of view, having determined to do it, it saves me an awful lot of energy wondering, 'Should I be doing other things? Is this the right thing to do?' ('Robert Fripp' 1979)

U2 co-producers Brian Eno and Daniel Lanois went as far as to make an ongoing rule to simplify decision-making processes. Very early in their working relationship, Eno proposed that if one of them made a suggestion, the other must agree with it. Lanois explained that to do so placed greater importance on team unity than the actual quality of any given idea. It was also a way of working that tended to get 'the ball rolling' quicker and prevented ideas from being 'suffocated' too early on. He concluded by adding that once an idea had been explored, the team tended to agree on whether or not it was worth pursuing (Massey 2009).

Intrinsic motivation, creativity and play

Amabile likens creativity to the limited field of a maze with multiple exits. Some pathways are long, winding and unfamiliar, and might lead to results that are rare, if not, brilliant. Just as likely, however, they might lead to dead ends. Other paths, though safer bets – well trodden and more direct – may lead to results that are generic and clichéd. When there is extrinsic pressure to get results, attention narrows as practitioners fix their sights on the end goal more intently. Any pathway that is overly long, or which might lead to a dead end, is now seen as a waste of time and energy. By contrast,

> if you are intrinsically motivated, you *enjoy being in the maze*. You enjoy playing in it, nosing around, trying out different pathways, exploring, thinking things through before blindly plunging ahead. You're not really concentrating on anything else but how much you enjoy the problem itself, how you like the challenge and the intrigue. Since you enjoy the activity of exploring the maze,

you will be likely to take full advantage of its possibilities. In other words you are likely to be creative. (1987: 230, italics in original)

Practitioners need to feel that they are investing their time and energy in response to 'the intrinsic properties of the task' (Amabile 1996: 91) that genuinely interest or excite them, rather than a force applied by an external agent. The example of Bob Dylan's playing with words in Chapter 1 is a great example of intrinsic motivation in action. Recombining, as he does, the words in a prolonged and an increasingly excited fashion, he takes advantage of the numerous creative pathways afforded by a limited field of attention: an end-in-itself. When, on the other hand, external influences are present that are perceived as being controlling, a clear 'difference between what the person *can* do and he [sic] *will* do' results (Amabile 1996: 93). Even extrinsic motivators that are positive (such as rewards) can lead to a compromised ability to problem solve:

> The outer presence and inner compulsion to conform arouse extrinsic, ego-involved motives in the problem solver. His [sic] main efforts tend to become directed towards the goals of being accepted and rewarded by the group, of avoiding rejection and punishment. The solution of the problem becomes of secondary relevance, and his task-involved motivation diminishes. In being concerned with goals extrinsic to the task itself, and particularly as rendered anxious about potential threats in the situation, his cognitive processes become less flexible, his insights less sensitive. (Crutchfield 1962: 125)

Amabile's thoughts regarding the positive impact of intrinsic motivation upon creativity has much in common with Apter's description of the paratelic (i.e. playful) state with its 'emphasis on immediate gratification wherever possible; a preference for spontaneity and freedom of action; a willingness to experiment and "mess around"; a disposition to fantasise and indulge in pretence and make-believe; and a tendency to prolong the activity wherever possible' (1991: 17). Similarly, Apter acknowledges, as does Amabile, the link between extrinsic motivation (both negative and positive) that focuses attention primarily on future goals and outcomes, and the narrowing of creative possibilities:

> If we consider creativity, we see that adding rewards to some activity, as well as making the activity seem like a chore, and therefore less enticing, tends to focus the activity on a future goal. This then narrows the possibilities of exploring divergent ideas and approaches. To put it another way, one is more likely to be original if one is allowed to go off on tangents and make new connections, however crazy these may seem at the outset. Experimenting and exploring in

ways that are not focused on a particular outcome are, in this respect, more likely to be innovative than those that are not. (Apter 2018: 106)

If extrinsic pressure from the social environment is strong enough, even those who might normally have a high level of intrinsic motivation may have their *joie de vivre* significantly impaired. In worse-case scenarios, where extrinsic forces imposed by a social field or political regime are unremitting and extreme, some sense of creative autonomy may still be possible if only as an imaginary reversal of power (Sutton-Smith 1979: 305–6). Soviet composer Dmitri Shostakovich (who lost many of his family and friends to the 'Great Terror' in the late 1930s) often feared for his and his family's lives as a result of the many 'unofficial' denunciations his innovative work received in the Stalinist regime mouthpiece Pravda. He was later denounced for not adequately propagating a sterilized utopian vision of Soviet life for the masses by Central Committee secretary Andrei Zhdanov: part of a wider policy aimed at weeding out any imperialist (think American) influences. Branded a 'formalist' (i.e. having made music deemed to be overly informed by his own aesthetic concerns), Shostakovich lost his teaching job, had many of his works banned and lived in fear, bag packed and waiting 'for his arrest at night out on the landing by the lift, so that at least his family wouldn't be disturbed' (Wilson 1994: 183). He later composed the 'Antiformalist Rayok', an unpublished satirical cantata that lampooned the Zhdanov decree and which he only ever performed for family and close friends. Like Shostakovich, Afrobeat innovator Fela Kuti paid a high price for his art. Daring to speak out against the political and societal injustices he saw around him in his homeland Nigeria during the 1970s, he was (at various times): jailed; had his property burnt down; received severe beatings; and lost his mother to violence (all) at the hands of the military regime he criticized and ridiculed in his music.

Creative constraints

Playframes can be designed equally well 'from the ground up' tabula rasa style (by reintroducing a limited array of elements with which to interact) or, conversely, by approaching a familiar situation with a view to eliminating select elements and creative pathways. Each approach effectively constrains choice as much as it facilitates. What matters most is that the terms of the frame are set in an atmosphere of positive social relationships, rather than out of habit, apathy or made begrudgingly in response to extrinsic pressure. When Talking

Heads co-founder David Byrne was asked what gets him in the 'creative zone', he responded by emphasizing the relationship between making (and adhering to) decisions, constraining choice and spontaneity:

> I usually have to have an assignment, and it could be an assignment that I give myself... which could be... 'I'm going to collaborate with another musician.' So that's the assignment. I have to figure out how to work with them, how to adapt what I do to what they do. Or it could be for a project like a theatre project or, sometimes, a record of songs. But often I try and have something where I go, 'This is your job. This is what you have to do. And it has to do this, and it has to do this.' That kind of motivates me. That kind of gets me going. If I just sat there and thought, 'Oh, you can do anything. You can write anything you want: about anything you want.' I think I'd be paralyzed. (*David Byrne Q&A* 2014)

Richard Hell describes his penchant for self-imposed restraints and their effect on his creative experience:

> My songs are almost like John Donne or Gerard Manley Hopkins, where the form is really strict and everything adds up. You make a statement in a stanza and then the implications are presented in the chorus, and then you make another statement that's consistent, that moves the discussion along a little further, in the next stanza, and then it gets summed up by the chorus again. It was very formal. People don't think of punk music as being like that, but my lyrics were really like clockwork. It doesn't mean it's cold or mechanistic – it's just that I liked having the constraints of the form. I imposed them on myself because it was fun. I always wrote the music first, but I wrote the lyrics to fit the construction of the music in this very exacting way. (Gollner 2015)

Constraints as simple as being economic in how one makes artistic statements can have a powerful impact on the reception of one's ideas, particularly given the limitations electronic media often impose. The current prevalence of the social-media application Twitter demonstrates how brevity and the popular interrelate, as did once, the seven-inch vinyl 'single' (two-to-three minutes per side being the norm) and its relationship with the AM radio broadcast format (and the latter's limited audio-quality). In the Stooges documentary film *Gimme Danger* (2016) Iggy Pop recalls how television personality Soupy Sales encouraged viewers to write to him but to limit their notes to twenty-five words or less. This, he said, had a marked influence on his approach to songwriting. Peter Gabriel similarly insists that, in his experience, adopting creative constraints is an effective way of inspiring a sense of challenge and fun in collaboration: 'The worst brief for an artist is to be told they can do anything. I have always believed that artists are a lot more creative if you tell them what they can't do. It's a drudge building something out of nothing and much more fun to explore ways of getting round the rules' (2010). Bandleader Miles Davis would, at times, tell his musicians what *not* to play, rather than what to play (*Celebrating a Masterpiece* 2008).

The presence of constraints does not always necessarily exert a positive influence upon creative action. In a study conducted by Herrmann, Goldschmidt and Miron-Spektor, it was found that the positive or negative influence of constraints was dependent upon whether or not they were *perceived* as being self-imposed or extrinsic in origin: even when 'utilizing the same constraint, of the same severity' (2018: 166). Self-imposed constraints were viewed as 'enabling', while extrinsic constraints were interpreted as coercing individuals into reaching a specific solution. It must be emphasized, however, that this observation relates specifically to the novelty-generation stage of creative action. Similarly, Amabile has conceded that when factors which might normally be expected to undermine intrinsic motivation are present, their influence may have a benign or even additive effect, provided they do not affect one's perceived sense of autonomy (Amabile and Pratt 2016). For example, external rewards can be viewed either negatively (as figurative 'carrots' used to induce certain behaviours) or positively (as 'no-strings-attached' thanks for a job well done).

Social dynamics have been highlighted as another factor influencing whether or not constraints will be perceived as obstacles or opportunities. In one field study (Rosso 2014) four groups were contrasted: two selected for demonstrating 'disabling dynamics' (described as being collectively fragmented and distrustful of each other's motives) with the other two demonstrating 'enabling dynamics', where members expressed a sense of interpersonal connectedness and an overall sense of clarity around shared goals. While constraints only added to the disabling groups' collective sense of frustration, the enabling groups viewed them positively. They were even willing to self-impose more. For the enabling groups, Rosso emphasized that communication was key, so that even when strong differences in opinion existed, they were dealt with explicitly rather than ignored. He continues:

> Teams experiencing enabling dynamics demonstrated an enhanced sense of playfulness, not just in the team dynamic but in their approach to challenging problems. These teams projected the aura of a group playing a game. The game (R&D) had clear rules and boundaries (constraints) and was very serious in its high stakes, but it was attractive in its challenges ... and enjoyable in the process

of playing. In such a 'game', freedom and constraint were not perceived as oppositional forces but as vital dualities of the creative process. As a result, these teams were not only willing to accept the constraints they faced, but they actively imposed constraints on themselves because they found them to enhance their creativity. In other words, they found freedom in constraint. (Rosso 2014: 577)

The playful reframing of experience does not so much remove constraints as ensure those present are perceived as a source of stimulation rather than frustration. Although playframing can be used to highlight the presence of and, in some cases, negotiate the temporary removal of selected real-world constraints, more often than not, extrinsic constraints are left in situ and their impact minimized by the foregrounding of explicitly negotiated/self-chosen playful constraints and challenges. Rules, roles and boundaries are voluntarily established or negotiated within play not only to coordinate action and harmonize goals but also to challenge power structures and provide respite from extrinsic pressure. While totally binding, playframe terms can be renegotiated time and again. Sutton-Smith goes as far as to stress that play should be considered 'as much the activity of oscillating in and out of [playframe] negotiations as it is the dramatic content that those negotiations allow' (Rosso 2014: 305). Approaching creative practice in terms of playframing also has the benefit of promoting intrinsic motivation, with situations defined as a figurative field of opportunity and challenge: a clearly defined field of play. Amabile emphasizes that challenge, intrinsic motivation and sustained task engagement go hand in hand (1996). Getzels and Csikszentmihalyi similarly emphasize how stimulation provided by 'the challenge of the problematic' (1976: 240) is a basic human neurogenic need.

Creative-risk taking

Risk can be written into playframes, just as might challenge. Creative-risk taking has been acknowledged as an important creativity-relevant skill (Amabile 1996) and one that is facilitated by adopting a playful (paratelic) frame of mind (Apter 1982, 1991). As drummer and composer Stewart Copeland asserts regarding his love of unscripted, spur-of-the-moment improvisations onstage: 'The worst musical train wreck hurts absolutely no one' (2009: 248). A telic (serious) framing of the same situation might cause performers to fear the consequences such a public *faux pas* might present in terms of influencing future ticket sales. A playful frame of mind, however – one in which paradoxical thought, ambiguity and risk are not only tolerated but experienced as pleasurable – is conducive to the flux-like processes inherent in creative thought and action. Robert Fripp of King Crimson once confided that his band's musical effectiveness was a function of their ability to take creative risks:

> If you work with hazard, the situation's not guaranteed. The point there is: 'We're all good players. We're all good pros. We'll make things safer. We'll put on a good performance.' And that's it. It's only mechanical – a very wonderful, smoothly working, efficient machine. But so what? It doesn't go beyond that. I like to work with very good professional musicians who go beyond being professional. It's only a level of craft. It takes you to the point from which you leap; you're very high up and you jump. And because you're high up you might fly a long way, or you might go straight down with a crash. You can either play safe and that won't happen; but neither will you take off and fly. Or, you build the hazard into the situation, so things can occur, and sometimes they might go wrong. (Mulhern 1986)

Minimalist composer Terry Riley concurs:

> I think that music has to have danger, you have to be right on the precipice to really be interested, not gliding along playing something you know. If you never get on the brink you're never going to learn what excitement you can rise to. You can only rise to great heights by danger and no great man [sic] has ever been safe. (Nyman 1999: 145)

It is not difficult to think of performers whose career trajectories and onstage behaviour has embodied Riley's advice, as has their approach to creative practice. Iggy Pop immediately comes to mind. It could be argued that those with personality *traits* (i.e. enduring characteristics) predisposed to dangerous behaviour have something of an advantage when it comes to taking creative risks. Adopting the paratelic *state* (i.e. a temporary condition) brings out the Iggy Pop in all of us, since doing so pushes consequences out of phenomenological view, turning any experiential 'car crash' into a 'roller-coaster ride'. Fortunately, in art and music all such joy rides need only be figurative. XTC co-founder and songwriter Andy Partridge comments, 'I like accidents. I like to put myself in the way of musical harm. I like being at the wheel of that musical car, and aiming it at the wall, just to see what shape the car's going to come out. It might come out an interesting shape that would have taken me forever to decide on otherwise' (Partridge and Bernhardt 2016).

Suspending habits and assumptions

Another way of exploiting creative pathways that might otherwise go unnoticed or seem inconsequential is to playfully question things one might normally accept as givens. Koestler states 'the discovery of hidden analogies . . . the bringing into consciousness of tacit axioms and habits of thought which were [previously] taken for granted; the un-covering of what has always been there' (1964: 120) is one of the great hallmarks of creativity, which he describes as 'an act of liberation – the defeat of habit by originality' (1964: 96). While ways of thinking that are rutted can be derailed by incongruity in imagination, there may even be times when one has no choice but to re-examine the very foundations of one's value system in response to some real-life incongruity. Gerald Casale of the band Devo recounts how being a witness to the Kent State Massacre in 1970 influenced his subsequent work as an artist and musician:

> witnessing the Kent State Shootings on May 4 1970, changed me. I was one way before that day on campus, standing there about 30 yards from the National Guard with their M1 rifles, and then I was another way after they shot. Until then I was pretty much a live and let live, somewhat pretentiously intellectual hippy . . . [later] My friends were actually encouraging me to join the Weather Underground – who were the students who were militarised by this action – but I knew there were only two outcomes to that: jail or death. I was probably too chickenshit for that, but I was committed from that time on to make my art my aggression, to those people who were the illegitimate authority who were destroying democracy and keeping people down. All the voter suppression, the racism, the military spending, imperialism, it really is all just one big gestalt.
> (Kitching 2018)

The result was a playful manifesto called De-Evolution: a bricolage of 'quack theories', 'conspiracy theories' and 'alternate information' with which to ludicrously challenge the core tenets of everyday science and religion. Casale has since observed that although the concept was tongue-in-cheek, in many ways the modern world seems to be devolving in a manner that very much resembles their provocations. Lead singer Mark Mothersbaugh recalls that Devo was not originally intended to be a recording band but a form of agitprop or art movement (Kitching 2018). As it turned out, it was the musical component of their work that provided the most effective channel into the public arena, after several years of developing their ideas and presentations. As well as gigging in their hometown of Akron, Ihio, the band dabbled in film-making from the beginning, even winning first prize at the 1977 Ann Arbor Film Festival (McKee 2012) for their short film *In the Beginning Was the End: The Truth About De-Evolution* (1976). The music that Devo made together was an attempt to ridicule and reject the bourgeois by creating an alternate world – one that rejected even their own previous musical identifications. Casale recalls:

> Mark I [*sic*] and I were very different but there was an underlying agreement on our world view, and we hated the same stuff. That's always important when you're young. Mark loved everything we told him about De-Evolution. He jumped in and the two of us agreed, from jamming twice, that we would not do the music we were previously doing. He would never do these progressive rock covers again and I would never do the blues again, but we would sit down and do something original, and as soon as it sounded like anything you've already heard, we had the right to tell the other one to stop it. We made that a rule, jokingly among ourselves, and we pretty much stuck to it, and this is how the Devo cannon [*sic*] of songs came about, between 1974, and when we erupted onto the world stage in 1978. (Kitching 2018)

The Oblique Strategies

One effective way of suspending habits and assumptions is to randomly disrupt or derail them. At times, it may be simply enough to shift one's focus or consider things from a different perspective. These are some of the approaches that producer Brian Eno and artist Peter Schmidt chose to adopt when they co-developed the 'Oblique Strategies' cards (Tamm 1995). Each card features a brief provocation intended to inspire a fresh approach to the creative task at hand. They can be consulted like an oracle, shuffled and chosen randomly whenever one feels a creative impasse has been reached, or just for the fun of it. The cards have been offered for sale as limited editions at times, with their number and content varying somewhat between editions. Websites also exist that offer randomly generated text derived from the original print editions (such as Harrison n.d.). Eno explains how the cards came about:

> The 'Oblique Strategies' evolved from me being in a number of working situations when the panic of the situation – particularly in studios – tended to make me quickly forget that there were other ways of working and that there were tangential ways of attacking problems that were in many senses more interesting than the direct head-on approach. If you're in a panic, you tend to

take the head-on approach because it seems to be the one that's going to yield the best results. Of course, that often isn't the case – it's just the most obvious and – apparently – reliable method. The function of the Oblique Strategies was, initially, to serve as a series of prompts which said, 'Don't forget that you could adopt *this* attitude', or 'Don't forget you could adopt *that* attitude.' (Taylor 2003)

Using the cards can be considered a form of playframing negotiation, since selecting a card is to choose to be influenced in some way by its advice or to consent wholesale to its terms. Dayal (2009) comments that when the cards contain directives, Eno does in fact follow them faithfully, even to the point of erasing whole song recordings if the card demands so. Examples include (all Harrison n.d.): 'discover your formulas and abandon them'; 'emphasise the flaws'; 'take a break'; 'ask your body'; 'think – inside the work – outside the work'; 'short circuit (example; a man eating peas with the idea that they will improve his virility shovels them straight into his lap)'; and 'do we need holes?' Perhaps, most pertinent to our discussion is, 'where's the edge? where does the frame start?'

The cards were used during the making of David Bowie's *Heroes* album (1977), one of four albums on which Eno and Bowie collaborated. Bowie explains that during the making of the album, Eno and himself spent most of their time together joking and laughing: 'I think out of all the time we spent recording, forty minutes out of every hour was spent just crying with laughter' (Sheppard 2009: 252). He goes on to add that the rules of each card were followed strictly: 'It was like a game. We took turns working on it; he'd do one overdub and I'd do the next. The idea was that each was to observe his Oblique Strategy as closely as he could. And as it turned out, they were entirely opposed to each other' (Sheppard 2009: 254).

In play, practitioners can use make-believe to reimagine the natural and social worlds as they see fit, adopting, discarding and swapping everyday roles in the process. As Sutton-Smith points out, role reversal is one of the key characteristics that differentiate play from other forms of social frame flexibility (1979: 317). 'Reverse roles' was the directive given by one Oblique Strategy selected during the making of David Bowie's 'Boys Keep Swinging' (1979a) on his next album *Lodger* (1979b). The resulting record sounded less slick than Bowie's usual fair and more like a garage band (so fashionable at the time), with drummer Dennis Davis playing bass, guitarist Carlos Alomar playing drums and so on (Sheppard 2009). Talking Heads did the same on their album

Speaking in Tongues (1983) with the band members swapping instrumental roles in order to get a more 'naive' sound and to keep things fresh.

Role-play and make-believe

Since Brian Sutton-Smith's theory of 'play-as-performance' (1979) reveals so much of the method behind what seems like the madness of play, now is a good time to reiterate its tenets. Irrespective of the actual number of participants involved, four roles are ever present in play: if only in imagination. These roles include the director(s) who establish, or negotiate, a safe communicational frame on behalf of real or imagined spectator(s) (this is the context); then we have the actor(s) and counter-actor(s) who engage in some form of contrastive action to the extent that the above frame affords (i.e. the dramatic text) (1979: 300–1). Even in solitary play, all four roles remain, though internalized. These roles are modelled upon the earliest experiences of play between adult and child and can be conceived as either 'actual or implicit characteristics' of play (1979: 298).

A playframe is therefore a context awaiting a text. When a 'director' suspends the ways of the real world for a time in play, a new context can be presented that opens up a range of alternate possibilities, limits and challenges for the 'actor(s)' and 'co-actor(s)' to respond to. Producer Brian Burton (aka Danger Mouse) explains how he reframed a situation in imagination for collaborator Karen O:

> So you can put her in a different environment and watch what happens.... What happens if you stick this person in this environment or this time period, and see how they act? I think about music that way: 'What would happen if Karen was alive at this point in time and was singing here?' It was like sticking an actress in an environment. (Sheffield 2019)

In this example, Danger Mouse uses framing to provoke new responses from an experienced artist. Famed theatre director Robert Wilson – who has collaborated with Laurie Anderson, Lou Reed, Tom Waits and David Byrne – describes how frames can be also used in a more facilitative manner, such as in the case of working with young artists:

> One key is always to listen. If you listen to the individual they pretty much will tell you the direction one should go. As a director, you're someone from the outside so you just give a frame for them. So, usually, I try to find a frame that I

think is appropriate or right for this individual and then you let that person fill it in. And the frame is not so important. It's how you fill in the frame; that's what's important. (*An Interview With Robert Wilson on 'Absolute Wilson'* 2006)

In popular music, roles can take many forms, relating to functions within the music-making and record-production processes (as mentioned previously) or even dramatic functions within the actual music and lyrics. The use of characters to inspire new perspectives or explore subject matter in a more relatable fashion is not uncommon in popular music. In terms of songwriting, Paul McCartney is notable for having written many musical vignettes that examine the lives of fictional everyday characters (e.g. 'Eleanor Rigby' (1966a); 'The Fool on the Hill' (1967b); and 'Ob-La-Di, Ob-La-Da' (1968a)). Similarly, Peter Gabriel, during his time with the band Genesis, invented not only convincing protagonists but, arguably, even more memorable dramatic foils. For these, he sang through each character's personae rather than about them: complete with highly individual, and often ludicrous, vocalizations. Notable examples include the Winkler in the song 'Get 'Em Out by Friday' (1972) and the Reverend in 'The Battle of Epping Forest' (1973). Arguably, the greatest and most prolific of all post-war songwriters to use characters in his work is Ray Davies of the Kinks. Davies's lyrics (and music) employ characters and their social, cultural and historical contexts in such a wide variety of ways – ranging from the music-hall satire of 'Plastic Man' (1969) to the thinly veiled autobiography of 'Two Sisters' (1967) to its US A-side, the sublimely cinematic 'Waterloo Sunset' (1967) and beyond – that an entire book would be necessary to do justice to this one aspect of his work.

Though broad themes or imagined vistas commonly provide musicians and composers with inspiration, at times they can also be used as impromptu cues with which to get collaborators to join in a game of musical make-believe. The resulting artefact may not necessarily evoke the same idea for the listener, but it nonetheless remains an effective strategy for coordinating collective action. Genesis guitarist Mike Rutherford shouted out, 'Pharaohs going down the Nile!' during a group jam session (Fielder and Sutcliffe 1984) as part of the writing process for the album *The Lamb Lies Down on Broadway* (1974b). He did so to encourage his bandmates to sustain and further develop a particular mood that he saw as promising. The resulting improvisation (caught on cassette tape by drummer Phil Collins) was later used during the song 'Fly on a Windshield' (1974a). Over the years, the band continued to give their taped improvisations titles encapsulating the material's mood. In addition to providing an effective means of locating material on their cassettes, it also ensured that future developments could be judged according to whether or not they added or detracted from the original mood.

At times, musicians take on (multiple) identities in a broader context than single songs in order to free themselves from the weight of their own musical legacy. One of the most famous examples of role-play and make-believe in popular music is the Beatles taking on the identity of Sgt. Pepper's Lonely Hearts Club Band in early 1967. It was a device that allowed the band to reject their own legacy and venture into musical territories that would otherwise be deemed not 'Beatle-ish'. David Bowie famously developed the concept even further during the 1970s, adopting and discarding various personae over the course of several albums: Ziggy Stardust; Aladdin Sane; Halloween Jack; and the Thin White Duke.

Parliament-Funkadelic bandleader and Brill Building alumnus George Clinton's use of characters was more like that of an eternal pantheon, observing that 'characters evolve but people are confined to their generation' (Rennison 2018). By creating an elaborate Afro-futuristic 'P-Funk' mythology, including alter-egos Dr Funkenstein and Sir Nose D'Voidoffunk, Clinton et al. were able to maintain a high level of creative freedom, navigating their way through sea changes in popular-music taste and integrating disparate influences over the years: 'It let us go wherever we wanted' (Rennison 2018). Even Parliament and Funkadelic – sibling bands with different musical and lyrical emphases – were but masks for what was, essentially, the same collective of musicians signed concurrently to two different record labels. Clinton's idea that personalities or genetic codes can transcend individuals and eras, he says, has its equivalent in modern-day record production: 'Samples from records are the same as DNA samples from lifeforms. . . . It's the same thing. Cloning became the thing. . . . It's the funk that is the clone and the character. . . . As long as that vehicle is there, P-Funk is still that' (Rennison 2018).

Framing creative practice using make-believe in order to promote creative freedom and longevity arguably reached its zenith in the form of a 'virtual' band created by Blur frontman Damon Albarn together with Tank Girl co-creator Jamie Hewlett. Described by Albarn as 'a genuine collective' (Elliot 2001), Gorillaz was initially created as a comment on the 'manufactured' pop bands of the time. It also functioned as a vehicle for Albarn to embrace a diverse new set of musical influences beyond the 'adolescent guitar band' paradigm he was losing interest in. Albarn confessed that singing 'through' a character like 2D allowed him to take creative risks that the public might otherwise balk at given his Britpop background, such as singing in styles like reggae (Elliot 2001). This sense of imaginary delegation is echoed by Hewlett when he commented: 'If you're going to pretend to be somebody you're not – which is the whole point of being a rock star – then why not just invent fake characters and have them do it all for you?' (Gaiman 2005).

Informed by a one-page manifesto (long since lost) and complete with the fictional band members 2D, Murdoc Niccals, Russel Hobbs and Noodle – each possessing elaborate backstories, as detailed in a ostensible 'autobiography' – Gorillaz has allowed Albarn to embrace remix culture and collaborate with artists as varied as Deltron 3030, reggae bassist Junior Dan, De La Soul, actor-director Dennis Hopper, mash-up producer Danger Mouse, Afrobeat-jazz drummer Tony Allen and, even, Elton John. The musical component of Gorillaz is, however, no more important than the band's fictious narrative, art, extensive body of animation and website: all overseen by Hewlitt. Both Albarn and Hewlitt admit to being more-than-happy to address new audiences through the medium of these characters: 'The older audience knows it's us two . . . but the best audience for Gorillaz is your 12 and 13-year-olds. They're probably getting the most enjoyment out of it, because they're not thinking, Oh it's those two wankers. There's different levels. If you're not interested in the characters you can just get into the music,' says Hewlitt (Elliot 2001). Albarn adds, 'I'm happy to be making music for kids. I don't give a fuck. I know who I am now, and I want to make music that people love. It's as simple as that' (Elliot 2001).

The Brill Building sound and bubblegum

The name *Gorillaz*, it would seem, is a thinly veiled reference to the prototypical 'manufactured' band, the Monkees. Starting out as an attempt by TV producers Bert Schneider and Bob Rafaelson to translate the energy and offbeat humour of the Beatles' *A Hard Day's Night* (1964) to the small screen, the series starred Davey Jones, Mickey Dolenz, Mike Nesmith and Peter Tork as an out-of-work pop band. In his capacity as Screen Gems music head Don Kirshner – who previously had success with his stable of Brill Building songwriters including Gerry Goffin and Carole King, Jeff Barry and Ellie Greenwich, Barry Mann and Cynthia Weil, and Neil Diamond (among notable others) – was responsible for organizing the music. The Brill Building 'sound' was not so much defined by a place – Kirshner's Aldon Music was located nearby at 1650 Broadway – or even a genre but an ethos. It was a return to the made-to-order music for teens by seasoned professionals, after the grass-roots recording artists of the rock 'n' roll era started to fall out of fashion.

While Kirshner's function was more akin to that of a record-label boss than a producer, he was still answerable to Rafaelson and Schneider (whose father, Abraham Schneider, was the president of Columbia Pictures). With the exception of a few token tracks written and produced by Nesmith, Kirshner was determined to tightly control all aspects of the music-production process, using the actors merely as singers. Tensions mounted when Nesmith complained that the public was being duped into thinking the music backing was being performed by the actors also (no mention of session players was featured on the record sleeves). Nesmith and Tork, soon followed by Dolenz and Jones, began to push for musical autonomy and Kirshner was eventually let go after Nesmith threatened to quit. The 'group' later realized, however, that Kirshner's contribution was perhaps more important than they had appreciated.

Some two years later, Kirshner was inspired to work with another 'virtual' band that, like the Monkees, had their own TV series aimed at a young audience. This time, there would be no risk of the talent revolting since they were animated cartoon characters. This new arrangement resulted in the hit 'Sugar, Sugar' (1969) written by Jeff Barry and Andy Kim and released as the Archies: the highest charting song of 1969 ('The Billboard Hot 100: 1969' 2007). When the Archies performed on *The Ed Sullivan Show*, an animated segment ('Sugar, Sugar' 1969) was broadcast to play along with the pretence that the performers on the record were cartoon characters. The success of the Archies resulted in a number of similar cartoon (and live action) children's TV shows featuring virtual bands including Josie and the Pussycats, the Groovy Goolies and the Partridge Family. These acts provided an effective conduit through which music-business people could service a market niche without the need to be tied down to any one 'face' or production team. This was, however, an approach to making and promoting records well established by makers of bubblegum music long before the Archies hit the scene.

The name *bubblegum* refers to a late 1960s marketing strategy spearheaded by Buddah Records promotions manager Neil Bogart, together with Jerry Kasenetz and Jeff Katz of 'Super K' productions. Together, they developed a working method where songwriters and producers were subcontracted to make catchy singles aimed at children and young teens in a garage-rock-meets-novelty-song style: think 'Louie Louie' by the Kingsmen (1963) meets '(How Much is That) Doggy in the Window' (1953). The twist, however, was that the records were released by 'bands' that didn't actually exist. While the songwriters who operated out of the Brill Building had to plug their wares to famous performers in order to make their income, Super K simply 'cut out the middle man', releasing directly to the public what might normally be considered 'demo' records (i.e. recordings passed on from publishers to performers, in place of sheet music, to show how the songs went). This isn't to say that the records were of lesser quality than might normally be the case – if anything, the opposite was true – but the emphasis was on servicing a perceived market demand rather than having to deal with would-be celebrities and their egos. As well as instilling a sense of competition between the various teams involved and providing feedback during the writing and record-production process to ensure that the songs all had a 'contrived innocence' to them, Kasenetz and Katz made up (and owned the rights to) all the names of the bands that supposedly performed on the records.

The genius of the bubblegum approach was that if a song did happen to be a hit, a group of young musicians could be put together to go out and play the songs in concert or on television as if it was they who were on the record. Tracks such as 'Yummy, Yummy, Yummy' (1968b), 'Chewy Chewy' (1968a), 'Sweeter than Sugar' (1969), 'Simon Says' (1967), '1, 2, 3, Red Light' (1968), 'Indian Giver' (1969) and 'Gimme Gimme Good Lovin'' (1969) were released under the monikers of the Ohio Express, 1910 Fruitgum Company and Crazy Elephant. Prominent writer/producers involved in the first wave of bubblegum between 1968 and 1972 included Jeff Barry and Andy Kim, Joey Levine, Artie Resnick, Ron Dante, Toni Wine and Ellie Greenwich. Another production team hired by Super K at the time included English songwriter Graham Gouldman and his colleagues, Kevin Godley, Lol Creme and Eric Stewart. Having, together, written and produced some twenty or so songs for Super K at their own fledgling Strawberry Studios facility in Stockport – all of which were released under a variety of pseudonyms (including Ohio Express and Crazy Elephant) – the team gained invaluable experience that helped inform their later chameleon-like, pan-genre approach to record production as the band 10cc in later years.

In the UK, bubblegum had a 'glam' element to it, with writers Nicky Chinn and Mike Chapman, and producer-writer Phil Wainman working with bands like Sweet, Mud and the Bay City Rollers. The Bay City Rollers were signed to the US label Bell Records, whose roster at the time also included the Partridge Family, David Cassidy, Tony Orlando and Dawn, Barry Manilow and ex-Monkees Davey Jones and Mickey Dolenz (as well as the entire Monkees' back catalogue). Bell eventually morphed into Arista Records with the help of ex-CBS Records head Clive Davis and was responsible for signing a number of key alternative and new-wave acts including Lou Reed and Patti Smith. Chapman later went on to produce hits for the CBGBs band Blondie, while the Bay City Rollers (along with the Brill Building sound that was such an obvious influence upon them) and bubblegum in general became key formative influences on another CBGBs act: the Ramones.

The Ramones adopted a highly stylized musical and visual approach including comic-book personae, with hair and wardrobe developed with their 'art director' Arturo Vega. The band also are noteworthy for having paved the way for punk rock internationally, as well as a number of bands that have adopted the band-as-caricature approach. The Cramps are one such act who seem to have jumped out of a 1960s B-movie/sexploitation flick and generally celebrate early rock 'n' roll's relationship with American taboos. Bands that have more recently taken up the Ramones mantle include the Aquabats – ostensible superheroes who battle monster villians onstage and have their own kids TV series – and Peelander-Z, who describe their approach as 'Japanese Action Comic Punk'. Peelander-Z look and sound something like equal parts the Wiggles, Japanese Manga and the Ramones, with each member boasting their own emblem colour and totem-animal costume. Like the Aquabats, Peelander-Z embody an approach to music that emphasizes the importance of fun and imagination. At their live shows, the band involves the audience both onstage and off, encouraging them to participate in their performances and even hosting TV-game-show-like contests.

Performance art and movement

In addition to using characters as a means of framing creative practice, other elements derived from the dramatic arts have also been used to good effect to help shape popular music. Performance artists such as Laurie Anderson, Meredith Monk and Mimi Goese have all made a name for themselves making very original music in a manner that breaks the mould of the serious singer-songwriter artist sitting deep in thought at their instrument dreaming up platitudes. These artists' music often emerges from a conceptual frame and in tandem with the movement of their bodies when performing. So much so that, at times, their music would be inconceivable divorced from physical expression such as dance, mimicry and other gestures. Monk and Goese's vocals have a particularly kinetic quality with melodies that seem to dance and leap in terms of pitch, rhythm and dynamics. Anderson's voice often tends more towards the monotone, sometimes engaging the audience with wry spoken-word observations that are not so far removed from stand-up comedy. At other times, she disguises her voice using vocoder synthesis to take on the 'viewpoint' of male characters or mimic voices of 'authority'. Movement (often amplified as larger-than-life back-drop silhouettes), dance and the reversive use of traditional instruments were a big part of Anderson's conceptual art/music since the early 1970s, including a suit fitted with internal drum machine triggers, a MIDI-keyboard necktie and a violin retrofitted with a tapehead bridge allowing her to play tape recordings fixed to her bow. Listening to these three artists' music alone makes less 'sense' than when their performances are experienced first-hand or via the medium of film or video. Cases in point include Anderson's 'Drum Dance/Smoke Rings' from her performance film *Home of the Brave* (1986), Monk's video for 'Turtle Dreams' (1983) and Goese's filmed performance of the song 'Second Skin' with her band Hugo Largo, complete with *faux* knife play (*Hugo Largo Profile* n.d.).

Even in more traditional band settings movement can be a key element for organizing performances and getting musicians to play together in a coherent and musical manner. Iggy Pop recalls how at early Stooges recording sessions his bandmates couldn't perform effectively unless he danced along as they played. The band were so used to playing that way onstage that without his idiosyncratic movements to cue them, the music just didn't have the same 'groove' (*Gimme Danger* 2016). Similarly, Bootsy Collins explains how playing for James Brown, and in Africa as a guest of Fela Kuti, both singers' bodies gave vital rhythmic cues for their musicians to match:

> [Fela Kuti's] rhythm was impeccable. Like James [Brown], every move he made, we had to watch. We had to make sure we had a hit for it . . . [*makes series of stab sounds*] We had that down, but we had to study the rhythm of his body. It wasn't that we were forced to do that. But if you wanted to be with James Brown, that's what you did. We loved doing it, just to see if we could do it. (Noz 2011, italics in original)

Actor, counter-actor and contrastive action

Playframing can help artists to face challenges, circumvent obstacles and adapt to change. When, through the eyes of play, life is understood as 'an endless series of oppositions . . . external (and sometimes internal forces) [that] one must fight' (Henricks 2008: 175) a degree of objectivity and detachment is possible that might otherwise be hard to attain. In play, such contests are experienced in a manner that is vivifying and life affirming. In fact, contrastive action can be understood as the powerhouse of play and expressive behaviours in general. Karen O concurs:

> That's something I've always liked to do in my work – something to push against. The wave against my surfboard is people saying, 'No, you can't do that.' You think I can't do that? I'll fucking do this in your face, motherfucker . . . 'Rebel outsider kids, unite!' Music is where I get to be that person. I'm a pretty shy, reserved, mild-mannered day-to-day person, but in that arena, that's where I get to be Destroyer and Defender of All. (Sheffield 2019)

In the following example, drummer Bill Bruford explains how he was invited to participate in a reformation of King Crimson in the mid-1990s that was to take the form of a 'double-trio' (i.e. two groups of guitar, bass and drums). Although initial efforts to co-ordinate his and co-drummer Pat Mastellotto's approaches were 'fairly fruitless', the answer to this particular creative challenge lay in reframing their outlook using a 'dramatic' premise. Bruford recounts:

> I said hello to Pat and Pat said hello to me and we really started work. I'd never heard of Pat before other than from the theme song of *Friends* [1994–2004] and I wouldn't have known that at the time. I didn't really know what to do with him nor him with me. We sat and practiced a bit and initially it was fairly fruitless and we couldn't think what to do until the penny dropped: what you do is adopt a character, a musical identity to make this work. Pat was essentially Ringo Starr connecting with the audience and I was essentially Jamie Muir or Elvin Jones upsetting, or terrorising or floating round and causing confusion with that connection. Once you'd adopted those kinds of characters and agreed that that was a great way to go then everything else is easy and after that everything fell into place. In a way it was a reversal of Jamie Muir's playing off of me on *Larks' Tongues In Aspic* [1973], I was the straight good boy and Muir was this creature from hell. I didn't know what to do with him or him with me. My function was to locate a beat and play it. So, something of a reversal and I think it worked really well. (Singleton 2016)

Given that roles in play can be actual or implicit, actors and counter-actors can take on many forms and degrees of complexity. As Henricks points out, 'People not only play with one another, they play with their own bodies and minds, with the elements of the physical environment, and even with cultural forms like ideas, norms, and language' (2008: 164). Anyone who has ever tried to make music using an unfamiliar software application (or instrument) will appreciate the true nature of opposition. As Zagorski-Thomas (2014) points out, technological actors are not passive recipients of one's best intentions but attempt to influence the user via their 'design scripts'. Machines can be as stubborn and quirky as any human collaborator.

Even within the music itself actors and co-actors play out a drama. Mertens describes traditional Western music as essentially 'dialectical' since 'development follows from the presence of a conflict between the opposites and finally leads to a situation of synthesis, in which conflicts are entirely or partially resolved. This can be called *narrative* by analogy with the evolution of a classical novel, in which the dénouement resolves the conflicts of the plot' ([1983] 2007: 17, italics in original). Mertens' discussion of the 'ups-and-downs' of conflict powering tonal music parallels Sutton-Smith's description of the drama (i.e. text) of play as involving '*a controllable and dialectical simulation of the moderately unmastered arousals and reductions of everyday life*' (1979: 309, italics in original).

When compositional elements are understood as 'actors' and 'counter-actors', it is possible for composers to emphasize their role as 'director' and 'audience', by-and-large, leaving the ensuing drama up to someone (or something) else: as have many experimental composers during the post-war period. This is why Brian Eno has stressed the importance of listening in his creative process (Tamm 1995). In the case of generative or 'algorithmic' music, these roles are taken to their extreme, so that the composer sets up the rules, roles and limits of the frame, and then sits back to observe the resulting process unfold. Even in a more traditional Western songwriting context, the analogy stills holds, given that a particular work might seem to emerge before the writer in imagination, as a result of its internal compositional dynamics. In this latter case, contrastive elements might include, among other things, musical motifs, 'call and response' phrases or lyrics – perhaps describing the interactions of a protagonist and antagonist. In arranging, the interplay of instruments with different pitch ranges and/or textures, similarly, provides interest via conflict. This can occur in a duel-like manner such as in a *concerto* and, to a lesser degree, within its modern-day (mini-) equivalent, the eight-bar *solo* (both of which feature single instruments struggling to overcome the might of a larger ensemble).

Biting off as much as you can chew

The art of record production can best be understood as a constellation of discreet creative problems, related tasks and subtasks. As Albin Zak states, record production combines 'musical and technological ideas and actions in a multifaceted creative process . . . each of which leaves its traces on the sounding musical surface . . . [including] songwriting, performance, arranging, recording and mixing' (2010b: 321). Before Bob Dylan and the Beatles ushered in the era of the singer-songwriter, each of these processes was handled by separate individuals (or teams) having little-to-no contact with each other. Today, in addition to integrating multiple musical roles within any given practitioner's DAW-based creative experience, technical activities also commonly form part of the process.

Realizing one's creative potential is not just a matter of acquiring domain-relevant skills and knowledge. It is also largely a matter of matching them to current challenge. Every time an individual or group sets about engaging a creative task, big or small, the opportunity exists to negotiate its terms. Those relating to the size, complexity and/or difficulty of tasks, in particular, can impact not just the quality of the experience but indicate which frame of mind is best suited to a particular chunk of the process. There are, of course, times when circumstances beyond one's control dictate which options are available. Nonetheless, understanding how task type, size and challenge level relate to knowledge, skills, motivation and group dynamics will help practitioners to figuratively bite off as much as they can comfortably chew, and in doing so, promote optimal experience rather than anxiety or boredom.

A componential model of creativity

Whether a music maker is involved in heavy metal, EDM, roots music, jazz, pop, R&B, punk or folk, the distinct stages of creative action will be the same. Amabile's social psychology of creativity (1983, 1996) presents a model of creative process involving a linear sequence of five discreet stages that transcends domain boundaries. It is a sequence that can apply to any number of separate tasks or subtasks nested within any given project – each, perhaps, with their own discreet goals. It is a framework that also 'describes the way in which cognitive abilities, personality characteristics, and social factors might contribute to different stages of creative [action]' (1983: 357). The five stages of creative process defined by Amabile are:

1. **Problem or Task Identification:** Engaged in response to external or internal stimuli.
2. **Preparation:** 'Building up and/or reactivating store of relevant information and response algorithms' (Amabile 1983: 367).
3. **Response Generation:** 'Search memory and immediate environment to generate response possibility' (Amabile 1983).
4. **Response Validation:** 'Test response possibility against factual knowledge and other criteria' (Amabile 1983).
5. **Outcome:** Either: complete success is verified (finish); failure (finish); or, if limited progress towards the goal is deemed promising, loop back to an earlier stage and continue on.

The confluence of social-environmental variables that affect creative process do so by influencing the three components discussed by Amabile (1996) and mentioned in Chapter 3 (i.e. task motivation, domain-relevant skills and creativity-relevant skills/processes) which, in turn, are each responsible for the success of specific stages. To illustrate, stages 1 and 3 are influenced by task motivation: 'the most important function of [which] is the control of attention' (Amabile 1983: 371). Adopting the paratelic (playful) state can be beneficial here since doing so temporarily frames activity as an end in itself. It also directs attention to include aspects of the direct environment and potentially useful elements that might otherwise be ignored if the perceived goal was the prime focus. Moreover, since creative individuals may start off with little-to-no idea of a clear creative problem to be solved, the process of finding it might involve the figurative kaleidoscope of playfulness. So too, abilities associated with playfulness such as cognitive flexibility and spontaneity, together with tolerance of ambiguity and paradox are beneficial in stage 3, since this is where novelty should be introduced. A telic (serious) frame of mind is better suited to stages 2 and 4, on the other hand, since they involve critical thinking informed by knowledge and experience pertaining to a specific domain. One could sum up by saying that stages 1 and 3 are appropriate zones for one's inner fool to stir things up and take risks. Stages 2 and 4, however, benefit from one's inner expert providing a broader 'network of possible wanderings' (Newell and Simon 1972: 82) and informing decisions about the usefulness of responses generated in stage 3.

Amabile's model makes good sense: define a goal; gather what one needs; try a variety of approaches; appraise your efforts; and, if you don't first succeed, try, try again (or quit while you're ahead). For those whose experience of creative practice is anything but clear-cut, Getzels and Csikszentmihalyi's (1976) observations regarding problem finding will come as something of a vindication. In this landmark longitudinal study, it was found that artists who had no clear idea of their goal (i.e. the creative problem needing to be solved or how they might solve it) when starting work were later judged (i.e. some eighteen years later) to be more successful, according to the standards of their artistic community, than those who had a fixed goal set in their minds at the outset (Csikszentmihalyi 1990: 277). In fact, the authors went as far as to split the students into two main groups, accordingly: the 'problem solvers', who produced more generic, unimaginative work; and the 'problem finders', who had to discover their own creative problem as it emerged out of play before they could solve it. While the former group looked 'on the problem as familiar and the [compositional] elements as new; the other [problem finders] look[ed] on the elements as familiar and the problem as new' (Getzels and Csikszentmihalyi 1976: 154).

In terms of understanding Amabile's model of creativity, what is crucial is that for problem finders, the creative problem only becomes evident when it emerges from the process of producing a response to it! And, perhaps, only after the problem has been solved!! This does not mean that a clear goal was not present from the outset but that it lay at a level below everyday consciousness (Getzels and Csikszentmihalyi 1976: 247). If, at the outset, one were to ask what the problem finder's goal was, their response might be nebulous at best. In such cases, it might be necessary to go through Amabile's stages more than once, with a slightly modified and better-defined goal emerging each time (in response to artefacts that arose in the previous iteration). Identifying, isolating and saving promising material that emerges from jam sessions for later use is a common practice among improvising musicians. The fact that one idea or artefact might seem fruitful while another doesn't shouldn't necessarily mean that an artist needs to articulate why, but merely that they trust their instinct to further develop it.

A key aspect of keeping creative process on track with regard to goals (conscious or otherwise) is feedback. The importance of moment-to-moment feedback in creative action cannot be overstated, not least of all because it is a precondition of flow (optimal experience). Csikszentmihalyi, who coined the term, states that only when attention is directed to intrinsic task-related feedback, rather than extrinsic factors, can this optimal state be attained. He adds that even in creative activities where clear goals are not obvious from the start, practitioners should be able to sense whether or not they are moving in a fruitful direction as they progress (1990: 55).

Miles Davis, one of the most influential performer-composer-bandleaders of the post-war era, was known for wandering the stage at concerts, sauntering up to his collaborators and staring at them as they played. This was his way of emphasizing that they should be focused on listening intently to the overall musical fabric as it emerged, together with their own contribution, instead of falling into the trap of playing prescribed 'licks' to impress the audience. This was not to say that relying on tropes or displays of virtuosity was undesirable, but rather that each phrase played should respond to a particular type of feedback. Davis, who often played with his back to the audience, was defiantly declaring what he saw as the primacy of the ensemble in the collective creative process. He was drawing his band member's attention away from the powerful influence audiences can exert and back towards the dynamic and ever-shifting musical drama unfolding on the stage. One could strongly argue that Davis was trying to encourage less of a 'performance' and more of a jam session, wordlessly emphasizing the importance of issues intrinsic to the musical task over the lure of extrinsic rewards and gratification (*Miles!* 2011).

Optimal experience

Csikszentmihalyi states that human beings divest a great deal of time and energy attempting to alleviate the anxiety and boredom that results when consciousness is disordered (1975). He stresses that even culture itself is a grand structure designed to ward off psychic chaos en masse. 'Optimal experience', or 'flow' for short, is a pleasurable state where 'information coming into awareness is congruent with goals [and] psychic energy flows effortlessly' (Csikszentmihalyi 1990: 39); skills are matched to challenge; and clear feedback is forthcoming. And since flow arises when goals are framed as ends-in-themselves, Csikszentmihalyi also refers to it as 'autotelic' experience. He adds that flow is more likely to be experienced by people with the ability and predisposition to playfully reframe experience and/or restructure their environment so that intrinsic motivation is maintained (i.e. those possessing an 'autotelic personality'). Similarly, 'autotelic activities' are described as those featuring a degree of novelty and challenge conducive to people testing and expanding the limits of their abilities (1975: 30). Either way, 'whether the structure is internal or external, the steps for experiencing flow are presumably the same; they involve the same process of delimiting reality, controlling some aspect of it, and responding to the feedback with a concentration that excludes anything else as irrelevant' (1975: 53–4). Flow can also occur in groups when individual goals are in harmony.

Although the concept of autotelic experience has much in common with Apter's paratelic experience, the two are not coterminous. Flow, for example, does not include states such as boredom (Apter 1982: 65) or unstructured negativism. Apter suggests that flow is, instead, one type of paratelic experience. Since both Apter and Csikszentmihalyi's approaches to adult play are phenomenological (i.e. concerning the experience of playfulness rather than specific activities), they transcend what Csikszentmihalyi argues is the arbitrary distinction between work and play. Therefore, when experiencing the autotelic and paratelic states, real-life consequences (even danger) may well be present, but they no longer inspire fear or anxiety.

Csikszentmihalyi makes another important distinction regarding flow states with different levels of complexity. He states that flow is a continuum ranging from 'macroflow' at one extreme, which can occur during structured activities of sufficient complexity (such as composing music) or where the stakes are high enough (like performing surgery or rock climbing), so that action and awareness merge to a high degree and self-consciousness abates, all the way to simple unstructured 'microflow' activities – 'like doodling or chewing gum' (1975: 54) – which, while far less enjoyable, nonetheless alleviate boredom and anxiety. The subjective dimensions of optimal experience include the following:

1. focus of attention (concentration): a merging of action and awareness in 'a limited stimulus field' (1975: 40);
2. clear goal(s) and immediate feedback: 'It is clear when you are doing right or wrong' (1979: 260);
3. time sense becomes warped;
4. feeling of heightened control, while feeling personally detached from the results of one's actions.

Workflow and playframes

Practitioners often refer their preferred patterns for going about creative tasks as their 'workflow'. Although most often expressed procedurally, workflows can also be embedded within workspaces conducive to carrying out predetermined operations in an efficient and reliable manner (as in the case of project-studio design and layout). In instances where projects have clear goals from the outset and a more or less predictable path to completion, a workflow is indeed an appropriate tool. In cases where creative goals are not yet clearly defined or where a heuristic approach is required (i.e. where there is no clear precedent to solution), however, then the 'one-size-fits-all' nature of a workflow might hinder the generation of many novel and/or appropriate creative pathways.

Whereas a workflow is by definition facilitative (often 'set and forget' in nature), a playframe's raison d'être is as much disruptive as it is enabling. A playframe will also be open to renegotiation in response to moment-to-moment feedback as the work emerges. Although playframes are more likely to resemble a set of provocations or proscriptions rather than the algorithms (i.e. set creative pathways) built into a workflow, they can still be saved for later use (e.g. as in the case of the Oblique Strategies). A playframe will also typically be a comparatively smaller affair, less monolithic and more likely to facilitate one-off tasks or subtasks than workflows. And although they are less efficient, the trouble taken to plan and implement a playframe's temporary rules, roles, restrictions and affordances will pay off in terms of the influence they exert over subsequent action. The caveat that playframes should be only be established temporarily, or within limited spatial zones, must be stressed if the negativism that is so often 'part and parcel' of playfulness in adults (Apter 1991; McDermott 1991) is to be contained within context-appropriate, safe and consensual boundaries. Workflows and playframes can therefore be used in combination, according to the creative needs of the moment.

Given that Csikszentmihalyi has theoretically unpacked the flow state and its preconditions, it would be a shame to not take advantage of this knowledge, so that playframing can be used to foster optimal experience. In particular, playframing can be an effective way to set up situations where all involved: have their skills and challenges optimally matched; have clear goals – or are given adequate autonomy in the case of problem finding so that they can follow their intuition; receive regular feedback (i.e. anything that signals the current state of play so that practitioners can tell if they are getting 'warmer' or 'colder': for example, an appropriately balanced headphone mix during recording); or have goals that are in harmony with their collaborators.

Playframing can also be used to lower or heighten the challenge bar and to limit options and incoming information to that which is relevant to the task at hand. As Csikszentmihalyi notes, 'One cannot enjoy doing the same thing at the same level for long. We grow either bored or frustrated: and then the desire to enjoy ourselves again pushes us to stretch our skills, or to discover new opportunities for using them' (1990: 75). In cases where an optimal skill-to-challenge balance is lost, it can be regained in the following fashion:

1. if skills are too high, then challenge can be increased (i.e. 'raise the challenge bar') or a handicap can be adopted;
2. if skills are too low: the challenge level can be decreased ('lower the bar'); collaborators with better-matched skills can be enlisted; or the situation can be reframed so that only sub-goals are addressed at the present time.

Another advantage of possessing an understanding of flow is that commissions, briefs and other extrinsic directives can be reframed in imagination so that their goals are used in the service of enjoying the activity: that is, work responsibilities can be transformed into fun challenges so that the *experience* is one of playfulness (with all its creative benefits).

The following chapter focuses on the topic of negotiation and how this matter relates to playframing.

5

Negotiations

Whenever practitioners set out to make music together, negotiations take place. This topic is discussed at length in Simon Zagorski-Thomas' *The Musicology of Record Production* (2014): a work informed by the triangulation of actor-network theory (ANT), social construction of technology (SCOT) and Csikszentmihalyi's systems model of creativity. According to Zagorski-Thomas, schemata derived from past experience and/or configuration by actors within a network influence how individuals think and act: to the extent that the environment (which includes other actors) affords it. In this context, configuration is defined as 'the alteration of a person's conceptual model of a phenomenon' (2014: 172). Further, 'All forms of configuration, and therefore power relationships, are negotiated. Persuasion, the creation of trust and any other social activity that involves the exercise of power or concerted activity can be seen as a process of aligning two sets of goals through reconfiguration' (2014: 152).

A key benefit of applying ANT to record production is how doing so addresses the issue of tacit assumptions and their influence upon perceptions, thoughts and action. The use of the term 'actor' is a potential source of confusion, however, since in ANT terms it can denote anything at all that 'acts or to which activity is granted by others' (Latour 1996). This can refer to humans, non-humans, the corporeal and, even, the incorporeal (e.g. 'background assumptions, methodologies, techniques, social rules and institutions, routines, experiments . . . [and] external objects', Detel 2001). The term 'actant' will be used herein to indicate actors as conceived by ANT and to differentiate them from the actors and co-actors described by Sutton-Smith (1979) as (explicit or implicit) characteristics of play.

While Zagorski-Thomas mentions Goffman's 'dramaturgy' (1956) as a schematic approach congruent with his own model, he does so merely in relation to role-playing, stating: 'members in a team activity need to negotiate the roles they perform not simply in terms of what one member chooses to do but also in respect to how the other members may choose to "play along" with that performance' (Zagorski-Thomas 2014: 161). Role-play and make-believe are not the only ways in which play can be used as a form of negotiation. Understanding drama in terms of contrastive action extends its relevance to include the dynamic interplay between humans and non-humans or even incorporeal actants such as machines, ideas, motifs, themes or any other aspect of composition or record production that can be identified.

Play as negotiation: The fine print

Play is, among other things, a form of power management, conceptual reorganization and an effective means of coordinating individuals' behaviour. Within play, elements that would otherwise be considered incompatible can be reconciled in a dialectic manner with potential to be 'vivifying and euphoric' (Sutton-Smith 1979: 309). It is these properties that make Sutton-Smith's theory of play-as-performance a powerful theoretical framework with which to unpack aspects of creative process related to negotiation, particularly where task motivation and creativity-relevant processes are integral. The process of playframing can also be used to influence how attention is directed and experience interpreted in creative-practice settings. As Csikszentmihalyi notes, 'Almost any description of the creative experience . . . includes experiential accounts that are in important respects analogous to those obtained from people at play' (1975: 37). Playframing addresses the underlying schemata that inform decision making, but in an oblique 'as if' manner. Sutton-Smith's theory can be applied equally well to verbal social negotiations or structural ones resulting in the manipulation of restrictions and affordances encountered within music-making environments.

Playframe negotiations will, at the very least, encourage participants to unselfconsciously focus on the present-moment concerns of task engagement and, preferably, ensure all concerned have access to what they need to get 'in the zone'. The latter entails: banishing from the frame issues irrelevant to the task at hand; structuring tasks and roles so that challenge is high enough to warrant deep concentration (together with immediate task-relevant feedback); ensuring all necessary tools are at the ready and optimally matched to the users' skills and preference; as well as distributing tasks and roles to reflect individuals' tastes and preferences. Although optimal experience (flow) is encouraged, boosting intrinsic motivation – even in a less-than-optimal manner – is the chief concern. Similarly, goals will be present, but it is the enjoyable experience of pursuing them that matters most since that is what determines how much time and effort will be devoted to tasks. As Apter states, when an activity is approached in a playful manner, 'the main thing is to travel hopefully, not necessarily to arrive' (1991: 16).

There is no correct or incorrect way that playframe negotiations might take place. They may be relatively formal (e.g. expressed as rules, verbal agreements, written terms of engagement or even as manifestos) or casual (e.g. using gestures or other subtle signs and acknowledgements). Playframe terms can be embedded within the design of procedural, physical or software systems and bespoke devices and instruments. They can also be used to disrupt patterns of behaviour and the usual intended use of devices. Group cohesion, inclusiveness and (at best) coordinated optimal experience (i.e. group flow) can be facilitated by harmonizing individual goals and encouraging tolerance of speculation. In cases where clearly defined goals have yet to emerge, playframe terms can be renegotiated as goals more clearly emerge out of successive iterations of playful interaction.

Irrespective of whether framing negotiations are extensive and detailed or, conversely, minimal and/or subtle, they should nonetheless be explicit. It should be acknowledged that within the bounds of the frame this situation is to be perceived as an end-in-itself, otherwise frustration awaits those not 'in on the game'. All involved should feel they have the potential to make a valuable contribution irrespective of how things play out. At times, this might entail sacrificing one's own level of activity – maybe 'leaving space', 'sitting out' or playing only 'in the pocket' – in order to support another individual or the group as a whole. The work of Stax Records' house band Booker T and the MGs is exemplary in this regard.

Even when music is made in solitude, music makers can choose how to frame task engagement so that extrinsic forces are either mitigated or aligned with intrinsic motivators in a 'synergistic' manner (Amabile and Pratt 2016). Once again, this can be done in imagination or by restructuring the task and/or environment. And since the project studio is inhabited by innumerable digital actants, solo practitioners can choose to reject or renegotiate the 'design scripts' configuring these inanimate counter-actors and the affordances they present (Zagorski-Thomas 2014).

Playframe terms can be set in a manner conducive to producing a certain class of divergent responses rather than a single 'best' one: within these limits free play can occur. Additional restrictions can be 'written into' the frame at any time to adjust the skill-to-challenge balance, level the playing field or to simply produce a different class of results. Depending upon time constraints, judgements (i.e. Amabile's stage 4: 'response validation' (1983, 1996)) can be made regarding the appropriateness or usefulness of artefacts at a later time, at set intervals or even concurrently by a third party (as might a producer or an orchestral conductor using gestures to encourage or discourage certain behaviours in real time). Producers Brian Eno and Daniel Lanois have both used feedback in the studio as a means of affecting artists' performances: setting up public address (PA) type foldback-speaker mixes instead of headphones; recording overdubs in the 'control room'; and, even, altering headphone mix cues in real time.

A playframe should also be understood to be a safe space and that, within it, creative-risk taking is encouraged. Participants can elect to leave the frame at any time and 'time out' called at any point. As well as forming subgroups in order to break tasks down into subtasks, these can also be used to align the frame of mind of participants in various ways. It should be kept in mind, however, that imbalances of power may be so great that, at times, those with the upper hand simply veto any attempt by others to veer from a predetermined (but perhaps unspoken) creative path or demarcation of roles. The following recollection by producer-engineer Hugh Padgham (from his time working with the Police on their 1983 album *Synchronicity*) is a case in point:

> [Stewart Copeland] said that he wanted to overdub a hi-hat on one of the songs.
> I didn't agree with him but due to the tensions flying around, I said, 'OK let's do it. Then I'll play it to Sting to see what he thinks after lunch.' So after lunch I play the song to Sting and he says, 'What's that fucking noise in there?' I said, 'It's a high-hat that Stewart recorded this morning – what do you think?' 'I think it's shit and I don't want it on MY song.'
> 'OK, well let's talk to Stewart and say we think it's unnecessary,' I said. 'No, I want you to erase it immediately now while I'm standing here,' he said. (Weiss 2018, upper-case emphasis in original)

Collaboration

Negotiating with collaborators entails defining creative goals, structuring activities and working environments, assigning roles and responsibilities, coordinating behaviour and so on. Each participant may or may not have a clear idea about these aims can best be achieved, but once points of view are voiced, the process of configuration begins in earnest. Zagorski-Thomas (2014) explains that configuration can occur in the following ways (n.b. the term 'actor' is used here in the ANT sense):

1. Suggest or invite the creation or reinforcement of a grouping or role between actors.
2. Reinforce a tentative or ambiguous aspect of the recipient's existing model.
3. Demonstrate – provide an example of activity that conflicts with some aspect of the recipient's model of a process.
4. Provide information that conflicts with some aspect of the recipient's model.
5. Suggest a narrative – by describing an event, person or thing in a way that involves a model of a process that differs from the one the recipient currently holds.
6. Exert physical control – this could be between human actors or could involve the design/physical structure of an object configuring an actor's behaviour or altering some aspect of their model.
7. Contradict some aspect of the recipient's existing model.
8. Give an instruction that causes the recipient to alter some aspect of their existing model. (Zagorski-Thomas 2014: 172–3)

Zagorski-Thomas continues, describing the various types of communication that can be used to configure actors socially:

1. language style of the spoken word;
2. musical sound (e.g. it might demonstrate the tonality or rhythm);
3. sound (timbre);
4. tone of voice;
5. passive/unconscious body language;
6. active gesture or movement;
7. language style of the written word;
8. other visual symbols (e.g. on a computer screen or music notation);
9. moving images. (Zagorski-Thomas 2014: 173)

If one accepts the premise that conflicting schemata in individuals form the ground against which all contrary positions are figured, then surely playfully reframing situations to temporarily but 'utterly suppress the ordinary meanings of the world' (Goffman [1974] 1986: 43) is a far easier course of action than trying to uncover and negate deeply embedded assumptions and habits one at a time. Furthermore, since the aim of response generation (stage 3) in creative process – which accounts for a great deal of collaborative activity – involves divergent production, there should be no reason that multiple viewpoints should impede that aspect of creative action. If anything, they will actually enhance the process – irrespective of which creative pathways end up 'paying off' – provided that activities are structured to handle divergence (where appropriate) and that tact, patience and goodwill prevail among participants. This is more likely to occur when an atmosphere of playfulness permeates proceedings.

In order to fully appreciate how framing negotiation in terms of play can impact the art of configuration, it is instructive to consider Goffman's ([1974] 1986) observations regarding play and how they might resonate with Zagorski-Thomas' description of options for configuration:

a. The playful act is so performed that its ordinary function is not realized. *The stronger and more competent participant restrains himself [sic] sufficiently to be a match for the weaker and less competent.*
b. *There is an exaggeration of the expansiveness of some acts.*
c. The sequence of activity that serves as a pattern is neither followed faithfully nor completed fully, but is subject to starting and stopping, to redoing, to discontinuation for a brief period of time, and to mixing with sequences from other routines.
d. A great deal of repetitiveness occurs.
e. *When more than one participant is to be involved, all must be freely willing to play, and anyone has the power to refuse an invitation to play or (if he is a participant) to terminate the play once it has begun.*
f. *Frequent role switching occurs during play, resulting in a mixing up of the dominance order found among players during occasions of literal activity.*
g. The play seems to be independent of any external needs of participants, *often continuing longer than would the actual behavior it is patterned after.*
h. Although playfulness can certainly be sustained by a solitary individual towards a surrogate of some kind, solitary playfulness will give way to social playfulness when a usable other appears, which, in many cases, can be a member of another species.
i. *Signs presumably are available to mark the beginning and termination of playfulness.* (Goffman's [1974] 1986: 41–3, italics added for emphasis)

A key benefit of using playframing as a negotiation tool is that conflicting viewpoints can be explored and reconciled in a manner resembling a fun game more than a serious power struggle. In the following example, Kevin Godley demonstrates how the four members of the band 10cc – all of whom were songwriters, instrumentalists and more-than-capable singers – were able to negotiate in a humorous manner that encouraged participation and a sense of competition without anxiety:

> For the most part it was an egoless situation. We created an environment whereby egos didn't intrude too much. It was really all about the work. It was really all about, 'Who's going to sing this?. . . . Well you start. You try it first. You go in the studio.' And someone would attempt to sing this song, and the others would stay in the control room. If it was shit, they'd hold up a sign that said, 'Next!'. . . . Like scoring figure skating, 'Four out of ten!' In other words, we tried everything and everyone. Everybody would get a shot, mainly vocals, because not everybody played every instrument, but mainly [for] vocals this process came into being. I would go in, and it wasn't my key. So, 'Next!' Eric would try it, and it was in his key, 'Right, you do it. But let's all have a go after it,' and it became self-evident which was going to work best. (Personal communication, 28 June 2018)

Negotiations can be also influenced in a less direct fashion by encouraging participants to adopt a playful frame of mind prior to working on music and, in doing so, removing barriers to cooperation and speculation. The Beastie Boys ensured that when they built their own G-Son studios in the early 1990s that the large studio/rehearsal space included a small basketball court and skate ramp so they could have fun in between jam sessions and recording (Levy 1998). As Ziv notes, creating a 'fun mood' is an important determining factor in how individuals interpret stimuli:

> The tension release aspect of laughter and its contagious effects can influence group cohesiveness. This in turn reduces social anxiety. We know that one of the greatest obstacles to divergent thinking is the fear of criticism from one's social environment. The pressures to be practical, logical and economic in our thinking are trademarks of our cultural values. If social anxiety is somewhat lessened, if judgmental attitudes are not taken as too menacing, 'adventurous', novel and original ideas are more easily expressed. (1989: 114)

Fields of play

Another benefit of playframing is that individual behaviours can be coordinated without necessarily converging towards a single predetermined goal. That creative practitioners should be afforded a degree of autonomy within limited boundaries has been a staple of post-war experimental music ever since John Cage – who described his approach as 'purposeless play' (1961) – argued in the early 1950s that composers could let go of control and share some their power with performers and the audience without putting themselves out of a job. Cage suggested that rather than filling up compositions with intentions, it might be more interesting to ask questions: with a given performance being just one of any number of possible answers (1961). And while it is individual composers who design these frames in the art-music tradition, popular-music acts like Sonic Youth have since demonstrated that experimental approaches can be set up in a collective manner. In Sonic Youth's case, this included the use of: 'prepared' guitars; bespoke non-traditional guitar tunings that varied from song to song; unconventional, playful (though often punishing) ways of extracting sounds from their instruments; and bespoke software systems programmed using the Max/MSP platform. Composer, musicologist and critic Michael Nyman writes:

> Experimental composers are . . . more excited by the prospect of outlining a *situation* in which sounds may occur, a *process* of generating action (sounding or otherwise), a *field* delineated by certain compositional 'rules'. . . . Experimental composers have evolved a vast number of processes to bring about 'acts the outcome of which are unknown' (Cage). The extent to which they are unknown (and to whom) is variable and depends on the specific process in question. Processes may range from a minimum of organization to a minimum of arbitrariness, proposing different relationships between chance and choice, presenting different kinds of options and obligations. (1999: 4, italics in original)

Nyman (1999: 6–9) goes on to list the predominant process types adopted in experimental music as follows:

1. **Chance determination processes:** systems within which random elements replace compositional intention.
2. **People processes:** performers may use suggested or mandatory material according to their own inclination or ability (within varying degrees of limit).

3. **Contextual processes:** 'concerned with actions dependent on unpredictable conditions and variables which arise within the musical continuity' (1999: 6).
4. **Repetition processes:** short musical or sonic events repeated at length, and usually foregrounded. Some of the materials often used include single notes, small melodic motifs, contrary-motion and parallel-fifth figures, *ostinati*, short chord progressions, arpeggios, spoken word, tape loops and echoes. These are combined, at times, with people and contextual processes, additive rhythms, cyclic patterns or ongoing 'phase' shifts as organizational techniques and so on. As with Op art, extensive repetition of simple figures can give rise to naturally occurring (in this case, psychoacoustic and acoustic) phenomena not actually present in the score, so that audiences (and the physical environment) can be considered active partners in the 'creation' of the music.
5. **Electronic processes:** ranging from those that utilize electronic systems to compositions where the system is the actual embodiment of it. That is, performers might be free to interact in any way they see fit with a circuit or system designed and built by the composer. Anything that occurs as a consequence can be considered a particular performance of that 'piece'.

As Eno points out, the music-as-process approach that stemmed from Cage and the Fluxus composers was embraced not by the music establishment but, instead, by young art students in the late 1960s (Nyman 1999). Serious musicians were interested in the 'difficult' atonal music and the exacting standards of serialist composers like Pierre Boulez, Karlheinz Stockhausen and Luciano Berio. Theirs was music that demanded subservience to the will of the composer, formidable technical skills and, despite rejecting 'tonal music' was, in fact, the logical culmination of the Western concert music tradition. Any music outside of that tradition (residing beyond the 'temple' of the concert hall, as it were) or, heaven forbid, was easy to play, pleasant sounding or unpredictable could not be trusted. Music with a capital 'M' was supposed to be about pure sound, not ideas or challenging perceptions. While Cage is unique in that he managed to coexist in both worlds (the serious and the playful) comfortably, his ideas were embraced and put into practice by those operating outside of the music establishment, while his actual compositions were what interested the bastions of the concert hall.

Nyman describes a seminal event that took place at Black Mountain College in 1952, as 'the first post-war mixed-media event', performed by John Cage, painter Robert Rauschenberg, pianist David Tudor, dancer/choreographer Merce Cunningham and the poets M. C. Richards and Charles Olsen. Interestingly, the various activities were organized simply on the basis of establishing temporal (and spatial) zones:

> For this star-studded occasion Cage provided a rhythmic structure, a series of time-brackets, or what Michael Kirby has called compartments. Once a performer's compartment had been signalled to start, he was free to act in any way he liked. The separate compartments were arranged to overlap one another so that a complex of differently timed, completely independent activities, each with its own time-space, was produced. (Nyman 1999: 72)

The concept that collaborative action can be about sharing ideas rather than having any one party controlling proceedings is well established in popular-music circles – particularly when players are invited to participate based upon respect for their previous work. Bootsy Collins suggests musical collaboration can be fun when players have respect for each other and possess the humility necessary to put the needs of the music first (as opposed to someone's ego). Furthermore, he likens leaders to servants rather than controllers:

> You can't control this creative force; nobody can. With all the examples we get, haven't we learned anything yet? It ain't about controlling nobody. It's about having fun with each other, sharing with each other, and not dictating. 'I own you.' 'No, you don't own me!' That's the crap we've been put on. It's not just musicians and artists, it's the world. But I think musicians and artists can help change that. That's what I'm looking forward to, is first for us to get that out of our minds. When you're in a studio, it ain't about dominating, unless you're called on. . . . Because certain times you have a thing and you want it to go a certain way. Nothing is wrong with that. But as long as you develop the attitude of service, the attitude of, 'What can I do for you today?' I walk in the studio and it's, 'What do you want me to do?' 'Oh man, we want you to just be you.' 'Well, that don't tell me nothing. What do you really want me to do?' That to me is where we can grow and be the leaders of tomorrow. Not controllers of them all, but leaders. (Noz 2011)

Record producer Daniel Lanois is one such 'leader' who has built a healthy career on being of service to his clients: 'When I go into the studio: head down; be creative; support the house philosophy; obey the house rules; deliver a masterpiece, and get on with your life' (*Daniel Lanois* 2012). If he adds his own musical parts to recordings, it is usually to accentuate certain grooves or provide supportive elements for the performers to build upon. It is in the mixing and sonic processing stages, however, where Lanois' personality usually gets to shine through.

Using spaces as physical fields of play is another key aspect of Lanois's approach to record production. His use of zones (together with electronic systems) is as structurally 'persuasive' as it is facilitative. Based on his own experience as a recording artist, Lanois is acutely aware of the influence various spaces and set-ups have upon practitioners' performance and frame of mind. Instead of describing traditional studio spaces in terms of control rooms and recording areas, he refers instead to the 'ideas room' (think overdubs and verbal debate/discussion) and 'engine room' (think loud, visceral performances and non-verbal interactions) respectively, in order to clarify the relationship between context and resultant text.

Lanois likes to build temporary studio set-ups in locations such as beautiful old houses, disused cinemas or anywhere that might inspire (or configure) the recording artist: even castles. This approach attempts to background technical considerations – resulting in something akin to a musical playground or 'boutique' studio experience – having finalized all technical issues before the artist arrives, so they can enjoy making sounds immediately and with as little distraction as possible (Scoppa 2010). Lanois confides that artists often feel that they owe him a good performance since he has already indulged them so, having constructed a bespoke space just for them. Rather than just provide one large monolithic performance space, Lanois also prepares performance subspaces he calls 'stations'. Each has its own idiosyncratic sound and may include, for example, a specific instrument plugged into a well-suited amplifier via a particular effect pedal, together with a certain microphone placed just so. Each station remains in an ongoing state of readiness and no small part of the chain may be borrowed to be used elsewhere. In this way, each station has its own unique and unchanging character, always available for when inspiration strikes, and so that performances can be captured easily and immediately (Massey 2009). With the noise of technological concerns and the unfamiliar blocked out, performers can focus on playing with whatever limited (but carefully crafted) options each station affords without distraction. Neil Young comments regarding his experience working within one such Lanois set-up: 'A lot of the sounds . . . were right there in the room. So I was immersed in the overall tone of the song from the beginning. Which meant . . . I was able to have a really good time' (Scoppa 2010: 36).

Another artist who understands the importance of capturing sonic events as they occur (just as one might catch a never-to-be-repeated moment with a photo Cartier-Bresson style) is Tom Waits:

> These days I want to be [in the studio] before anyone has had a musical thought. . . . If you are making a record you are the one saying 'action', and you are the one saying 'cut' and you have to be sure that the most interesting thing is not going on outside the frame. I try to pay attention to what people are doing the moment they come into the room. If they are just goofing around before we begin that may be the best thing they do all day. I have to be waiting. (Adams 2011)

Playing the field

If Csikszentmihalyi's systems model of creativity tells us anything, it is that the interactions between a person, domain and field are a form of collaboration:

> before a person can introduce a creative variation, he or she must have access to a domain and must want to learn to perform according to its rules. This implies that motivation is important. But it also suggests a number of additional factors that are usually ignored, for instance, that cognitive and motivational factors interact with the state of the domain and the field. (1999: 327)

One of the greatest challenges arts practitioners have to face is to attempt to introduce novelty into their chosen domain(s). Usually, such efforts are met with resistance from the field, since part of its role is to determine which artefacts and concepts will (and will not) be accepted and integrated into the domain. As Gardner acknowledges, 'Judgements of creativity are inherently communal' (1994: 145). It is worthwhile noting that Csikszentmihalyi (1999) acknowledges that since the general public's access to the domain of popular music is greater than, say, the world of science, the former's field is less able to enforce its judgements.

At times, a field might not only applaud innovation but celebrate the innovator as well. In some extraordinary cases, ideas and products can have such an impact that the domain receiving them must change in no small way in order to accommodate them. In humanistic terms, Taylor (1975b) refers to this process as 'transactualization' (i.e. a cultural extension of individual self-actualization). Feldman concurs: 'We know that domains change because they are transformed by great creative effort . . . the unique interplay between a remarkable individual's mind and a domain's most challenging problems' (1999: 178). People can influence domains in more subtle ways as well. The 'misuse' of technology is a good example. Eno describes how using devices in ways not originally intended by the designer can bring about a 'constant dance' between artists and technologists:

> as soon as the technology sits there, then some person . . . comes along and thinks, 'Hmm, you know you could do something else with that that nobody's ever done before.' So then they do that. And then, of course, somebody else, a technology designer, says, 'Oh, the tool they're using for that could be much better. I'll redesign the tool.' And then this person says, 'OK, that's a new tool.' (Warren 2013)

Just as technology is often reappropriated, symbols and memes can be 'misused' as a means of increasing an artist's standing in the wider sociocultural context of creativity. So-called reality television – like the publicity stunts of yesteryear – is one popular way of indirectly 'gatecrashing' the domain of one's choice. Another, more imaginative 'in' can be the use of make-believe and mimicry. David Bowie is one such artist who, having collaborated with dancer, mime artist and choreographer Lindsay Kemp in the late 1960s, decided to employ performance-art concepts to increase the impact of his music. It was, however, a process that took considerable time and experimentation to implement successfully. Despite having had a hit record some two years earlier, by 1971, Bowie had yet to become a star. 'Space Oddity' (1969), the song that had briefly propelled him into the spotlight, tapped into the space-race *zeitgeist* near its climax, with the moon landing imminent. Moreover, both the song and the record's production ingeniously mined the fear, uncertainty and claustrophobia that shadowed mankind's collective aspirations for the 'final frontier' (the song was inspired by the film *2001: A Space Odyssey* (1968)). If Bowie had succeeded in connecting with the public's imagination that one time, he had yet to learn how to do so in a manner that he found creatively satisfying. This disconnect can be attributed to the fact that his first three LPs 'were vehicles for self-analysis and bitter reflections on the culture around him. They spoke *for* him, but not *to* anybody' (Dogett 2011: 10, italics in original).

Invigorated after a short American radio tour, Bowie began toying with the theme of celebrity on his upcoming album *Hunky Dory* (1971). While the album was well received critically, Bowie's big breakthrough had to wait until the follow-up *The Rise and Fall of Ziggy Stardust and the Spiders from Mars* (1972), when he resolved to not only sing about fame but actually embody it: onstage and off. Together with his close collaborator, photographer Mick Rock,

Bowie embarked on what Rock describes as a 'propaganda' campaign including publicity photos, promotional 'film clips' (i.e. videos) and the hiring of real bodyguards (despite having no real need for them). Rock remembers, 'It was all designed to give people the idea, "Who's this guy? Well, we don't know who he is, but he's got these bodyguards and a personal photographer. He must be a big deal!"' (*Shot!* 2016). The ruse worked, and soon after, Bowie was no longer a pop music 'king for a day' but a long-reigning one:

> Little of the music on those albums was beyond the imagination of Bowie's peers; much of it was overtly indebted to his predecessors, especially the Beatles and the Rolling Stones. What marked Bowie out as a unique talent were the themes of his songs, and the way in which he sold them (and himself). Nobody had ever manipulated the tools of pop stardom so blatantly, and with such stunning impact. (Doggett 2011: 10)

Flux this shit!

Just as flow (optimal experience) depends on certain readily identifiable preconditions, it is social, cultural and historical factors – as much as any one individual's efforts – that determine whether or not a person or group's interactions with the domain and field will amount to a healthy flow of ideas:

> In order to establish and preserve criteria, a field must have a minimum of organization. However, it is often the case that instead of serving the domain, members of the field devote most of their energies to serving themselves, making it difficult for new ideas to be evaluated on their merits. . . . If a historical period is stagnant, it is probably not because there were no potentially creative individuals around, but because of the ineptitude of the relevant fields. (Csikszentmihalyi 1999: 326)

When members of the field take *themselves* too seriously – as sentinels of time-honoured, immutable institutions rather than part of a larger process – the time is ripe for someone to come along and give them a 'good kick in the pants'. Dada and punk are obvious examples of groups of artists that revolted against the status quo. Less well known and harder to define perhaps (but arguably more influential) was the international multi- and interdisciplinary network of creative individuals known as Fluxus.

Fluxus was informed by a truly rebellious and often jokey DIY ethos. If John Cage's ideas were about changing one's inner experience, rather than the institution in which one operated, then Fluxus (named in reference to 'flow' and 'effluent') was more about saying 'It's not *me*; it's *you* [the field] who's the problem!' Inspired by Cage, Dada and Duchamp, Fluxus artists had in common a desire to purge the world of 'constipated' arts institutions, their 'Europanism', the fetishism of artworks and commercialized culture. Practical, low-cost 'living art' and 'anti-art' made for, and by, everyday people was the order of the day: made using whatever materials and means they had at their disposal. Writing in *The New York Times*, art critic Ken Johnson (2011) described Fluxus in a fashion that bears a striking resemblance to Sutton-Smith's (1979) discussion of playframe negotiation – albeit on a global scale:

> What Fluxus was is a matter of some debate. Was it an art movement, an anti-art movement, a sociopolitical movement or, as the artists themselves tended to protest, not a movement at all?. . . . You could think of Fluxus as an international, utopian conspiracy to alter the world's collective consciousness in favor of noncompetitive fun and games and other peaceable and pleasurable pursuits. Their weapons of choice were feeble jokes, verbal and visual puns, satiric publications and instructions for absurd performances. Bypassing the commercial gallery system, Fluxus novelties were meant to be sold cheaply by mail and in artist-run stores . . . [Fluxus used] silliness to liberate the viewer from the usual categories of knowledge and the structures of power that keep them in place. (Johnson 2011)

Fluxus works took on any number of forms: often ephemeral. When products were made, they were usually provocative, if not bewildering. Piss and shit were sold as collectables, as were fluxkits (something like mini-art-compendiums-meet-goodie-bags) often containing small plastic boxes adorned with black-and-white labels – usually designed and assembled by colour-blind Fluxus 'founder' George Maciunas – and housing small conceptual collections like Shigeko Kubota's 'Flux Medicine' (*c.* 1968: actual and placebo medicines), Ken Friedman's 'A Flux Corsage' (*c.* 1968: seeds) and George Brecht's 'Games and Puzzles' (*c.* 1968: four plastic balls and two instruction cards). Other prominent names associated with Fluxus include Yoko Ono, La Monte Young, Nam June Paik, Benjamin Patterson, Alison Knowles, John Cale (of the Velvet Underground), George Brecht, Joseph Beuys and John Cage.

Unforced errors: Part 1

One of the more memorable and long-standing musical descendants of Cage and Fluxus was co-founded in 1970, by a group of fine art students and staff (including experimental composer Gavin Bryars) at Portsmouth Polytechnic. Throughout its ten-year performance history, the Portsmouth Sinfonia delighted, confused and infuriated concertgoers in equal measure. In order to fully appreciate the significance of this ensemble, one should keep in mind that symphony orchestras are feted cultural mini-institutions that bar entry to all but the most talented, celebrated and well connected. For a group of art students, dilettantes and otherwise interested parties – most of whom had little-to-no previous experience with their chosen instruments or score-reading ability – to bluff their way through much-loved classical repertoire was one thing, but to be guided by a conductor who possessed no feeling for rhythm whatsoever (or conducting for that matter) was truly audacious. Add to this 'injury' the insult that the Sinfonia became something of a cultural phenomenon, playing the Royal Albert Hall and releasing albums on major record labels (i.e. Columbia and Phillips) one is left to wonder how they managed to gatecrash their way into the art-music world.

Although it might be tempting to blame the Sinfonia's notoriety on their having a publicist, the fact remains that they were entertaining. They played light 'popular classics' such as Rossini's 'William Tell Overture' (c. 1828) and Johann Strauss's 'Blue Danube Waltz' (composed 1866) – along with concert material that had entered the public's awareness, such as Richard Strauss's 'Introduction' to *Also Sprach Zarathustra* – often arranged in truncated form (retaining just the 'well-known bits', Nyman 1999: 161). Keys, too, were changed if too many 'sharps' or 'flats' made playing overly challenging. The audience's familiarity with the repertoire was a crucial element of the experiment, since their sense of anticipation, when confounded, produced a funny (ha ha) effect rather than a funny (peculiar) one.

Despite being marketed as 'the world's worst orchestra' and winning *Rolling Stone* magazine's comedy album of the year in 1975, the orchestra was no gag or stunt. Anyone could join, provided they played to the best of their ability (whatever that might amount to) and attend rehearsals regularly. Other than that, performers were encouraged to move out of their comfort zone. If they had prior musical experience, they should play an instrument they weren't so familiar with. The rules and ethos informing the Sinfonia constitute 'textbook' experimental music (people) process since the will of the composer was distorted by 'unforced errors' inherent in the performers well-intentioned, but technically limited, renditions. Nyman explains:

> What one hears at a Sinfonia concert is familiar music, seriously dislocated (to a greater or lesser extent). The originals may be recognized only by their rhythmic

> content or there may occasionally be more than a whiff of familiarity about a tune. Rhythm in the Sinfonia is something not to be relied upon; most players get lost, are not sufficiently in control of their instruments to keep up the pace, may suddenly telescope half a dozen bars into one, or lose their place. Pitch too is a very volatile element; as some players will most probably, if unintentionally, be playing wrong notes, the vertical combination will be unpredictable... rather, pitch shape and melodic contour may be preserved. (1999: 162)

As in Cages' compositions, all these 'uncontrolled variables' (Nyman 1999: 162) result in no two performances of a given work ever sounding the same. And true to the Fluxus approach, everyday folk were given a cultural platform previously reserved for only a select few initiates.

In addition to Gavin Bryars' involvement, other notable Sinfonia members over the years included composer Michael Nyman, Brian Eno (who produced the Sinfonia's first two albums) and Clive Langer. Langer – who later went to co-produce artists including Madness, Elvis Costello and the Attractions, David Bowie, Morissey and They Might Be Giants with partner Alan Winstanley – feels that the Sinfonia might just have paved the way for the punk music phenomenon that erupted in Britain in 1976, and that it definitely influenced his own subsequent foray into pop music:

> [The Porstmouth Sinfonia] was just pre-punk... so there was a bit of punk ethic about it.... It had a lot of influence on [Langer's band] Deaf School.... We started this band in Liverpool Art College and we recruited people who were interesting looking rather than being great musicians. Again, a kind of pre-punk ethic... it kind of coincided with the idea that maybe we were a bit tone deaf, we weren't great musicians but we wanted to start an interesting musical band. (*In Living Memory* 2011)

Whether or not the Portsmouth Sinfonia actually inspired the advent of punk in the UK, both had in common an 'If *they* can do this, then *I* can certainly do this!' DIY ethos: one that creatively reinvigorated and democratized the British music scene in ways unseen since the late 1950s (with the skiffle craze) and early 1960s (with the rise of the Beatles).

While punk in the UK was a crucial development in popular-music history, arguably, its greatest legacy was that it cleared the way for a diverse array of post-punk acts to follow in the late 1970s/early 1980s. With limited musical skills and bare-bones production no longer seen as a handicap, small independent ('indie') record labels sprang up not only in London (e.g. Rough Trade, Mute and Do It) but as far afield as Glasgow (Postcard); Edinburgh (Fast Product); Manchester (Factory); Melbourne, Australia (Missing Link); Christchurch, New Zealand (Flying Nun); and in the United States, Atlanta, Georgia (DB RECS and Hib-Tone). If punk mirrored Dada in being nihilistic, reactionary and highly unstable, then post-punk stepped into the void punk left behind and took full advantage of the room to stretch out creatively. For a while (1978–84), it seemed like the proverbial lunatics had taken over the asylum, with bands like the Go Betweens, Joy Division, the Birthday Party and the Verlaines being lauded by the British music press, while indie bands Adam and the Ants, the B-52's, Depeche Mode and the Human League went on to enjoy chart success and their 'five minutes' of fame. In the case of R.E.M. and the Smiths, their impact went far beyond what anyone could have possibly imagined.

Working alone

While one has a greater degree of autonomy when working alone compared to working in a collaborative context, it is still necessary to deal with any number of actants, each of which influence proceedings in ways ranging from subtle to the formidable. Not least of these are one's current skill set and preconceptions regarding music making in general. Other common actants might include project briefs, available tools and facilities. While non-human actants won't talk things through with you (not yet, anyway) they will, nonetheless, exert pressure and constrain (as well as afford) action. In fact, an actant's power is never greater than when the practitioner is unaware of its influence.

One effective way of improving negotiation skills with non-human actants is to become familiar with them in situations where results don't matter. Although study can be beneficial, the act of doing arguably brings greater familiarity and provides a foundation for later playful interaction and true spontaneity (rather than impulsivity). This is because play occurs in settings that are familiar. In situations that are new, phases of exploration are required first before play can occur. Methodical approaches to navigating domain-skill issues such as workshopping or études (i.e. 'studies', where specific technical skills necessary to master a given genre, or composition, are isolated and repeated in many permutations: often within a quasi-compositional context) can provide the necessary familiarity and mapping out of the territory in question into manageable chunks. Simply choosing what stimuli is allowed into consciousness and providing a new context for it is a negotiation between practitioner and domain.

Playframing, too, presents an opportunity to conceptually isolate any actant and explore/play with it in a manner similar to études. If the prospect of devoting one's attention to a decontextualized component of the minutiae of one's craft seems boring then good. The Dylan example discussed in Chapter 1 is illustrative of the fact that play and playfulness depend on one's ability to isolate information, no matter how arbitrary, and familiarize oneself with it first as a foundation. Only then, can recontextualization through play begin. The more unstimulating the setting, the more necessary it becomes to bring-your-own (BYO) stimulation in the form of playfulness (i.e. how one chooses to structure the experience). To this end, anything that provides a context for performance and reception (i.e. the communicative aspect of play, whether between two or more people or even just in imagination, like the proverbial child singing with a brush 'microphone' in front of the mirror) can be thought of as a frame since it cues how the experience should be interpreted. As musician and filmmaker Jim Jarmusch observes, 'Genres are just frames – you can put whatever you want inside them' (Fear 2019).

Technology

The studio-as-instrument paradigm, today embodied in the ubiquitous DAW, has integrated the once separate acts of recording, editing and mixing music into a seamless process together with performance and (commonly) composition. While the logistics of record production in traditional studio complexes placed considerable pressure on practitioners, the tension was further exacerbated by the, often, contradictory goals of performers and technical staff (Zagorski-Thomas 2014). Working in a do-it-yourself (DIY) capacity with the aid of a computer can be far less stressful (depending on whether or not the software/hardware is equipped to facilitate your aims), if not fun. Less formal working environments and less time constraints can lead to novel approaches and happy accidents. Valerie Frissen writes:

> Playing with technologies has always been an important driving force behind technological transformation. This is even more the case in the digital era, which has given rise to a lively Do-It-Yourself (DIY) culture, in which amateurs and ordinary users have become prominent players in the technological game ... play offers an interesting angle to understand the characteristics of this DIY culture. In the digital DIY culture technology is used and tinkered with in an open-ended

way. In the process of playing around, new connections, ideas, and applications spring up. Improvisation, trial and error, and playing with the rules characterize these practices. Digital DIY practices are highly socially driven: collaboration and communication with others is a crucial element. The motivation of a digital DIY enthusiast is not so much to produce serious, intentional innovations, but is more intrinsically shaped by the fun and enjoyment of tinkering itself, which can be quite an absorbing pastime. Innovations are often just the accidental results of such processes. (2015: 149)

In the case of 'real' instruments, a fair degree of the time and effort spent learning how to play is dedicated to physically manipulating the device. Depending upon the design of the instrument in question – which is largely dependent upon how it excites air using either strings (chordophones), tubes (aerophones) or membranes and such (membranophones and idiophones) – corresponding fine motor skills need to be developed. Doing so to a level where consistently pleasing musical results are the norm can take years, even in the case of electric versions of the above (which often retain the essential design characteristics of their acoustic counterparts). Making music using DAW software capable of producing sound via synthesis, sampling and recordings has freed contemporary musicians from the tyranny of unforgiving, and inflexible, traditional instruments. These can be triggered in any number of simple ways, using either sequencers or in real time with trigger pads and small keyboards (i.e. computer or piano-style). Working with digital devices, however, can subtly, and unduly, influence the ways in which practitioners approach creative problems. Brian Eno explains:

There's still quite a lot of hate going on for me in working with computers. . . . You have to stay aware when you start working with a computer that you're on a very tilted playing field. You're more likely to do some things than others. It can be very interesting when you try to do something that isn't within the normal inclination of the computer. (Tingen 2005)

This idea is echoed by composer-performer Anna Meredith, who sees the computer as part facilitator, part tyrant:

I loved the fact that I was self-sufficient. That I could make this thing and then press spacebar and it would play. That felt great. So, it just felt like an evolving idea of getting more confident with working out how to make electronics work for me . . . and not let the idea of using software, or hardware, dictate what the music had to be. (*Anna Meredith* 2019)

Zagorski-Thomas (after Akrich and Latour 1992) frames the struggle between man and machine in terms of the 'antiprogram', which denotes a 'choice between subscribing to the program and using the technology in the manner it was designed, or de-inscribing oneself from the technology: rejecting or renegotiating the program' (Zagorski-Thomas 2014: 140). As James Gardner observes, examples of people renegotiating the design program of recording technology are nothing new: 'It's worth remembering that the phonograph was designed as an accessible recording device as well as one for playback, and instances of speedshifting, reversing, overdubbing and re-recording have all been documented as far back as the 1870s and 80s. As soon as sound could be stored and played back, people starting messing about with it' (*These Hopeful Machines* 2013).

It is not always necessary to engage with technology disruptively in order to assert one's will. Simply choosing one tool over another (i.e. one that is capable of performing the same task but in a dissimilar manner) can be an effective form of negotiation. Recently, a new generation of third-party 'plugins' have emerged that integrate seamlessly with the major DAW platforms but allow users to engage complex sound synthesis and effects processing with little-to-no understanding of the underlying principles involved. Their interfaces are often bold, colourful and irreverent, and include feedback in the form of playful animations. Instead of presenting one monolithic device with a multitude of controls over generic parameters (as is often the case with a DAW's inbuilt synthesizers and effects), some third-party plug-ins resemble the simple guitar effect pedals of the 1970s. That is, they do one thing well, have a minimum of controls and offer many different low-cost units to choose from.

The downside to all this new-found freedom is the sheer volume of software and hardware devices to be auditioned and integrated into one's 'workflow'. It is no small act of will to seek out and adopt devices appropriate to one's musical aims and matched to current skills. Developers are also starting to recognize the need for software that doesn't just make sounds but helps musicians to access materials (such as samples stored in different folder hierarchies) using intuitive, interactive audiovisual recall systems.

Kraftwerk and Kling Klang

One group that exemplifies an informed approach to negotiating with technology is Kraftwerk. Throughout the 1970s, Kraftwerk spent a great deal of time and effort tending to the creative-practice environment (Kling Klang Studios) they built and continually modified over the years. Despite humble beginnings, the studio was nonetheless crucial to the band's musical development, which was based around group improvisation. The original basic recording set-up provided a means to scrutinize their jam sessions for fruitful material and afforded the band greater creative autonomy via 'in-house' recording of their albums: although other, better-equipped studios were used for mixing. Much of the money the band made was invested back into the studio and, over time, Kling Klang grew into a largely self-sufficient creative haven.

Not unlike the Bauhaus before them, Kraftwerk – together with key collaborators engineer Conny Plank (up until 1975) and artist Emil Schult, a student of Fluxus artist Joseph Beuys – developed an environment where art, craft and technology came together as an integrated whole and where the facilitation of spontaneity and nuanced musical expression was key. After the creative and commercial success of their seminal album *Autobahn* (1974) – which the band saw as something of a blueprint for all future work – equipment and performance set-ups were designed to channel their creative energy towards specific designated themes, if not tone poems, and often featuring technological and kinetic *anaphones* (i.e. musical representations of actual sounds encountered in life). In addition to musical systems, visual prompts were adopted as a means of framing and harmonizing their individual creative efforts towards a unified field of play. Bespoke devices dedicated to facilitating the musical aims of each project were also put together with the help of friends trained in the relevant technologies (and, later, by employees) in workshop spaces adjoining the studio.

The ongoing development of Kling Klang, which the band likened to the tending of a garden, was done in a carefully considered fashion, since they were acutely aware that not only did they play their instruments but their instruments, in turn, influenced how, and what, they played. A similar amount of deliberation informed how Kraftwerk presented themselves as self-effacing men-machine hybrids onstage, inspired, in part, by the work of British 'sculptors' Gilbert and George:

> We started off 'Kling Klang' studio in 1970, which really marked the beginning of Kraftwerk. The studio was, in fact, just an empty room in a workshop premises that was a part of an industrial area in Dusseldorf. . . . We don't regard ourselves just as musicians but as Musik-Arbeiter (musical workers), and we designed and built up our complete portable studio set. . . . The physical layout of the equipment, besides being functional, was to imply the idea of the 'man-machine' . . . [where]

the music does not become dominated by one or the other. For example, some people perform with their musical machines built up high around them in an impressive way – we prefer the low profile image, bringing man and machine together in a 'friendly partnership' of musical creation. (Beecher 1981: 62–3)

Kraftwerk and Kling Klang became so inseparable that by 1981, the entire studio set-up could be taken out on tour as a multi-media live-performance rig. Today, the same can be achieved using personal computers running Max/MSP, Pure Data, processing or openFrameworks programming environments, with hardware interfaces based around Arduino or Raspberry Pi microprocessors.

Fag ends and lollipops

At the age of eighteen, Daphne Oram rejected an offer to study at the Royal College of Music in favour of becoming a sound-balance engineer at the British Broadcasting Corporation (BBC). Perhaps best known as the first director of the BBC's Radiophonic Workshop (which she co-founded in 1957 after many years of lobbying), Oram was also a successful freelance electronic composer, inventor, early champion of *musique concrète*, theorist and educator.

Employed to perform rudimentary tasks during wartime such as 'shadowing' performances of classical concert music (i.e. keeping a vinyl recording of the same work manually in sync with the orchestra should a sudden evacuation be necessary – the recording could then be 'punched in' as if the orchestra was still playing), Oram often stayed back after hours, building makeshift studios out of whatever equipment was at hand: only to have to disassemble them each time. The Radiophonic Workshop was put together in much the same way by reappropriating BBC surplus or junk equipment (referred to by the staff as 'fag ends'). The Army surplus shops of Lisle Street, Soho, were another ready source of cheap electronics 'plunder' at the time (noise generators, filters, tubes, etc.). This is how the electronic music of the 1950s and 1960s was put together before the advent of commercial synthesizers, with test equipment used as simple oscillators. Tape edits of their recorded tones were required if they were to be strung together into melodies, and noise into rhythms. Occasionally, purpose-built treats such as vocoders ('lollipops') were gifted to appease the director (Marshall 2008). Less than a year after establishing the workshop, however, Oram left to set up her own freelance studio due to frustration with an overly restrictive BBC bureaucracy.

What is remarkable about Oram is how she gave such careful consideration to the problem of interfacing humans with machines, along with the impact this relationship had upon creativity. Her musings led her to independently design and co-develop what she called the Oramics Machine (daphneoram.org n.d.) – an unwieldy-but-powerful electronic music device programmed by painting lines, dots and shapes onto small glass panels and clear film stock. In addition to allowing both digital (i.e. dots for pitch) and analogue data input (i.e. lines capable of continuously controlling vibrato, note duration/rhythm, timbre, envelope amplitude and dynamics), a key design aim of the machine was immediate audio-visual feedback and intuitive reprogramming capabilities. Given that sound synthesis using old test oscillators together with *musique concrète* tape-editing techniques was the electronic music norm in the early 1960s – a process demanding detailed planning and tedious trial and error to pull off – Oram's system was a giant leap forward. She listed the interface capabilities of her design as including 'humanizing factors' such as:

1. Freehand drawing of all instructions.
2. Facilities for drawing, separately, the instructions for each parameter.
3. A monitoring system to allow immediate, or almost immediate, 'feedback' of the result.
4. Easy access to the separate parameter instructions so that, after monitoring, alterations can be made and the results re-monitored. (1972: 96–7)

Perhaps even more extraordinary is that in her 1972 book *An Individual Note of Music, Sound and Electronics* Oram grapples with many of the same concepts that Csikszentmihalyi deals with in his writing regarding both flow and creativity as a social-cultural-historical system. Oram's approach is more philosophical, however, likening the plight of creative individuals to the laws of electromagnetism and electron flow in circuit design:

> We find that each electronic device requires the right type of outlet if it is going to function well. The manufacturer of the device has designed it with a certain type of output which must be matched by the input of the equipment to which it is linked. . . . The electronic amplifier can, I think, be seen as an analogy of the dilemma of many inventors, composers, writers and artists, and perhaps, more especially, such an analogy emphasises the dilemma of some of our university students. 'Signals' are being crammed into the student, crammed in at a fearsome rate, ready for the future when he [*sic*] will correlate and amplify them. But what of the future outlets? Where are the matched impedances ready to

receive these signals?. . . . The composer, also, relies on the impedances that are offered to him. He, too, will have to warp his individuality, or resort to distortion or even 'destruction', if he cannot find 'circuits' which have input impedances corresponding to his output . . . we, as members of the listening public, have each our own individuality to blame . . . for we are providing the outlets and he is matching to them.

[Conversely] . . . when we offer no impedances at all – a sort of musical 'super welfare state' – we are providing the worst type of outlets . . . for, if all is acceptable, mediocrity will flow profusely; the normal musical output of a gifted composer may then appear to be an insignificant trickle . . . only those outputs boosted by the most blatant gimmicks and the most publicised 'happenings' will make any effect at all. (1972: 117–19)

The following section features a case study of the Talking Heads' 1980 album *Remain in Light*.

Case study

Remain in Light

Talking Heads, Brian Eno and *Remain in Light*

Talking Heads

By the time Talking Heads set to work on their album *Remain in Light* (1980b), they had already released three critically acclaimed albums (two co-produced with Brian Eno), toured the world and were generally considered to be at the vanguard of the new-wave music scene. They hadn't always been considered so hip, though. Starting out in the mid-1970s as regulars at CBGBs in Manhattan's Bowery district, the band was regarded the club's 'in-joke, the in-house court jesters', a group that couldn't possibly translate to the broader stage of 'show-biz' (Gittins 2004: 20). Part of Eno's attraction to Talking Heads was that their music didn't seem to emanate from a clearly defined or concretized sense of identity. Instead, it was his impression that their approach (as with many of the New York no-wave bands of the time) 'proceed[ed] from a "what would happen if" orientation . . . a rarified kind of research' (Tamm 1995: 25).

Listening to the band's early material captured on video at CBGBs in 1975 (since removed from YouTube) reveals a 'bare bones' three-piece sound consisting solely of unadorned voice, guitar, bass and drums, with nary a power chord to be heard. 'Quirky' is an apt descriptor. Lead singer David Byrne's vocal delivery sounds not so much anxious as perplexed, with little sense of the deep-felt emotionality and sonic projection one would expect from singers of the time. In fact, he mostly mumbles into the microphone as if conversing with a friend. All the while, the music backing is equal parts clockwork stiffness and a funk of sorts. The band's demeanour and songs come across, at first, as ironic. On closer inspection, they appear sincere, instead displaying a defiantly naive disregard for sociocultural conventions.

One might well imagine the early Talking Heads as a band that fell to earth. Disguised as a mild-mannered bubblegum group, no one would have been any the wiser had they been using the medium of song to report back to the Mothership. For Byrne anyway – a Scottish immigrant growing up in Canada and, later, the United States – the analogy is perhaps justified. Gittins sums up Byrne's early modus operandi as follows: '[He] doubts empirical givens, questioning external realities' (2004: 67). Rather than see himself as strange Byrne explains: 'I prefer to see my viewpoints and behaviour as sensible reactions to the goofy things around me' (2004: 28). His lyrics scrutinize so much that people take for granted: love and animals included. Even subject matter as pedestrian as air or paper is examined free of their usual associations and assumptions regarding their benign state.

Just as Byrne's lyrics question the usual perspectives adopted in popular song, so did the band's music. Their early sound was an attempt at musical reductionism taken to the extreme. They were clear about what they didn't want to sound like, avoiding most rock-music clichés to the point where their arrangements were 'just the bare-bones musical elements needed to lay out a song. Nothing more' (Byrne 2012: 39). As the band began to introduce more layering into their music, with the addition of ex-Modern Lovers keyboardist and guitarist Jerry Harrison, it was, again, often done in ways that were surprising. A bass guitar might play notes unrelated to the tonic of the song's key (e.g. in the track 'Animals' (1979a)). Sections of a vocal melody might consist of little more than a single-note jumping back and forth by an octave (e.g. in the track 'Mind' (1979f)); or, a clear sense of pulse to orientate dancers with an accented backbeat (i.e. beats two and four) might be conspicuous in its absence (e.g. as in the track 'Drugs' (1979b)).

Eno

Talking Heads co-producer Brian Eno studied painting in the mid-1960s, attending the Ipswich Art School during 1964 and 1966. His training was typical for the time, encouraged by his educators to emphasize process over product: 'it was the height of the 1960s avant-garde philosophy that the residue left by an artistic gesture was less important than the conceptual nature of the gesture itself' (Tamm 1995: 34). His appreciation of experimental music included the work of composers such as John Cage, Steve Reich, Cornelius Cardew and Gavin Bryars.

Although Eno enthusiastically embraced the concept of process as a kind of product in its own right – fashioning works that might constitute little more than a list of instructions for others to carry out – he never totally abandoned the idea that creative artefacts should also be aesthetically rewarding. Nonetheless, much of Eno's creative output over the last fifty or so years – whether as a composer, record producer, artist or app developer – is conspicuous in its conceptual foundations. His is a particular type of conceptual approach, however: one that has been described as 'creative play' (Garbarini 1988b). Collaborator Leo Abrahams notes that Eno's creative agenda is to simultaneously produce artefacts that are 'culturally worthwhile' but to have fun in the process. He likens Eno's influence on the atmosphere of recording sessions to that of a dinner-party guest who is really fun and able to lift the mood of the whole room (Dayal 2009: 56). While Eno was credited as a co-producer on previous Talking Heads records, on *Remain in Light* he saw himself as a de facto fifth member of the band.

Remain in Light

While Talking Heads' first two albums featured songs written almost exclusively by David Byrne, their third release *Fear of Music* ((1979c), henceforth *FOM*) featured collaborations between Byrne and keyboardist-guitarist Jerry Harrison, along with a group improvisation that gave rise to the song 'Life During Wartime' (1979e). With *Remain in Light* (henceforth *RIL*), Talking Heads and Eno were determined to reimagine themselves, rejecting their previous stylistic innovations and working methods. As Tina Weymouth recalls: 'We threw everything that we had previously learnt out of the window on *Remain In Light*. . . . We decided to fly without a net' (Gittins 2004: 63).

No songs on *RIL* were written prior to the album's recording sessions. Jerry Harrison explains: 'we incorporated the idea of writing in the studio, trying to capture the innocent, uncertain charm of the first time we played a song, that sense of exploration' (Thomson 2010: 42). Group jam sessions were recorded, with spontaneity taking precedence over polish; short sections identified as worthy were then re-recorded, replayed over at length (with one musician overdubbing at a time) as if looped. After the initial grooves were completed, the intention was for the band to have a break and reconvene a few weeks later for more overdubs. The resulting (layered) tracks could then be arranged by cueing and muting individual instruments in much the same way one might today using a DAW like Ableton Live. There was a problem, though. The backing tracks the band made together during the initial sessions were so fresh and new that, for a while, they couldn't work out how to turn them into finished songs.

Byrne has since credited Eno's positivity as being a key factor in keeping the project afloat and energizing the band despite the uncertainty of abandoning their previous ways of working: 'Besides being a fifth band member on this record, Brian is a wonderful enthusiast. He sells the excitement and potential of working in a new way – the upside of stepping into the unknown, experimenting and seeing what might happen' (*David Byrne interview* 2017). Byrne eventually solved the problem of how to add vocals to this 'fluid beat music . . . [with] no obvious cadences to attach words to' (Gittins 2004: 65), when he reflected that religious ecstasy was expressed in some cultures through secular song and dance. As a result, *legato* (i.e. flowing) vocal melodies – otherworldly and impersonal – were used as 'choruses' in contrast to *sprechstimme* (i.e. half-spoken, half-sung) 'verses' reminiscent of the more anxious David Byrne vocals of old. Group chants, rapping, spoken word and mimicry of the television evangelists featured on Byrne and Eno's then unreleased *My Life in the Bush of Ghosts* project (1981) also feature prominently. All of these various vocal 'sections' could then be layered together and cued (at times, sounding simultaneously) in much the same manner as the instrumental backing.

Another key aspect of *RIL*'s sound arises from Eno and the band's admiration of the music of West African 'Afrobeat' bandleader (and cultural icon) Fela Kuti. While the band was acutely aware they could never (nor they would attempt to) copy Afrobeat convincingly, the style, nonetheless, inspired them to experiment with new musical approaches they might not otherwise have contemplated. Drummer Chris Frantz recalls:

> I've noticed that Brian often says or takes credit for introducing us to African rhythms and sensibilities, but in fact in 1974, like three years before we met him – maybe even 1973 – we would go up from Providence up to Cambridge, Massachusetts where there was this very interesting Multikulti store where you could buy dashiki, or you could buy Indian spices for cooking Indian food, or you could buy some nice bongos, or you could get a Fela Kuti album or a Chief Commander Ebenezer Obey album, or a King Sunny Adé. My favorite of course was Manu Dibango.
>
> So we had these records in our collection, even when we were in college. If you are an art student you want to get stimulated. The African music and the African sensibility was very stimulating to a WASP guy like me. We never felt like we could even approximate what Fela did with his band, but we could use it as a source of inspiration and a way to do something unpredictable for us. (Benji B 2014)

Bass player Tina Weymouth continues, explaining the initial impetus for the *RIL* approach:

> So when David and Brian Eno went off to do their record [*My Life in the Bush of Ghosts* (1981)] we thought, 'Oh, what are we going to go now?' We started jamming in our loft and we went to see Brian Eno. He said, 'What are you up to?' We said, 'Oh we're having these great jams. Come on over. Why don't you play with us?' He said, 'Oh I don't know how to play anything.' So we said, 'Well, it doesn't matter. We're all going to switch instruments.' When David heard that Brian was going to jam with us, then he came running back.
>
> So we were always doing that, creating new situations and circumstances to keep it interesting for everybody to be part of. Instead of sitting down and writing a song and saying, 'OK, this is what we're going to.' We usually jammed songs anyway, but this was really totally trying to reduce everything to two cords [*sic*] if possible. If we're going to make another cord it was going to be by creating another layer. It became much more interesting, much more like jazz in that way. (Benji B 2014)

With *RIL*, the traditional demarcation between writers, musicians and technicians was also broken down. Jerry Harrison recalls that Eno encouraged the band to think of the studio as an extension of their instruments and that it, too, could be 'played':

> If you look back at photos of the Beatles's engineers, they're wearing white lab coats. They were totally behind the glass. You didn't go in there. The musicians were in the other room and being captured by technicians. Maybe if you were lucky they would play the music back through speakers. Eno broke that barrier down. Everything was an instrument. (Ivie 2020)

Interview with Jerry Harrison (21 February 2019)

Marshall Heiser: With *RIL*, Talking Heads started with a blank canvas in two ways: You started out without any material written prior to the sessions, and you were using a new creative process. What motivated such a risky approach at that time in your career?

Jerry Harrison: Well, on *FOM* we had decided to record the album where we rehearsed, because we felt that we were comfortable there and it would have a different sound than going into a normal recording studio. So we often thought that by changing the surroundings or changing the process it would force us to do new things. So *RIL* was a continuation of that, but I would say that more specifically that by *RIL* we had also noticed there was something that happened sometimes the first time you ever played a song. It had a delicacy or a tentativeness that we liked and the more familiar with it you were that it took on maybe more self-confidence. And, of course, for some songs it just got better and better and better. But there was also a delicacy to capturing something in the moment it was created. So, that was the concept of *RIL*. And, I think that we all had been listening to 'I Zimbra' (1979d) which we had recorded on *FOM* [and] almost didn't make the album, because we didn't have any lyrics for it. We were all on our way to Australia and New Zealand for a tour. We were going to go from there, from Perth to Europe, have a couple of weeks off and play at, I think, Pink Pop [Festival] or something like that in Denmark. I remember, we were in the recording studio, basically listening to the whole album and I said, 'Could we just listen to that track that we never quite finished?' and we put it on. It was like, 'This has *got* to go on the record!' So, David and I rearranged our travel and came back from Perth on a thirty-hour flight to New York and, in the meantime, Brian came up with that Dadaist poem by Hugo Ball, which became the lyrics. We recognized that pushing ourselves, we'll say, in a more African direction was something that we were all really excited about. So that was also an underlying sort of template for where we wanted to go.

MH: Can risk taking be beneficial to creative practice do you think? And, if so, when? And, when isn't it useful?

Harrison: Well, I definitely think it can be very useful. And I would say that the most common time that it's useful is [when] people fall into ruts all the time and their music begins to sound similar, or the same, or uninspired. And I think that the process of people trying to recreate whatever their last hit record was, is deleterious to the process of experimentation. I think when bands made one album every year or more, I mean, if we think about Talking Heads, we made an album and toured the world every year from 1977 until really after *RIL* when we all made a solo record [laughs] and then we did *Speaking in Tongues* (1983). You know, we were pretty busy. But I think that people trying to eek out every last sale out of their albums. It's taking two or three years because they go around the world and have to build that much momentum for the album. The record companies want you to try and duplicate those sales of ten or so million records, and, of course, when you have record sales like that, or course, it's very exciting and you *do* want to do it. But I think, the time between records then, you are chasing your tail a little bit. If you look back to something like the Rolling Stones, or the Beatles, or the Who, not to mention the Talking Heads, you wouldn't have wanted the Beatles to remake *Rubber Soul* (1965) like four times in a row. That was a great experiment, but you were, like, looking forward to where they went. And I think that the fan base wanted something new and you could go someplace. The Who went to *The Who Sell Out* (1967) and then they went to *Live at Leeds* (1970) and then they went to *Tommy* (1969) [*sic*]. Look at these great changes in direction and that's what people expected. And they were disappointed if there was not change. And that didn't mean that one record didn't come back and you'd say, 'Well, that one's really my favourite.' And then, people'd revisit old territory as they got to be a more mature band. But there was a desire and a need, and an expectation of experimentation. And I think that when people started to try and duplicate albums of ten or eleven million sales they became conservative. And that conservative impulse actually made their creative output really less interesting. We were fortunate at a time when people were making records on a regular basis and people wanted us to change. And then, on *RIL* we used this sort of method, by using the [mixing] board as the way that we switched between parts, of theses layered parts, we kind of used the board as a compositional tool. And we would add this part to this part of the song or this part to the other part of the song. It did create a very challenging thing for David in particular, because, of course, none of the lyrics had been written and since it was such a modal record, there was often not that many chord changes and that lack of chord changes created a challenge in creating interesting vocal melodies. When we did a similar process on *Speaking in Tongues* [1983] we made sure to build in chord changes so that there would be the variety of places to go with your voice to create much more interesting melodies.

MH: There were two blocks of sessions for *RIL*, the first being at Compass Point Studios in Nassau and then Sigma Sound in New York. You've said previously that the first sessions flowed really easily, whereas the second sessions were 'nightmarishly hard' (Thompson 2010). Was that because of the things you've just mentioned, or were there other factors that made it very difficult?

Harrison: Well, we were doing the lyrics at that part of the recording, so, yes, there was that. But, I also think that there was a momentum in the Bahamas, and had we just kept going, we may have had a much easier time. And, by taking three weeks off and coming back to New York, there was a very hot summer, and it was such a different atmosphere that when we started to get into it, maybe we were just in a different mood. So I personally think that it was quite a mistake for us to stop. I mean, I'm very proud of the record. Maybe it wouldn't have been anywhere near as good. I could be totally wrong. It could be just the opposite. But, it felt to me like we got kind of stuck. And what happened then was that one of the ways that David, I think, became more involved with the songs is we started to layer new guitar parts and sometime bass parts and various other musical parts as an easier way of having it be fresh in our mind. And this created some issues because Chris and Tina were not sitting around the studio as much as, say, David and I were. And so they were not as understanding of the difficulty of the process of writing the lyrics. So then, they started to feel frustrated, 'cos suddenly parts that they really loved would seem to be no longer very active in the song, or gone altogether. And there was also such an 'All for one and one for all' feeling in the Bahamas. When you're at Compass Point, you might go swimming, but there's basically, you sort of go to the studio and that's it. Whereas, in New York we all had our own places where we lived and you have the distractions of everyday life, your girlfriend or whatever else is in your life that you need to deal with. That being said, the album came out amazing. So we kind of got the momentum going, and also, by being in New York, I saw that Adrian Belew was playing at the Mudd Club and went down and talked to him and got him to come up and play those amazing solos he plays on the record, and I brought in Nona Hendryx. Had we stayed in the Bahamas, those two things wouldn't have happened. And so, I think that that was essential. It had gotten into be in such a hurry, it was really funny, and I remember Eno going, 'Oh I don't want anyone else to sing on it, I'll just sing the background parts. Everybody else sings out of tune.' And I went, 'You'll be so happy to have Nona. I *know* you'll really love it.' And he was very excited by it. He would sing with her at times. You know, they hit it off. And she, of course, had a great deal of experience having been in Labelle, that she knew how to come up with really good background parts and fit in and just is such a polished and wonderful singer.

MH: It's interesting because, as a listener, those two textures of Nona Hendryx's voice and Adrian Belew's guitar are quintessential aspects of the album, from a listener's point of view.

Harrison: Absolutely.

MH: When you said it was 'nightmarishly hard' in New York, is that perhaps a bit of an overstatement, or was it really 'pressure-cooker' stressful?

Harrison: Well, there was a deadline to get it done, 'cos we had decided to do these shows. And that was actually quite amazing because David and I sat down and said, 'Well, how many people do we need to perform these songs?' And we kind of came up with this list which included a second bass player, another keyboard player, another guitar player, background singers, percussion. And I went out and I was able to hire Adrian and Bernie Worrell, and I had been doing a record with Buster Jones and Dolette McDonald. So, I came back in the afternoon, I said: 'We have the most amazing band!' and it was all done in like three hours, except for the percussionist. Then Bernie recommended Steve Scales. But then David went off to California and mixed a few songs with Dave Jerden, and I stayed with Eno and John Potoker at Sigma Sound . . . and I started rehearsals in Long Island City with this big band because we did these two shows, one in Central Park, but the first one up at the Heatwave festival in Toronto where we unveiled the idea of the big band. So we basically had these two sort of much higher paying shows than we normally had. So we did it as an experiment. And then, it was just so much fun and so wonderful that we knew that we had to continue with that and then we found a way to. . . . I think it was the only time we ever borrowed any money from Warner Brothers was to pay for that touring band in the very beginning.

MH: Looking at video footage of the live shows, there's one in Rome in particular that's on the internet, songs like 'The Great Curve' (1980c), there's a sense of jubilance, elation, almost ecstasy that's coming from both the band and the audience. Was that how it felt at the time?

Harrison: It was. It was just amazing. No one had ever seen . . . it became quite common, the Police and many, many other bands, even the Rolling Stones, people started copying us and having background singers and always having percussion. People just started to realize how it could enhance even a kind of traditional rock band. But we were the first ones to totally integrate it into our sound. One of the other things about that tour was that we lined up on stage in a line in the same way that King Sunny Adé did, which meant that there were times when the left side of the stage and the right side of the stage almost were going off in their own directions. Especially, because we had interlocking bass players, you know, so if you were on one side you'd hear Tina and if you were on the other side you'd hear Buster more. And so, there were some very sort of abstract things that started happening as well. But it was so much fun! And that was a just great band. And I think that that Rome show is really terrific.

MH: So, you went from a situation where there was a lot of pressure and then to a situation where you must have felt a real sense of relief. Was it almost like going through a dark tunnel and coming out to the light at the other end?

Harrison: I don't know if I'd put it quite that way. One of the things that I say was so difficult in New York is don't forget it seemed so difficult because it was in contrast to what just seemed to just flow naturally in the Bahamas. So like you know it's sort of as if you were swimming with the river behind you and suddenly you came around a turn and the river was facing you. And it was just that contrast as much as anything that I wanted to reflect. I think, one of the things for myself as a member, there was a little bit of a mixed feeling when I put the whole band together because I knew that to a degree it would change the focus of the audience's attention. When we were a four piece, we always toured with all the lights on onstage, all white lights. So people could always see what all four members of the band were doing at all times. And, as is often the case, people have a favourite member of the band. And, of course, people focus on the singing. But when the band got larger, you might say, I knew my role would seem less clear, but I took a great deal of pleasure and satisfaction in that I had actually put this whole band together. And we also, at times, would give the musicians who had joined us some of the more interesting parts to play even though we had played them on the record, because we wanted them excited and involved.

MH: You booked Sigma Sound because you'd produced some sessions for Nona Hendryx at that studio. Did you choose that studio because of the famous Philly sound? Were you hoping that the studio itself would influence the sound of the recordings, the performances of the musicians, and even, maybe, their frame of mind because of the studios' heritage?

Harrison: No, it was mainly that I was doing the negotiations between a few studios and I was able to convince Sigma Sound that they never got any rock acts, and that we could be a loss leader for them so that they could expand their clientele [both laugh]. So, I negotiated just an unbelievably great rate.

MH: I'm glad you've cleared that up! [both laugh]. Before *RIL*, Talking Heads was already a band that questioned so many of the 'givens' of what a song or what a band could be. Regarding that process, I suppose it's a reductive process: you rule out all the things that you don't want to be at the start . . .

Harrison: Yes.

MH: … So, how does it feel when you're filling in the blanks?

Harrison: Well, I think that one of the biggest things was that we knew we didn't want to be blues-based. So certain things were sort of off-limits. That was the main thing. I think that one of the things that coming from painting we all realized that interesting paintings definitely come from restricting the mediums with which you're allowed to work. So, I think that we applied that to music. And, I think that another thing that was very clear from the similarity with music is that in painting at that time period there were a lot of painters who would do things with super-high and very jarring changes between parts of the canvas. And, I think that we did that with music. If you look at something like 'Artists Only' (1978a) the connections between the sections of the song are dramatically different. So that influenced us. Actually, when I joined the band I feel that I helped make those connections a little bit more graceful. But it was a debate that I had with myself to say, 'Is this an improvement for me to make that happen, or am I spoiling something that's so jagged and weird that maybe it *should* be like that?'

MH: *RIL* necessitated a metamorphosis of the band, it was almost like the band became another band, but it also represented a metamorphosis of popular music in general in the wake of that album. Is that too big a claim to make?

Harrison: No, I think that's exactly right. I think it was a really groundbreaking record and, as I said, you can look at a lot of bands who then ended up expanding their sound to include background singers or percussion or various other things. Often they seemed more like an addition, rather than actually inherent to the sound. As well as, you know, this introduction of the influences of African music, we were certainly amongst the first to do that. I think it was also very important that on *RIL*, though we were influenced, it is still us playing them. It wasn't like we hired a bunch of people from another country and they played the parts the way they always did. It went through the filter of our abilities to try and play with that feel. It may have been less precise but it also made it 'us'.

MH: Do you feel that perhaps *RIL* has had an influence on the way people make records today with DAWs, samplers, looping and whatnot?

Harrison: I think, yes. I think that maybe people started to understand that they could write starting with a groove and a feeling and then building from there. But I think that anytime that people did things by themselves they automatically were a little – although sometimes it was all planned out, I think that when Steve Winwood made a solo record, he'd already planned out what all the parts were, so to speak, and they were more traditional parts – but there's just no way that if you're sitting there and you're hearing just this line or that line that you're not going to be influenced by 'Well, I'd like to try doing this.' The other thing about that method of recording is that you're trying to make every part seem really interesting. When you hear them all at once, all together, as long as they're doing the job they need to do, that's all it needs to do. This also can be dangerous, because you'll end up making everything a little too complicated. So I think that it does affect the thought process of how you're doing it. And, you have to be disciplined about it. You must throw some things that you really love out, and you have to make decisions between, 'Is this going to be more dominant or is *this* going to be more dominant?'

MH: So, there so many more decisions to make since you're not only a performer, but you're a writer, arranger, recordist . . .

Harrison: Right.

MH: . . . producer as well. Is that too much to expect from modern musicians?

Harrison: Oh, I don't think that I'd go that far. I do think that there's an awful lot of people [who do] one hour of recording and five hours of editing, and I think that that's not the best way to go. I think there's become a loss of forcing yourself to play the thing the way you wanted it, [knowing] that you can fix it, or somebody else can fix it and make it fine. I think that that's taken away from the musicianship of people, but also the things that happen just when you're forcing yourself to play the music.

Unforced errors: Part 2

That, in 1980, New Yorkers Talking Heads should dare attempt to play in the manner of a popular-music hybrid emerging out of West Africa was an audacious act. And that they should be comfortable with the fact that they couldn't really replicate it accurately was bolder still. Brian Eno's deep admiration of the work of Fela Kuti and Tony Allen, along with his having been a player in the Portsmouth Sinfonia, perhaps explains why such liberties were not only tolerated but actively encouraged. The band were well aware that the sound of *RIL* resulted from them trying something new, getting it wrong and being OK with the naive charm of the results. That was the first half of the process anyway.

Back in New York, what followed was the recognition by Byrne (together with Eno and Harrison) that his old ways of framing musical experience were ill-equipped to fashion songs out of the tapestry-like, modal grooves. Further, in addition to the challenge of having to find an 'in' to this new material, the existing backing tracks had to be reworked somewhat in order to accommodate Byrne and Eno's attempts to confront the material on its own terms and keep the process of-the-moment. This is not unlike the proverbial old mixing conundrum of blending the instruments in the mix first, only to find that when the vocals are finally added (last) that the backing-track balance no longer works.

Validation and vindication

Angélique Kidjo tells the story (Currin 2018) of hearing the track 'Once in a Lifetime' (1980a) at a party while she was a music student in Paris. When she tried to tell her friends that the song was 'African' music they responded incredulously, saying that something so sophisticated could not possibly come out of Africa. Kidjo had sensed something about the record the others were deaf to. The music, while perhaps not immediately connoting 'African' to Western ears of the time (in 1983), presented a way of framing experience which to her 'seemed natural' and validated her cultural experience: 'With my sense of solitude and loneliness and longing, that song brought me back home for the rest of the party' (Currin 2018). It would seem that while the Talking Heads had toyed with Afrobeat in much the same way that the Portsmouth Sinfonia had toyed with Western classical music (i.e. as unapologetic novices), they had gotten much more than they bargained for. Byrne, for one, was forced to find the answers regarding how to proceed not only by immersing himself in the sounds of contemporary West-African popular music and the new 'rap' music that was being released at the time but by re-examining his own assumptions about the role of music (and music making) in society. The fact that Kidjo saw the results – which represented a more thoroughly communal approach than Talking Heads had previously attempted – as a kind of validation rather than an act of asymmetric cultural exchange or exploitation testifies to the fidelity of the band and Eno's intentions (as opposed to their Afrobeat 'chops'). She has since commented:

> People don't realize the privilege of their freedom. The dictatorship in Benin was very difficult for me as a free artist. Music from all around the world stopped coming in the middle of the '70s. They said no more music from the outside, so the radio and TV became propaganda. Every artist was summoned to write propaganda. I refused. . . . I get tired of people who call themselves purists. Before you start talking about 'purity', look at yourself: Are you pure? What is pure in your surroundings? What is pure in nature? The rhetoric of purity, that's what brought Hitler to power – looking for a pure race. We are not perfect, and that's why we are brothers and sisters. The fact that we keep ourselves divided is exactly what the people in power want us to do. The more divided you are, the more power you give them, and the more they can kill you. . . . David Byrne did an interview when [*RIL*] was released, telling people to listen to Fela Kuti and to read books about African music. What he learned by reading those books was

the way drums are used in West Africa. The repetitive patterns of the drums bring you to a trance. That's where the idea of looping comes in place, like the bassline that played the same all through one song. People told them it was too pretentious, but the Talking Heads were very honest from the get-go. From the moment you give credit to the people who inspire you, and you don't copy their songs, it's not cultural appropriation, it's cultural expression. (Currin 2018)

While *RIL* is clearly influenced by Afrobeat, it cannot be considered Afrobeat per se. Nonetheless, it is indebted to it in the same way that so much of experimental music is indebted to John Cage's (limited) understanding and interpretation of Zen Buddhist concepts and Dada:

> neither Dada nor Zen is a fixed tangible. They change; and in quite different ways in different places and times, they invigorate action. What was Dada in the 1920's is now, with the exception of the work of Marcel Duchamp, just art. What I do, I do not wish blamed on Zen, though without my engagement with Zen (attendance at lectures by Alan Watts and D. T. Suzuki, reading of the literature) I doubt whether I would have done what I have done. I am told that Alan Watts has questioned the relation between my work and Zen. I mention this in order to free Zen of any responsibility for my actions. (1961: xi)

Peak experience or infantile escapism?

In his 2012 book *How Music Works*, David Byrne reflects upon how *RIL* influenced his own experience as a performer and collaborator:

> I knew the music we'd just recorded was less angsty than the stuff we'd done previously. It was about surrender, ecstasy and transcendence, and the live performance tended to really bring those qualities to the forefront. It wasn't just an intellectual conceit: I could feel lifted and transported on stage. I think audiences sometimes felt this too. . . . It may seem paradoxical, but the more integral everyone was, the more everyone gave up some individuality and surrendered to the music. It was a living, breathing model of a more ideal society, an ephemeral utopia that everyone, even the audience, felt was being manifested in front of them, if only for a brief period. . . . As I experienced it, this was not just a musical transformation but also a psychic one. (2012: 48–9)

Byrne's views are in sharp contrast with those voiced by composer Wim Mertens. In the latter's critique of the use of repetition in the work of American minimalist composers ([1983] 2007), he describes phenomenological states arising in listeners similar to those linked to autotelic (optimal) experience (Csikszentmihalyi 1975, 1990) and Abraham Maslow's well-known humanist take on what he described as 'peak experience' (1964). Somewhat incredulously, Mertens was either wholly ignorant of positive psychology at the time or (more probably) simply chose to ignore it, instead preferring to frame these states in terms of the historically significant, but comparatively archaic, Freudian psychoanalytic model of unconscious libidinal processes:

> The ecstatic state induced by this music, which could also be called a state of innocence, an hypnotic state, or a religious state, is created by an independent libido, freed of all restrictions of reality. Repetitive music only appears to succeed when the listener consciously discards his [sic] dialectical way of listening. Ecstasy in other words can only occur when the ego can let go.
>
> Repetitive music can lead to psychological regression. The so-called religious experience of repetitive music is in fact a camouflaged erotic experience. One can speak of a controlled pseudo-satisfaction because the abandoning of dialectical time does not really happen but is only imaginary. The libido, freed from the external world, turns towards the ego to obtain imaginary satisfaction. Freud defined this as a regression and a 'return to the infantile experience of hallucinatory satisfaction'.
>
> To what extent the ecstatic dimension is consciously pursued and to what extent it may even be the main purpose of composing repetitive music, is not clear. It is certainly one of the main reasons for its popularity. The drug-like experience and the imaginary satisfaction it brings about are even more obvious in disco music and space rock, the popular derivatives of repetitive music. This music at least leaves no room for doubt about its intentions. The same criticism of imaginary satisfaction can be equally applied to the whole of the non-dialectical movement. Processes of production without negativity are utopian and historically unrealistic, like the absolute libido in repetitive music. (Mertens [1983] 2007: 124)

Summary and conclusion

There are a number of reasons why Talking Heads and Brian Eno's album *Remain in Light* has been chosen as the subject of a case study. These are:

1. the band's ability to question 'givens' and tacit assumptions informing their creative system: both in song lyrics and in consciously negotiating what form their band might (and might not) take;

2. their choosing, as a group, to abandon their old ways of approaching music making;
3. the inclusion of an array of influences, tropes and processes from outside the mainstream popular-music domain of the time (c. 1980);
4. the band not being attached to emulating a new influence faithfully;
5. the line between co-producer as facilitator and band member was acknowledged as being blurred;
6. use of the studio-as-an-instrument (in particular, using the mixing board as an arrangement tool);
7. the creation of music that was more repetitive in nature and less dialectic: that is, (i) 'layering up' tracks rather than playing through tension/release-type chord changes, and (ii) foregrounding rhythm and backgrounding tonal harmony;
8. the 'distribution' of the playful frame of mind (i.e. Eno acted as a cheerleader of sorts) in order to: (i) coax uninhibited performances out of the band (in the Bahamas); and (ii) attenuate the stress of addressing creative tasks with no clear precedents (back in New York);
9. that the project took on a 'life of its own' (i.e. problem finding), with the team able to follow where each track seemed to want to go (even though doing so created tension between the members who wanted to respect the integrity of the original backing tracks and those who felt obliged to develop them further: at times, beyond recognition);
10. the end product necessitated the band changing its original form (expanding from a four-piece new-wave band to a nine-piece 'fourth-world' funk ensemble);
11. the band's metamorphosis was echoed by a domain-level 'transactualization': spreading out via critical acclaim in the rock-music press, positive audience responses to the tour and, later, through MTV video play and song placements in motion pictures.

Judging by the growing number of articles being written in praise of *RIL* recently – particularly in late 2020 in acknowledgement of the album's fortieth anniversary – it is a work that continues to resonate with media commentators and critics. That artists as diverse as Thom Yorke, Peter Gabriel and Angélique Kidjo also continue to sing the album's praises, similarly, attests to its ongoing influence. Further, in 2017, *RIL* was recognized by the United States Library of Congress for inclusion in the National Recording Registry as culturally, historically or aesthetically significant. One must not underestimate, however, the considerable cross-cultural, interpersonal, technical and heuristic challenges that informed *RIL*. Those challenges, along with the novel responses made by Talking Heads, Brian Eno and their collaborators – some of which necessitated a reappraisal of their preconceptions about musical collaboration, record production and sociocultural norms – made for an album that sounds, arguably, much more at home in the twenty-first century than it ever did in the 1980s.

The way so many project-studio-based musicians approach their craft today has been, no doubt, influenced by the rise of DJing, hip-hop culture and, more recently, the democratization of technology. When *RIL* was being made in 1980 none of these phenomena had yet made an impact upon mainstream culture. They were, however, to become integral parts of the mainstream of the future. Perhaps, *RIL* belonged not so much to the real world of 1980 as an imaginary one collaborator Jon Hassell referred to at the time (together with Eno and Byrne) as the 'Fourth World': a region with music that might just sound like 'a [funky] field recording or unearthing of anthropology of the future' (Sheppard 2009: 322).

6

Beyond the frame

Are you experienced?

The chief aim of this monograph has been to explore experiences and behaviours that, while integral to creative practice, have largely been ignored by popular-music and record-production scholarship. Given the recent trend in emphasizing the sociocultural nature of creativity, it should not be surprising that the inner experience of individual musicians has been relegated to a mere footnote in the literature. When experience *is* discussed, it is usually with regard to reception and perception of existing musical texts, rather than the motivation to create. And yet, Mihalyi Csikszentmihalyi – one of the key figures in proffering a sociocultural interpretation of creativity – never intended for the individual or phenomenological concerns to be written out of the creative landscape but, instead, contextualized within it.

Moreover, it has also been activities linked to productivity rather than recreation in popular-music creative practice that have, overwhelmingly, been the focus of attention to date. In his seminal tome *Between Boredom and Anxiety: The Experience of Play in Work and Games* (1975), Csikszentmihalyi identified two factors that might explain this latter, more pervasive, bias. The first, as he so economically puts it, is that 'Something that cannot be defined can safely be ignored' (1975: 197). It would seem that umbrella terms like 'play' and, indeed, 'creativity' denote easily recognizable, but nonetheless, complex multidimensional phenomena. Such unwieldy, catch-all descriptors are far too vague to facilitate any truly systematic exploration. Constructs like play need to be made 'operational' (i.e. measurable) and conceptualized with a nuanced (i.e. componential) vocabulary if they are to be integrated into our current map of 'reality'. It is now the best part of forty years since Amabile, Apter, Csikszentmihalyi, Lieberman and Sutton-Smith (among others) have each addressed these issues separately, though in a largely congruent manner.

The second issue raised by Csikszentmihalyi relates to a group of widely held tacit assumptions regarding the supposed irreconcilable nature (and comparative value) of work and play. That is, that (a) work is more important than play; (b) play is more enjoyable than work; and (c) enjoyment is synonymous with pleasure. These are of course oversimplifications:

> The satisfaction of basic needs may be a prerequisite for experiencing enjoyment, but by itself is not enough to give a sense of fulfillment. One needs to grow, to develop new skills, to take on new challenges to maintain a self-concept as a fully functioning human being. When skills are stunted or when opportunities for action are reduced, people will turn to pleasure as the only meaningful experience available. Or they will work harder for extrinsic rewards, to accumulate some tangible feedback for their existence. Status, power, and money are signs that one is competent, that one is acquiring control. But these are secondary rewards that matter only when the primary enjoyment that could be had from action itself is not available. (Csikszentmihalyi 1975: 198–9)

While the issues of componentialization and cross-discipline coherence have been dealt with in previous chapters, the issue of how the productive and recreational relate (along with their associated frames of mind) is the subject of this chapter.

The good, the bad and the useless

Based upon his ideas regarding the relationship of motivation and personality to the fulfilment of human needs, Abraham Maslow made some important distinctions between behaviours that can be described as either coping ('instrumental, adaptive, functional and purposive') or expressive (non-instrumental or, as Henricks 2008 calls it, 'consummational'). Although Maslow (1954) was well aware that human behaviour is far more nuanced than what such sharp theoretical dichotomies might suggest, his observations got the conversation going about behaviours that might seem to have no relevance to survival:

> In its preoccupation with practical results, with technology and means, [contemporary psychology] has notoriously little to say, for example, about beauty, art, fun, play, wonder, awe, joy, love, happiness, and other 'useless' reactions and end-experiences. It is therefore of little or no service to the artist, the musician, the poet, the novelist, to the humanist, the connoisseur, the

axiologist, the theologian, or to other end- or enjoyment-oriented individuals. (1954: 131)

Complicating matters further is the fact that any given behaviour may have multiple determining factors, not least of all, motivations and purposes that are not static:

> Clearly creative behavior, like painting, is like any other behavior in having multiple determinants. It may be seen in innately creative people whether they are satisfied or not, happy or unhappy, hungry or sated. Also it is clear that creative activity may be compensatory, ameliorative, or purely economic. . . . In any case, here too we must distinguish, in a dynamic fashion, the overt behavior itself from its various motivations or purposes. (1954: 46)

This paradox was not lost on composer John Cage:

> And what is the purpose of writing music? One is, of course, not dealing with purposes but dealing with sounds. Or the answer must take the form of a paradox: a purposeful purposelessness or a purposeless play. This play, however, is an affirmation of life – not an attempt to bring order out of chaos nor to suggest improvements in creation, but simply a way of waking up to the very life we're living, which is so excellent once one gets one's mind and one's desires out of the way and lets it act of its own accord. (1961: 12)

It would appear that human behaviour is anything but predictable. Even in situations where it might be in an individual's best interest to choose a course of action that provides the greatest long-term benefit with the least possible effort, it is not uncommon for some to reject the obvious well-trodden pathways to need-fulfilment and seek out novelty for its own sake. At the height of their international fame, one half of the band 10cc (Kevin Godley and Lol Creme) turned their backs on the 'sure thing' of ongoing chart success, touring and financial security to leave the band, and invest their own money into a fourteen-month recording project that sent them broke and flopped. While Godley felt, in hindsight, that doing so was an act of indulgence, to this day, Creme is defiant in his assertion that it was well worth it, so that the duo could follow the musical challenges that interested them: 'just having fun in the studio and making music do things for us that it has never done for us before. Keeping it exciting' (Doherty 1977: 45). Creme went on to contrast their new-found freedom with the motivating factors they experienced in 10cc: 'It was no longer exciting in the confines of writing hit songs, or writing commercials because you're going to get paid a lot of bread to do them. That's a horrible reason for doing anything' (Doherty 1977: 45). While this is an extreme case, it highlights the powerful influence of motivation upon creative action.

Today, we live in an era where some in power admonish academia that it has a responsibility to channel research in ways that foster innovation, provide practical benefits, can be readily monetized and, in general, focus on the 'useful' (i.e. science, technology, engineering and mathematics: STEM) and shun the 'useless' (i.e. the arts). This might seem like sound advice, to get serious about addressing pressing needs. And yet, creativity research has long since shown that without sufficient intrinsic motivation, pathways to innovation are severely constricted. Moreover, innovation in STEM fields can depend equally upon researchers having the freedom to play with ideas and concepts that seem to have no useful application at the present time, just as might artists and musicians:

> From industry, there is considerable evidence that the most important advances in technology come not from the formal Research and Development process, but from what Thomas Peters calls 'skunkworks' – small groups of renegade scientists or technicians who are left to their own devices. Often they persist on a 'bootleg' project that passionately interests them even when told not to do so. (Amabile 1987: 225)

There is no reason that governments should not have their proverbial cake and eat it too, when it comes to embracing arts education funding. In Britain, state-funded art and design schools first appeared in the early nineteenth century, both in London and regional (manufacturing) centres, in order to meet the needs of industry. It shouldn't be surprising, however, given the Romantic spirit of the times that these same fledgling institutions imparted not only practical knowledge and skills but an appreciation of aesthetics (Banks and Oakley 2016). That is, the *useless* soon entered the picture. A proliferation of art school and 'living maintenance' grants in the 1960s – part of a larger post-war governmental push towards expanding the scope of free education – allowed working-class youth who otherwise might never have had the opportunity to engage in post-secondary studies (such as Pete Townshend, John Lennon, Keith Richards, Ray Davies, Brian Eno and the list goes on) to learn about established traditions and techniques which, in turn, they would be encouraged to rebel against (Frith and Horne 1987). By this stage, the aim of an UK state-funded arts education was not just pragmatic but (according to the Robbins Report to the Committee on

Higher Education published in 1963) to 'cultivate' members of society. Banks and Oakley (after Strand 1987) proclaim: 'How students applied themselves to that study, or what they did after it, was regarded as no more or less significant as opening up the possibility for mass participation and engagement with aesthetic education' (2016: 6). They continue:

> the traditional tension between art and commerce, free aesthetics and purposeful industry, takes on a particularly productive cast from the 1960s. Open and diverse institutions, producing both radical and innovative art and design, and serving a plurality of commercial tastes and markets appeared to be in the ascendancy – offering gains all round. But note that the art school was regarded by Frith and Horne [1987] less a conveyor belt or production line for fully-formed creative industry 'talent', and more as an indeterminate context for the cultivation of a type – the creative or artistic personality – whose 'career path', was regarded as an extrinsic and external matter. As Beck and Cornford (2012: 60) aver, the art school was less a sausage factory and more a 'condition of possibility' whose principal benefits were more 'environmental and affective' than instrumentally educative. (Banks and Oakley 2016: 12)

That an arts graduate's career path should be an 'extrinsic and external matter' is not a matter of wilful ignorance but an acknowledgement of the difference between algorithmic and heuristic pathways – a distinction that can apply to one's life journey as readily as it might to a simple creative project. Anyhow, regardless of where an arts graduate's professional life may take them, there will always be room for work and play. As it turns out, work (i.e. associated with the 'instrumental': towards an end) and play (i.e. 'consummational': an end-in-itself) are not the mutually exclusive categories they might, at first, appear to be. Work activities can be approached in a playful manner, just as play activities can be addressed in all seriousness, with an 'eye on the prize'. Apart from baseline personal preferences for certain types of activities, the most fulfilling experiences of all, it would seem, are made possible by engaging those same activities as ends in themselves: regardless of whether or not the context is one of work or play. That is, work and play can be reconciled by addressing the *experience* of playfulness in adults (as opposed to objectively observing play activities). Cultivating creative personalities and autotelic personalities – that is, persons within whom the desire to immerse themselves in their craft and seek out innovation is habitual, even in the face of little-to-no extrinsic rewards – must surely be in any non-authoritarian government's best interest.

Iterations and oscillations

When it comes to creative process, the playful frame of mind is but one side of the figurative coin. Hadamard (1945: 29) identifies two ways of thinking that work in tandem to generate practical new ideas: 'cognito' (meaning to 'shake together') and 'intelligo' (meaning to 'select among'). Getzels elaborates: 'one refers to letting ideas, memories, impulses, fantasies rise freely; the other refers to the process of choosing among the combination those patterns which have significance in reality. The "cognitio" component of creative thinking seems predominantly an impulsive, sub-conscious, playful, divergent process, the "intelligo" component predominantly a reflective, conscious, directed, convergent process' (1975: 333). More recently, Csikszentmihalyi (1999) has observed that the serious business of critiquing playful responses to a creative problem, while involving convergent thinking skills, memory and so forth, must also be informed by experience with the symbolic systems, technologies and history of any given domain. Without an understanding of the values held by the relevant field, one would be ill-equipped to develop creative problems that are personally satisfying and which the field might also acknowledge as innovative, practical and timely.

During various stages of creative action it is normal and natural to switch back and forth between the paratelic (playful) and telic (serious) interpretation of experience. Apter explains that only one state can be adopted at a time and that 'we reverse backwards and forwards between these contrasting ways of "being in the world", the movement from one to the other producing a kind of systole and diastole of everyday existence' (1991: 15): hence the name *Reversal Theory*. This is not only to be expected but desirable, since, as mentioned in Chapter 4, different stages of iterative creative process benefit from the application of different skills, processes and motivating factors (Amabile 1983, 1996). Apter likens the oscillation between telic and paratelic frames in response to one's environment to the adaptability of organisms in nature:

> it is possible to assert that to be healthy is to be unstable – to be able to move between different kinds of personality to suit the occasion. . . . If biodiversity is necessary to the health of an ecological system, then what we might call 'psychodiversity' is just as important to the health of the individual: it allows him or her to adapt to ever-changing and relatively unpredictable environments, and also to have a life which is rich with experiential diversity and allows for the expression of all sides of his or her personality. (2003: 474–5)

Practitioners engaged in playframing must come up for serious air from time to time, in order to contextualize their efforts within the bigger picture of a project or brief, or to communicate (often in precise domain-specific terms) with other parties focused intently on the 'endgame'. There are also times when practitioners need to explore new relevant information that may come to light. As novel facets of a situation become evident, playframes can be renegotiated to factor in these new findings (Sutton-Smith 1979: 306). Practitioners might also need to engage in further research, skill-building, or acquire new tools as part of a 'preparation' stage for the next iteration of playful engagement. Oscillations between exploratory and playful frames will, quite possibly, be as common as those between serious and playful ones, though the distinction is subtler. While play and exploration are both intrinsically motivated, playful ('ludic') behaviour utilizes past experience, is dependent upon mood and involves 'conceptual reorganization and consolidation' (Hutt 1979: 192). Exploratory ('epistemic') behaviour, on the other hand, seeks out new information, knowledge or skills. Or, to put it another way: play makes the familiar strange, while exploration makes the strange familiar.

Maslow, for one, was aware of the synergistic nature of playful and serious modes of thought: 'Fantasy, dreaming, symbolism, unconscious thinking, infantile, emotional thinking, psychoanalytic free association, are all productive in their own way. Healthy people come to many of their conclusions and decisions with the aid of these techniques, traditionally opposed to rationality but in actuality synergic with it' (1954: 286). Psychoanalyst and art historian Ernst Kris also famously noted that regression to infantile modes of thought in the service of the ego are common to wit and creativity in art, involving 'a continual interplay between creation and criticism, manifested in the painter's alternation of working on the canvas and stepping back to observe the effect' (1952: 253). He warned, however, that regression and control must be balanced if unintelligible or uninspired products are to be avoided.

It is possible to see such playful regression at work in the creative process and products of songwriters such as Syd Barrett, John Lennon (particularly during his psychedelic period) and Brian Wilson. The work of Syd Barrett is particularly illuminating, since he released records from 1966 to 1967, together with Pink Floyd and producers Joe Boyd and, later, Norman Smith, that achieved a healthy balance between regression and control. These can be contrasted with his later, mercurial solo records (*The Madcap Laughs*, 1970c, and *Barrett* 1970a) – both recorded after his significant mental health issues had arisen –

in which regression all but ruled supreme. Playwright and friend David Gale contextualizes Syd's regressive tendencies within the larger movement of 1960s rebellion: 'The times were feverish and Syd was a creature of those times.... You have to remember that the systematic and wilful suspension of rationality was widespread' (Chapman 2010: 181). Many of Barrett's unconventional artistic approaches and behaviours, often attributed to his deteriorating mental state, were also linked – well before these issues arose mid-year 1967 – to an idiosyncratic sense of humour, penchant for playfulness and love of process-orientated experimental art and music (Chapman 2010).

The reluctant rock star

It would not be too great a stretch to claim that Syd Barrett's small-but-groundbreaking recorded output and sudden descent into obscurity has granted him almost mythic status, arguably surpassed only by that of pre-war blues guitarist Robert Johnson. While I do not wish to attempt to explain away or reduce Barrett's legacy, his biography is rich with anecdotal evidence of how factors associated with the playful frame of mind (such as divergent thinking, holding off on closing creative options for extended periods, and suspending rationality) can bring about chaos, as much as innovation.

Syd wanted the process of music making to be fun – a reward in itself – as painting had been for him (Chapman 2010: 295). In this way, his stance exemplifies Apter's (1982) concept of the paratelic frame of mind. Unfortunately, he tended to adopt that frame of mind habitually, often in highly inappropriate circumstances. At first, he was unable to decide if all the adulation and fame experienced as a pop star was a blessing or a curse. By the end of 1967, though, he saw Pink Floyd's career in a mostly negative light, referring to it as 'the job'. The situation was further exacerbated, mid-year onwards, by increasing signs of alleged (undiagnosed) drug-onset mental illness. Claims that Syd may have been suffering from schizophrenia were difficult to confirm at the time, given the intensity of the band's music-business commitments (including a hectic and haphazard touring schedule), and a history of child-like, prankish and often-provocative behaviour he demonstrated as a youth growing up in Cambridge.

Barrett's tricky, divergent approach to making music – rather more like game playing than by-rote performances – frustrated his fair share of collaborators. Several have noted that his performance of songs in the studio varied markedly each and every time he played. Soft Machine's Mike Ratledge, who backed Syd on the solo track 'No Good Trying' (1970b) recounts, 'Nothing was ever the same. I wouldn't have minded if it was uniformly irregular but it changed from take to take. In the end you just had to watch his hands to see what he was doing' (Chapman 2010: 238). Producer Norman Smith is even more emphatic in his recollection of recording sessions with Syd: 'It was sheer hell. There are no pleasant memories. I always left with a headache. Syd was undisciplined and would simply never sing the same thing twice' (Jones 1996). Pink Floyd band members Nick Mason and Roger Waters have since recalled, with both frustration and amusement, a flux-like song-cum-prank played by Barrett called 'Have You Got It Yet?' (unreleased), where they were given the impression he was teaching them a new song. Over the course of an hour, the piece – with lyrics consisting only of the title repeated over and over – changed subtly each time Barrett played it, so they couldn't possibly ever 'get it' (Miles 2006: 117).

In time, Syd's playful, child-like approach to creativity regressed to a point where only 'unruly torrents of wordplay that only rarely yielded up their inner logic' materialized (Chapman 2010: 237). A track like 'Octopus' (1969), while mostly upbeat and carnivalesque, is as disturbing as it is disorientating at times, like ruminations from inside an allegorical womb, with Syd unable or unwilling to find words to relate his experience. Photographer Mick Rock, who at one time shared a flat with Barrett, has since said, 'My experience of Syd was that his legendary withdrawal from daily human intercourse was a matter of choice not necessity' (Jones 1996). Either way, Barrett spent the remainder of his life in his native Cambridge living with a fair degree of autonomy, coupled with some daily-living support from his mother and sister, and royalty cheques from his Pink Floyd work.

While he never returned to music, Syd sustained his passion for painting. Clearly, the activity itself was more important to him than the product, since he would destroy each and every work after it was completed (Chapman 2010). If such behaviour seems strange, then an observation made during Getzels and Csikszentmihalyi's longitudinal study of artists might go some way to explain it:

> Despite the fact that almost no one can make either a reputation or living from painting, the artists studied were almost fanatically devoted to their work. . . . Yet as soon as they finished a painting or sculpture, they seemed to lose all interest in it. Nor were they interested much in each other's paintings or in great masterpieces . . . and seemed to be generally bored or baffled by talk about the aesthetic qualities of the works they or their friends produced. . . . Slowly it

became obvious that something in the activity of painting itself kept them going. The process of making their products was so enjoyable that they were ready to sacrifice a great deal for the chance of continuing to do so . . . the artistic process added up to a structured experience which was almost addictive in its fascination. (Csikszentmihalyi 1975: xi–ii)

Singer-songwriter Mitski echoes the above statement, even going to the extent of explaining her continuing desire to make music as if it were some kind of unrequited love:

I'm revealing a big secret . . . but a lot of my songs are just about music and trying to pursue it, and not feeling loved by it. A lot of the 'yous' in my songs are abstract ideas about music. . . . I will neglect everything else, including me as a person, just to get to keep making music. . . . And even if it actually sometimes hurts, it doesn't matter as long as I get to be a musician. (Schnipper 2018)

Mitski goes on to state that the business of being a musician and a public figure entails so much more than simply being creative. It seems that the trade-off for the rare privilege of being able to devote oneself to the pursuit of music making in a professional capacity is that, after tending to everything else, there is not that much time left to actually do it:

I thought that if I worked really hard at this, then eventually I'd get to the point where I can just spend all my time making music. But I've found that the more I do this, the less time I get to spend on music. Around 10% of my time – less than that – I'm actually making music or playing music. Most of my time it's press and travel and admin stuff: answering emails and just being a business person, putting out fires. It's just being a working adult. No one gets to just do what they like to do all day. We have to make a living first, and then maybe in our spare time we get to do the thing that we love. So I'm not complaining, I know that's just reality. But for some reason I had some fantasy in my mind that, 'Well, if I work really hard at this, then eventually I'll get to make music the way I want to, all the time.' I'm finding that's not the case. (McDermott 2018)

Pathologies of play

Adopting the paratelic frame can be addictive (just as can flow or peak experience). So much so that, at times, it can be tempting to adopt it in ways that might be too dominant (i.e. adopted too often), inappropriate, wilfully ignorant of real-life consequences, or made at the expense of others. When such poor judgement or compulsion occurs, what started out as fun and games soon enough starts to resemble pathology (Apter 1991). In the following quote, Kevin Godley emphasizes the allure of immersing oneself in creative pursuits and how doing so feels like being in another world. The world he describes exists within the 'protective bubble' of adult playfulness. He warns, however, that the real world and all its duties, relationships and daily-living considerations remains regardless, and requires our participation:

> an artist lives in two worlds. There's the world of what's going on up here [points to head].... I sometimes have difficulty with [the real] world, but I'm aware that I have to live in it. I occasionally pay a bill [laughs] and do something that belongs in this world. I have relationships with people. I'm married. I live somewhere. I quite enjoy aspects of the real world, but sitting down here and making music and filming things, and so on and so forth, is really where I feel happiest, in the world that doesn't exist yet, in the world that I'm constantly conjuring. (Personal communication, 28 June 2018)

The fine line between playfulness and pathology shouldn't be surprising when one considers that humour, play and neuroses all have in common a sense of 'confinement', with the 'wider realm of reality' being ignored for a time. It is the length of time this confinement endures that, in part, distinguishes them from each other: a joke might only last for moments, minutes at most; a game for an hour or so, while the neurotic is confined, at length, to a pathological field of 'enforced play' (Elitzur 1990a). The cliché that artists should live in their own 'unknowable internal landscape' and the rest of the world be damned is, according to McIntyre, a hangover from the nineteenth-century Romantic movement (2007). It was a 'position [which] paradoxically left the supposedly free-willed self-expressive individual at the mercy of their own creative drives; drives that must be obeyed to the point of insanity' (2007: 3). Wu-Tang Clan's RZA, on the other hand, finds that being in-the-moment and open to the world around you, with all its ups and downs, can be a joy when approached with the right frame of mind:

> Quincy Jones ... said to ODB [Ol' Dirty Bastard], 'When it rains, get wet.' In my early days of success, it rained, and I wasn't paying attention to everything that was going on. But in this round of life, I am looking to responsibly get wet. I just really let myself be encompassed by the moments that I was enjoying instead of introverting myself, like, go into a city, stay in my room, go to work, come back, start writing, start working more. Not understanding that there's

a certain joy to the situation that you gotta absorb, so that rain is that joy. (Newman 2019)

Pop idles

In addition to playfulness, artists and thinkers, over the years, have identified several other common cognitive and experiential phenomena they claim are beneficial to creativity. Some describe aspects of their creative journey in terms of being a conduit of ideas rather than their source. Claxton likens this receptive aspect of creative practice – one that is tolerant of uncertainty – to 'gathering and inspecting the fruits of intuition without bruising them or avidly turning them into jams and pies' (1997: 81). Keith Richards of the Rolling Stones describes his songwriting experience as something akin to a television picking up a signal with its antenna: 'if there's any songs out there, they'll come through you' (Garbarini 1988a: 63). David Byrne of Talking Heads similarly states that many songwriters believe 'the writer taps into something universal. . . . It doesn't reflect my petty concerns or desires or problems' (Zollo 1997: 497). In both examples, the artist displays a willingness to acquiesce a degree of conscious control over the shaping of their ideas. They also share a sense of detachment from the products of their creative process, not knowing what might emerge, or indeed, if anything necessarily will.

Cognitive incubation

Simply 'doing nothing' can be beneficial to artists after extended periods of concerted mental activity seem to have produced no satisfactory answer to a creative problem. A sudden and unexpected flash of 'illumination' that comes long after work on a problem has ceased (Amabile 1996: 101) is a phenomenon well acknowledged by creativity scholars. This is often referred to as (cognitive) 'incubation' (see Claxton 1997; Fulgosi and Guilford 1968; Getzels and Jackson 1962; Hadamard 1945; Lieberman 1977). It is a process that can occur in both the short and long term (e.g. taking minutes, hours, days or even weeks). Ringo Starr describes how short-term cognitive incubation worked for the Beatles:

> We'd struggle with [a song], sometimes well into the night, and then we'd break for a cuppa' tea or something, or walk around the room or go up on the roof. Then we'd come back in and it would all magically mesh together – just like that.

You'd been struggling for six hours and then suddenly everyone came together and it fell into place. (Garbarini 1988c: 47)

Guilford goes as far as to claim, 'I doubt that any recognized creative person would deny the fact that incubation occurs and is frequently helpful' (1975: 55).

In situations where people feel rushed, pressured, threatened or even simply judged or ridiculed by their peers, they often revert back to old 'performance scripts' and algorithmic approaches that provide quick, though formulaic, results. In such stressful situations individuals may also be less likely to speculate, pay attention to emergent patterns or leave creative options open long enough to draw the full benefits of combinatorial play (Amabile 1983, 1996; Claxton 1997; Prince 1975). The protective frame of play can therefore encourage cognitive incubation by creating a psychological zone of nonchalance and detachment. Adopting a playful frame of mind can also provide similar benefits to taking a break, since play temporarily suspends certain information-processing functions. Hutt explains: 'play serves a physiological function in the awake organism analogous to that of REM sleep. During play there is temporary suspension of the cortical information-processing functions – the nervous system may be described as "idling", in the sense of an electromechanical engine, while at the same time allowing metabolic restitutive functions to take place' (1979: 181).

Fringe consciousness

Barry Miles (1998), a friend of Paul McCartney's since the mid-1960s, remarks how both Lennon and McCartney were skilled at entering a state of mind where ideas came to them from the fringes of consciousness: 'a half-trance state' (1998: 467). The creativity scholar Graham Wallas (after William James) discusses the elusiveness of such hazy fields of 'fringe-consciousness', likening it to peripheral vision:

> The field of vision of our eyes consists of a small circle of full 'focal' vision, surrounded by an irregular area of peripheral vision which is increasingly vague as the limit of vision is neared. We are usually unaware of the existence of peripheral vision, because as soon as anything interesting presents itself there we have a strong natural tendency to turn the focus of vision in its direction. Using these terms, we can say that one reason why we tend to ignore the mental events in our peripheral consciousness is that we have a strong tendency to bring them into focal consciousness as soon as they are interesting to us, but that we can

sometimes, by a severe effort, keep them in the periphery of consciousness, and observe them there. (Hadamard 1945: 25–6)

Miles gives the example of how this ability assisted the flow in McCartney's songwriting: 'When he gets a good melody, Paul often just blocks it in with any old words that spring to mind' (1998: 281). For instance, singer-songwriter Donovan recalls McCartney playing him the song 'Eleanor Rigby' (1966a) as a work in progress in 1966 with the title 'Ola Na Tungee' (Miles 1998: 281). In this way, McCartney could keep the flux-like momentum of melodic invention going, without switching over to a more focused, logical frame of mind or getting caught up in less pressing details that could be refined later. This is not to say that lyrics are any less important than the melodic content of a song, but rather that the rhythm and phonetic flow of the words, moreso than their literal meaning, can provide a solid structural basis for an emergent melody.

Shirley Manson of the band Garbage is another singer-songwriter who appreciates the value of not letting critical thinking get in the way of the flow of lyrical ideas as they emerge:

> I don't overthink anymore, I just try to really be in the moment – which is a challenge for me, at the best of times – but I've certainly managed to become better at that practice in the studio, where I just try not to overthink about how people will receive it, will they understand it, has it told the story? Instead, I just try to approach it like I would with poetry: to capture the feeling of what it is I'm trying to say. (Slater 2020)

The value of boredom

Boredom is not only unavoidable but a necessary part of record production. At times, recording musicians might endure lengthy periods of trying out variations and different approaches with little progress being made. As is clear from the Dylan example in Chapter 1, it is possible to be playful even though a situation is not a stimulating one. The paratelic state can include boredom (Apter 1991) just as for those people with an autotelic (playful) personality, optimal experience (flow) can arise out of situations where others might be bored or anxious. As Sutton-Smith observes, when 'objects become uninteresting, play responses increase in number apparently because the subject seeks now to increase stimulation which the objects no longer provide by themselves' (1979: 299). John Cage has gone as far as saying that 'the way to get ideas is to do something boring. For instance, composing in such a way the process of composing is boring induces ideas. They fly into one's head like birds' (1961: 12).

Playframes can be set to ensure that wherever possible, participant numbers are limited to only those that need to be present, so those involved don't feel overly self-conscious when proceedings take longer than expected or necessary lulls occur. During the making of Peter Gabriel's 1986 album *So*, only three people were involved in the development of the song's basic formal structures (i.e. co-producer Daniel Lanois, Gabriel and guitarist David Rhodes). Lanois likened the process to steering a small canoe, rather than a large ship or barge, allowing the team to make changes easily, without any loss of face or inconvenience to other players, who were brought in at a later time to add their parts as overdubs (Massey 2009: 21).

It is not uncommon for artists to feel vulnerable when creating and, therefore, they might wish to structure their working environment in such a way that they can operate without distraction. Doing so is conducive to attaining the deep concentration necessary to attain flow. DJ Shadow is one such practitioner who prefers to keep things private and personal when he creates:

> **To make music, I need isolation, focus and quiet.** I'm not the kind of person who can make beats on the back of the bus. It's difficult for me to do collaborations because I don't like there to be anyone else in the room. I need to be in my own space and to organise things in a way that makes sense to me. . . . **It takes me about two hours to get into the creative zone.** A spiritual jazz musician, I can't remember who, described it as a 'god frequency'. It isn't accessible when there's a lot of noise and chaos or when your mind is cluttered. It doesn't work if your day is broken up by meetings and appointments. I have to strip away all the social media, all the distractions, in order to tap into that frequency. (Fox 2016, bold emphasis in original)

Artefacts of play

Iterations of creative process, together with oscillations between serious and playful frames of mind, can be rapid and subtle enough (particularly in the flow state) to escape detection, while, at other times, stages such as 'preparation' (stage 2) may be clear enough due to an obvious lack of experience or domain skills that need addressing before further progress can be made. In this latter instance, considerable time and effort may be necessary to assess precisely what one is lacking and develop strategies for bridging the gap.

When it is clear that one is attending exclusively to 'response generation' tasks (stage 3) and novelty is the aim, then a very different class of skills and processes are called for, such as keeping options open longer, suspending critical thinking and fixing attention in the present moment (i.e. focusing on matters intrinsic to the task, rather than on future rewards). All of these aims can be achieved by adopting the playful frame of mind. It is somewhat paradoxical that, at such times, a creative goal is best attained by not focusing on it. This is since the greater the number of possible creative pathways that are trialled, and the more attention is directed to elements within the environment that may, or may not, end up being related to the task at hand, the more response possibilities will be generated which can then be scrutinized in the following stage (4). When iterations of these stages cycle over in quick succession, the process might appear more like a zig-zag motion towards the end goal than a logical linear path. While the eventual path to completion will seem obvious enough in retrospect – just as a joke's punch line is obvious after the telling – during the process of creation, it might be anyone's guess as to which pathways lead to satisfying results and which do not.

The recent plethora of Beatles album reissues including multiple 'outtakes' and different versions of songs stand as a testament to the band's creative process in the studio (as chronicled in Mark Lewisohn's *The Complete Beatles Recording Sessions* 1988). Theirs was an approach that benefited from trying wildly divergent approaches to any given track, and recording multiple 'takes' of the band playing together during the course of a session, where seemingly inconsequential arrangement ideas often emerged and were refined during subsequent takes. Some of these elements later became key facets of the finished recording. At other times, tracks were abandoned and returned to again much later, using a very different approach.

In their later studio years, the Beatles often started sessions at night and persevered long into the early hours of the morning in order to develop and refine their ideas as much as their performances, building on past experience and moving beyond their own previous standards of innovation with each release. While this empirical approach to shaping arrangements onsite paid off creatively, it was time-consuming and taxing for the technical staff. Beatles engineer Geoff Emerick complained that the band often didn't turn up at the studio until hours after their allotted studio-session start time. Nevertheless, the engineering staff were always at the ready regardless and were also the last to leave. Talking in 1968, producer George Martin was more sympathetic in his appraisal of the situation, acknowledging that such privilege was one of the spoils of the Beatles' fame. It was also reflective of a wider social, cultural and political awakening of youth power on the international stage: 'It's rather like the students revolting in France. Youth is realising its power. I was very much the boss and they were the pupils. This naturally changed with their success and power. They want more say about what goes on' (Howlett 2018).

Artefacts that emerge as a by-product of playful engagement with creative tasks can best be understood as 'artefacts of play' rather than mere creative products. While the distinction may seem subtle, or even pointless, it is anything but. It is not uncommon for fruitful ideas to arise out of play and only in retrospect does their value (in terms of wider application) become apparent. As Apter explains: 'This is not to say that activity in the playful state cannot have serious consequences, only that these consequences were not what the person had in mind at the time of carrying out the activity' (2018: 105).

A simple example of creative practice where artefacts of play are commonly generated is in the rehearsal room during group improvisation. If a tape recorder is activated and then forgotten about, the results can later be reviewed and anything 'promising' can be saved for integration into a future creative product. Kate Pierson of the B-52's recalls using such a strategy: 'we sometimes jam for hours or even days on something and then we sort of take the best parts in a very long process of listening and then collage those pieces together' (Schnee 2015). Cindy Wilson elaborates: 'the thing is, it's very labour intensive when you do it that way, 'cos you have to go back and listen to all the jamming and everything. But, that way you get an interesting and not predictable melody or harmony. Kate and I came out with some outrageous harmonies, just the weirdness and serendipity of jamming that way' (Pearson 2021).

In a similar manner, Brian Eno creates many hours of material that may or may not be used in a 'finished' product, explaining that until he has a deadline to meet, much of his work is in a state of flux. Whether or not one of his creative artefacts will be used (or how) depends upon yet-undetermined creative goals:

> My daughter recently . . . was looking at my archive, where I have 2,809 unreleased pieces of music, and she said, 'Dad, how do you actually finish any of these?' And I said, 'When there's a deadline.' And that's really true, but I'll tell you why that's true. When there's a deadline, there's also a destination, a context, a reason for something. And that's what makes me finish it. Up until that point,

it's an experiment. It's sitting on my shelf, and I can take it down again, as I often do, work on it again, put it back on, take it out two years later, work on it some more. So, everything's in progress until there's a reason to finish it for me. (Warren 2013)

Seminal hip-hop act De La Soul even went to the extraordinary effort (on their 2016 kickstarter-financed album *and the Anonymous Nobody*) of recording over 200 hours of multi-genre jam sessions with their ten-piece live band the Rhythm Roots Allstars over a three-year period. They later scrutinized the material and looped choice sections into 'beds' for their forthcoming tracks (Bollinger 2016; Cohen 2016) just as they might if sampling someone else's material. By sampling their own band instead, they retained ownership of their new album and avoided any possible clearance issues: something that had plagued them in the past. Despite De La Soul's first album (*3 Feet High and Rising* 1989) being inducted into the US Library of Congress' National Recording Registry, that very record – along with other early titles of theirs – is no longer commercially available due to the potential threat of litigation.

The 'comping' of vocal takes is another simple example of how recorded performances can be approached as by-product of play rather than serious attempts at 'perfection'. This common recording strategy, where a singer does multiple uninterrupted takes (often three or so) in quick succession, allows the performer to immerse themselves in the flow of the whole track. The takes can then be immediately reviewed and quickly compiled into one 'master' take. Since there is less pressure to come up with a best take immediately, the singer might even feel playful enough to take creative risks and try different approaches each time around. The resulting master doesn't need to be used in the final mix necessarily. Instead, it can be used primarily as feedback. Chances are, by listening to the playful compilation take, the singer might be inspired to approach subsequent takes in ways they might otherwise have not considered.

The following section presents a case study of Brian Wilson and the Beach Boys' (unfinished) *SMiLE* project.

Case study

The struggle behind the *SMiLE*

Part 1: Brian fucks with the formula!

One of the most well-documented recording projects in the history of rock music is one that was never actually completed. *SMiLE* was to be the follow-up album to the Beach Boys' first million-selling single 'Good Vibrations' (1966a). Described by its producer, Brian Wilson of the Beach Boys, as a 'pocket symphony', the record had taken an unprecedented seven months to complete (Leaf 1993). Likewise, with *SMiLE*, Wilson resolved to take his time. Conducting some eighty-or-so sessions between August 1966 and May 1967, he adopted the same mosaic-like compositional technique used to good effect on 'Good Vibrations' but extended to the scale of an entire album. Despite being eagerly awaited by fans, contemporary musicians and the band's record label alike – with Wilson working at his creative peak (Badman 2004; Bell 2004) – the project was scrapped after ten months of sessions had produced approximately fifty hours of tape.

Such extravagance must be understood in context of the times. Nineteen sixty-six was the year 'psychedelia' first entered the lexicon of popular culture (DeRogatis 2003), and rock music's status as a disposable distraction for teens was being challenged by artists like Dylan and the Beatles with their albums *Blonde on Blonde* (1966) and *Revolver* (1966b) respectively. Newcomers such as the Mothers of Invention, the Doors and the Pink Floyd were taking similar creative risks, pushing the boundaries of what popular music was capable of expressing, integrating musical and conceptual elements derived from outside of the domain. It was also the year that Wilson and the Beach Boys' collective status of passé was suddenly upgraded to progressive, thanks to their album *Pet Sounds* (1966b). Compared to previous efforts, the work sold poorly in the United States but nonetheless exerted a strong influence over the English music scene of the time (Abbott 2001). As a fledgling new member of the rock avant-garde, Wilson decided to surround himself with a 'hip' new group of collaborators while the Beach Boys were on tour promoting *Pet Sounds*. This was his attempt to buffer himself from those wanting a return to the formulaic songwriting and production style of earlier Beach Boys' records.

In contrast to the previously high-pressure, production-line manner in which he was obliged to deliver a new album every few months, Wilson was determined to take a more unhurried approach with *SMiLE*. This time, he wanted to focus on creative process as something to be enjoyed. The overall mood of the project (at first titled 'Dumb Angel') was both comic and spiritual. That is, Wilson believed that laughter lowered people's ego defences, opening them up to new experiences and perspectives (*Beautiful Dreamer* 2004). To this end, a variety of imaginative and child-like means were employed to inspire a playful frame of mind in both himself and those whose help he had enlisted. Some in the Beach Boys camp however – including publicist Derek Taylor, Beach Boy Mike Love and Wilson's father-cum-manager Murry – were less than sympathetic to his new approach and (increasingly) unpredictable whims, wondering where all this fun and games might be leading the band. Furthermore (sometimes lyricist) Mike Love openly resented Wilson's collaboration with new lyricist Van Dyke Parks (Priore 1997, 2005).

Instead of working on whole songs with clear large-scale syntactical structures, the *SMiLE* sessions were intentionally limited to recording short interchangeable fragments or 'modules'. These audio passages – many of which lasted only seconds – were somewhat analogous to single motion picture 'takes', with content ranging from musical (instrumental or vocal) to spoken word or, even, sound effects and role-playing. While it is commonplace for filmmakers to shoot scene takes according to a storyboarded structure, Wilson approached each fragment as an 'end-in-itself' (with near enough not good enough) as much as he did as a musical 'function'. In this manner, any number of larger structures and divergent moods could be produced through the process of combining and re-combining the modules in a variety of sequences (Doggett 2003). It was not uncommon for the syntactical basis of key modules to be returned to several times, either reinterpreted with a divergent new arrangement or merely refined: though not always for the better.

Although *SMiLE* was to contain songs in the traditional sense, it is difficult to say exactly where one starts and another ends. They are not always mutually exclusive entities but rather constitute a loosely unified group of interchangeable sound recordings and musical themes. Listening to the session tapes, it is possible to hear how an incidental idea might emerge in the context of one song, only to turn up again, months later, as the centrepiece of another. Wilson states, regarding the recording of 'Good Vibrations': 'we got so into it that the more we created, the more we wanted to create ... there was no real set direction we were going in' (Zollo 1997: 131). The process itself was clearly of-the-moment.

The problem with SMiLE was that Wilson never actually got around to the secondary process of combining the modules into an acceptable sequence. He clearly possessed the skills necessary to create an abundance of material, but stitching it all together was a challenge too great at the time. In fact, not one song was completed to his satisfaction by May 1967, when the project was finally scrapped. Regardless, many of the SMiLE modules have since surfaced in piecemeal releases by the band and as unauthorized 'bootleg' compilations. By far, the most significant release was in 2004 when Wilson and Van Dyke Parks finally sequenced a three-movement 'symphonic' configuration released by Nonesuch Records. This time, however, Wilson called upon his own backing band rather than the Beach Boys to re-record the various fragments. Not to be left behind, the Beach Boys' original record company Capitol Records eventually released over seven hours of original 1960s session 'highlights' in 2011 as *The Beach Boys: The Smile Sessions* (referred to herein as the 2011 boxset). This material, together with published session logs (Badman 2004; Slowinski and Boyd 2011) and anecdotal evidence gleaned from a variety of print, film and audio sources, constitutes a formidable body of data, making analysis of the original project today a more viable proposition.

SMiLE can be said to have failed long before it succeeded, in part, since it was an artistic and technical overreach, with Wilson employing non-linear production methods decades before DAW technology streamlined the process. As it turns out, the multiplicity of forms the SMiLE session material took on over some forty years at the hands of Wilson, the Beach Boys, Capitol and fans alike provides invaluable insight into the relationship of the parts to the whole within composition and record production in general. It also highlights the crucial role that DAW technology plays in today's decidedly non-linear record-production process.

Mid-1960s record-production practice

According to the Beatles' producer George Martin, the 'ultimate aim' of record making in the 1950s and early 1960s was to produce audio facsimiles of live performances that were 'as accurate as possible' (Badman 2000: 256). In the case of rock music, records at that time were all about capturing a 'vibe' or 'feel' – the proverbial 'lightning in a bottle' – with arrangements and sound-balance issues having to be sorted out before committing to tape. Recording sessions were generally conducted in three-hour blocks and, according to Helen Shapiro (an English pop starlet of the early 1960s), it wasn't uncommon to 'easily' record four songs in a single session. Editing was used extensively but was overwhelmingly a linear affair involving 'the splicing together of the best pieces, no matter how small' (Southall, Vince and Rouse 2002: 65) in order to maintain the illusion of a complete, unadulterated performance.

This isn't to say that there weren't exceptions to the rule. Certain record-production auteurs existed who had somehow attained a high level of creative autonomy (and autocracy). Phil Spector – famous for his 'wall of sound' – was one notable American example whose records seemingly defied the limits of sonic reality and conventions of ensemble performance. In England, Joe Meek was a similarly innovative and eccentric maverick. During the years 1964–5, Spector's influence on Wilson cannot be overstated. He later admitted, 'When I got really familiar with Spector's work. Then I started to see the point of making records. You design the experience to be a record rather than just a song. It's the record that people listen to' (Leaf 1990). Wilson even went to the extent of adopting Spector's session musicians ('The Wrecking Crew'), studio (Gold Star in Hollywood) and engineer (Larry Levine), in his effort to emulate his work.

With Spector's influence well and truly assimilated by early 1966, Wilson found his own production voice with the album *Pet Sounds* (1966b). It is as a whole that the album succeeds, sustaining a reflective mood from start to finish, and best listened to in one uninterrupted sitting. When the disc ends, one gets the feeling of having come back to 'reality' – not unlike surfacing from a darkened cinema after watching a beautiful, deftly paced movie. *Pet Sounds* diverges from previous Beach Boys' efforts in several ways. Its sound field has a relatively heightened sense of depth and 'warmth', with the songs employing more inventive use of harmony and chord voicings than was previously the case. The prominent use of percussion is another key feature (as opposed to the driving drum backbeats of yesteryear) with the orchestrations echoing the quirkiness of 'exotica' bandleader Les Baxter and the 'cool' of Burt Bacharach moreso than Spector's teen fanfares.

Although less successful than previous Beach Boys releases in the United States, *Pet Sounds* established a new market for the band in the UK and Europe.

Just as Spector had once set the production benchmark for Wilson, the young Beach Boy was now setting the standard for his trans-Atlantic contemporaries. Artists including the Who, Eric Clapton with Cream, and, in particular, Paul McCartney were all singing *Pet Sounds'* praises (Leaf 1990; Abbott 2001). In fact, McCartney and Beatles producer George Martin both cited the album as a major influence and inspiration for the *Sgt. Pepper's Lonely Hearts Club Band* album (1967a). Martin has since gone as far as to describe *Pet Sounds* as 'the criterion of excellence' in the popular-music world (*An All-Star Tribute to Brian Wilson* 2001). One major benefit of this new-found peer and critical acclaim was that Capitol trusted Wilson and his new stylistic direction. Knowing full well that the label would finance and promote his next effort regardless, Wilson, for a time at least, felt free to take even greater creative risks. And take risks, he did. By October 1966, as Beach Boy Bruce Johnston recalls, his own reaction to the first commercial fruits of Wilson's indulgence was, 'When we finally heard "Good Vibrations" edited and mixed, we thought we were going to have the biggest hit in the world or the career was over' (Abbott 2001: 113).

What is *SMiLE*?

Trying to describe *SMiLE* isn't an easy task, simply because it has no definitive form and content. For several decades, it was a most elusive thing, seemingly changing its size and shape as the years progressed. David Anderle once observed: 'It was pieces of music. That's why I've had trouble over these years, in terms of people trying to put a *SMiLE* record together. It's my recollection that Brian was still experimenting with units of music. Just from the musical point of view, there never was a *SMiLE*. As a finished product' (Boyd 2011). What *can* be said about *SMiLE* is that it isn't a specific album, nor is it a particular group of songs. Possibly the best term offered yet to describe the project is that of 'sonic menagerie' (Wolfe 2011). According to Mark Linett – the person chiefly responsible for collating the session tapes since 1988 – all that remains from the eighty-or-so sessions conducted between 3 August 1966 and 18 May 1967 is 'a bunch of bits and pieces – a few songs that were more or less completed later' ('#118 – Mark Linett Beach Boys SMiLE Part One' 2011). By the time the project was scrapped, Wilson states that he'd recorded more than enough backing tracks to fill an entire album, but the Beach Boys hadn't sung on most of these at that point (McCulley 2003: 198).

Wilson once described his compositional process as emerging from playing with 'feels': 'I go to the piano and play "feels". "Feels" are specific rhythm patterns, fragments of ideas. Once they're out of my head and into the open air. I can see them and touch them firmly. Then the song starts to blossom and become a real thing' (Leaf 1990: 8). Evoking the senses of touch and sight as metaphors for shaping ideas here (or was it true synaesthesia at work?) is noteworthy. Wilson's modular record-production technique – first used during the 'Good Vibrations' sessions – can be understood as a logical extension of his earlier 'feels' approach. In fact, the *SMiLE* modules can be defined as primary artefacts of a compositional process not unlike *musique concrète*. Long before any final song form had been envisaged, succinct musical ideas, manifest as ephemeral sound waves, were concretized via magnetic flux patterns acting upon black oxide adhered to pieces of mylar tape. These strips could then be scrutinized, torn apart and recombined like pieces of clay shaped by an artist's hand. This empirical process was so dependent upon recording technology that, as Eno asserts (Tamm 1995: 41), it constituted a new popular-music artform altogether. Admittedly, the Beatles had already applied *musique concrète* techniques as embellishment to their track 'Tomorrow Never Knows' (1966c) released some months before 'Good Vibrations' came out. However, the latter track itself actually *emerged* from such a process.

The somewhat tenuous relationship between the songs written by Wilson and Van Dyke Parks and their manifestations as recordings finds a parallel in the Russian Formalist distinction between a unifying, overriding abstract pattern (*fabula*) and the specific linear sequencing of the various substructures inspired by it (*syuzhet* (Holmberg 1996)). *SMiLE*'s main, unifying theme was, arguably, the national myth of 'relentless European expansion across America, westward from Plymouth Rock to Hawaii' (Badman 2004: 151). This explains the abundance of 'tack' pianos (mimicking the saloon pianos of Hollywood Westerns) and ukuleles, along with imaginative references to Americana like the 'iron horse', evoked vocally and musically in the track 'Cabinessence' (1969). Much of the material recorded has little however, if anything, to do with the Americana theme. And even if it did, a theme is not quite a story. There are no central characters. No Black Jack Daveys or House Carpenters populate the *SMiLE* pantheon. Nor do any specific pilgrims progress onwards westward from Plymouth Rock with whom the listener can relate. Names arise but only in passing. It's the potential experience rather than actual resulting narratives that hold *SMiLE* together. Such open-endedness would eventually play a key part in the project's undoing, however. Even a work as inscrutable as Joyce's *Ulysses* (1922) – similarly famous for its playfully divergent perspectives and styles – was a retelling of Homer's *The Odyssey* (1990), featuring key episodes based upon that epic's structure (though compressed into the twenty-four-hour sequence of 16 June 1904: 'Bloomsday'). The mention of actual events that took place on that day in real Dublin locations further supports an otherwise fragmented text, making it more manageable for both writer and reader alike.

What does *SMiLE* sound like?

If *SMiLE* is best considered a sonic menagerie, then describing how 'it' sounds is a pointless exercise. Rather, it's preferable to describe the many musical inhabitants of this complex macrocosm. The music might sound at one moment not unlike a homophonic version of a Carlo Gesualdo madrigal, filled with manneristic, unpredictable chromatic turns (though treated with a typically glissandi-laden Beach Boys' approach), only to morph into a cheesy doo-wop ditty the next. Other modules sound like young men pretending to be animals, or performing an 'underwater' chant populated by word-beasts such as 'swim swim fishy', 'underwater current', 'jellyfish', 'shark', 'dolphin', 'goldfish' and 'eel'. Some fragments are reminiscent of a wild-west movie score or the Beach Boys faking a group orgasm. A musical sound painting of a steam locomotive gives way elsewhere to a spoken word skit about a man trapped inside a microphone. Some modules feature the guttural chanting of cartoon-esque cavemen or a group of French horns 'talking' and 'laughing' with each other.

What is consistent about *SMiLE* is that it usually sounds playful or 'colourful' – not unlike what you might expect to hear in an animated *Sesame Street* (1969–present) segment. The music often, simultaneously, employs instrumental and vocal elements that are widely varied with respect to timbre and pitch range, combining them in a somewhat contrary 'interlocking' fashion. That is, they fit but also feel autonomous. A plethora of sound densities result from these combinations. The vocal arrangements create a kind of 'tapestry' of sound, using a wide range of pitch centres, antiphonal effects, rhythmic variations, juxtapositions of *legato* and *staccato* figures, rounders-like echoes and vocal effects not usually associated with mid-1960s rock records. Harpsichords and tack pianos abound (often played in unison). Mallets are also used extensively, as is quirky, echoey percussion. *SMiLE* exemplifies an ongoing naive, playful search for novel ways of recombining elements. It could just as well be titled, 'Things to do for composers on a rainy day.'

When one compares *SMiLE* – and indeed *Pet Sounds* – to earlier Beach Boys records, their unique sense of rhythm becomes evident. Whereas, the Beach Boys surf and hotrod songs displayed a constant, rollicking sense of metre and pulse well suited to dancing, *SMiLE* never lets the listener settle into a groove for too long. Even the most well-known version of 'Heroes and Villains' – the *Smiley Smile* version (1967a) – only runs for forty seconds before the strident, Spector-esque instrumental backing disappears, leaving only a barbershop quartet-like *ritardando* cadence and then silence, which is broken by a genteel eighteenth-century dance feel (the ever-present 'Bicycle Rider' theme).

SMiLE sounds in many ways 'visual'. That is, many of the modules constitute 'word painting' or allude to visual concepts or physical entities. For example, the four elements are evoked in the tracks 'Wind Chimes', 'Fire', the earthen 'Vega-Tables' and 'Cool Cool Water' (aka 'I Love to Say Da Da' and 'In Blue Hawaii'). By lyricist Van Dyke Parks's own admission, the project was approached in 'cartoon terms. To me it was a musical cartoon' (Priore 2005: 102). *SMiLE*'s individual modules are indeed analogous to cartoon panels, though each module is like a panel without a fixed narrative to attach itself to. Like Roy Lichtenstein's Pop-art painting 'Drowning Girl' (1963), each module seems to have been granted a sense of autonomy from the start. They are detached as in 'not linked', as well as possessing a zen-like lack of emotional charge, being meditations upon a scene, rather than commentaries. Whether or not the modules are embedded within a larger whole is a secondary concern. And their sense of singularity is evident in the disjointed and abrupt fashion with which they're often spliced together.

The boldness of 'Good Vibrations' (1966a) and *SMiLE*'s many jumpcut edits is, indeed, their most striking characteristic. Due to the relative lack of multitracking options in 1960s-era record-making practice, modern-day listeners might be surprised to learn that tape editing was at that time a fine art and extensively used as a means of compiling the best takes from recording sessions into a seamless, sequential whole. Pink Floyd manager Peter Jenner recalls that EMI Records engineers in 1967 were so expert at the art of editing it was impossible to discern a tape splice even in the most delicate of instrumental passages (Cavanagh 2003: 48). *SMiLE*'s highly noticeable edits, therefore, must be acknowledged as compositional statements in themselves, giving the music a sonic signature every bit as noticeable as the performances themselves. There was no way this music could be 'real'. Wilson was therefore echoing the techniques of *musique concrète* and seemed to be breaking the audio 'fourth wall' – if there can be said to be such a thing.

One gets the impression with *SMiLE* of a seemingly inexhaustible source of creativity and inspiration that is nonetheless defiantly anti-intellectual and of-the-moment. Wilson's child-like ability to find wonder in the ordinary fills this musical cornucopia unselfconsciously to the brim. No idea seems too silly, or incidental, to be tried out, and no one version of any idea seems to be accepted as definitive: everything is 'fair game'. Wilson recently chose the following words to describe the project: 'Childhood. Freedom. A rejection of adult rules and adult conformity. Our message was, "Adults keep out. This is about the spirit of youth"' (Myers 2011). It was this rejection of the usual 'rules of the game' that ultimately caused *SMiLE* to remain in a state of limbo for so long, since the verse/chorus/middle-eight schtick of mid-1960s pop-song convention clearly wouldn't suffice. That isn't to say *SMiLE* required structures of great sophistication. Rather, a means of organization which honoured the regressive nature of the modules and their reluctance to form unequivocally meaningful statements was required. This lack of clear, logical meaning was a key problem for Mike Love, as epitomized by his reaction to Van Dyke Parks's lyrics, particularly for 'Cabin Essence' and 'Surf's Up'. He simply couldn't fathom what all this was supposed to mean and fretted that Beach Boys fans would feel the same (Badman 2004: 149, 163; Priore 2005). The fact is that *SMiLE*'s many musical and lyrical elements don't really mean anything. Its modules, when considered as discreet units, represent a return to the pre-grammatical, non-linear and analogical (as opposed to logical) thinking of early childhood (Meares 2005): they are artefacts of play.

Technology and frame of mind

Notwithstanding the practice of linear editing – commonplace ever since magnetic tape replaced direct-to-disc recording (Southall, Vince and Rouse 2002) – multitrack recording, though long extant by the late 1960s, facilitated a means of joining together many disparate musical utterances 'as if' they were one (albeit, now in a concurrent manner). Such developments in technology alone, however, didn't inspire practitioners to fully exploit the potential of the medium. Instead, a thoroughly playful frame of mind also informed such fanciful productions as 'Good Vibrations' (1966a), *SMiLE* and the Beatles' *Sgt. Pepper's Lonely Hearts Club Band* (1967a). And in doing so, these key works ushered in new standards of popular-music record making (Miles 1998; *Beautiful Dreamer* 2004). It would now be required of listeners to suspend their disbelief regarding the obvious acoustic implausibility of records. If this were not the case, then the Beatles should have attempted a tape-loop filled 'Tomorrow Never Knows' (1966c) in late 1963 when four-track recording was first made available to them, instead of the energetic live 'rave-up' performance of 'I Want to Hold Your Hand' (1963).

Not surprisingly perhaps, in today's world where analogue tape recording is all but a memory, turning original compositions into record productions – even for skilled musicians – has less in common with traditional real-time performance than the process of filmmaking (with all of its storyboarding, multiple takes, various camera angles and editing). This synchronization of separate audio events to create the impression of concurrency, or sequentially using 'cut and paste' functions, can now be achieved with programs as rudimentary as GarageBand. Nor, is it uncommon for novices to combine their own audio recordings with virtual instruments in software, sequenced either in real time (using the computer keyboard to input notes) or stepwise fashion. When mixed together, these independent parts should, at best, integrate sufficiently to create the illusion of a unified musical event.

If the proliferation in recent years of low-cost DAWs is to facilitate anything more than greater convenience for practitioners, a corresponding challenging of certain tacit assumptions regarding creative process must be forthcoming. The many options for manipulating sound events facilitated by DAW technology (i.e. multitrack recording, non-linear editing, looping and automated mixing) potentialize a process of combinatorial play. Such an approach, however, is equally dependent upon a frame of mind where 'implications beyond the present moment' are temporarily banished from awareness (Apter 1991: 14). In this way, using a program like Logic Pro (where the central editing window is a linear timeline-based one, modelled on the piano rolls of yesteryear) might produce very different results to those made using a truly non-linear approach to accessing and triggering audio files, such as the 'Session View' window featured in the Ableton Live. Here, multiple loops and samples each have their own discreet 'cue' commands, allowing them to be resynchronized and playfully (re)combined 'on the fly' in real time, before the serious task of committing to any set linear organization rears its head.

The parts and the whole: Non-linearity, regression and emergence

The 2011 boxset demonstrates that since the release of Wilson's 'symphonic' remake in 2004 there are now, arguably, two *SMiLE*s – the linear and the non-linear versions. These could also be described, respectively, as the quasi-narrative and the ludic versions. The original modules (as featured on the 2011 boxset CDs 2 to 5) are like the many rooms within *Steppenwolf*'s 'Theatre of the Mind' – for madmen only (Hesse [1927] 2015). Willingness is required on the listener's part to leave preconceptions of linear flow behind and take each module as a discreet experience, just as one might take the separate rooms of a funhouse. They possess no logical connection. In their unorganized state, one module doesn't modify or contextualize the other, in order to form a statement or argument. They resonate rather than respond to each other – like pictures hanging side-by-side on the same wall.

In *The Metaphor of Play* psychiatrist Russell Meares contrasts the 'inner' non-linear language of playful thought with the linear language of mundane public discourse. He writes: 'The language of the playing child has a peculiar form. It shows abbreviations, it jumps, and it is not grammatical. It moves by analogy, resemblance, and other associations' (2005: 38). Similarly, Givón uses the term 'pre-grammatical' to describe a form of communication common to both 'pidgin' speech and that of young children at an early stage of language acquisition (Robert and Chapouthier 2006: 165). Here, words are starkly juxtaposed rather than integrated into the complex syntactical relationships of true language. Koestler explains that pre-grammatical communication is inherently visual, like the unfolding panels in a cartoon strip, and states that the reason that the highest compliment possible is to call a thinker 'visionary' stems from the fact that 'true creativity often starts where language ends' (1964: 177):

> the poet who reverts to the pictorial mode of thought is regressing to an older and lower level of the mental hierarchy – as we do every night when we dream, as mental patients do when they regress to infantile fantasies. But the poet, unlike the dreamer in his sleep, alternates between two different levels of the mental hierarchy. . . . The poet thinks both in images and verbal concepts, at the same time and in quick alternation. . . . The dreamer floats among the phantom shapes of the hoary deep; the poet is a skin-diver with a breathing tube. (1964: 168)

Equipped with ProTools digital editing facilities, and urged on by supportive and nurturing (new) family, friends and co-artists, Wilson finally displayed the artistic agility of Koestler's proverbial, masterly skin-diver (*Beautiful Dreamer* 2004). The 2004 'symphonic' sequencing of *SMiLE* displays a complexity that none of the parts themselves could hint at. Its overall affect is an emergent property, displaying a surprising sense of flow, given the varied and disjointed nature of the modules. Capra states: 'Emergence results in the creation of novelty, and this novelty is often qualitatively different from the phenomena out of which it emerged' (2002: 36). There is a necessary trade-off, however. Something grand is gained, but the *SMiLE*-as-game phenomenon has perhaps since been overshadowed by the aesthetically successful integration of the modules. What for so long had been a lively subject of speculation and a source of interactivity was now in danger of being mistaken for an audio fossil. Similarly, Meares suggests, 'Words for affect are dead metaphors' (2005: 182). It could be argued that the 'symphonic' *SMiLE* constitutes – as does any 'finished' work of art – dead play: concretized process. The 2011 boxset has clearly addressed this situation by including both the 2004 linear sequence and the separate modules.

Feedback

Emergent works can be described as 'dissipative structures' (Prigogine and Stengers 1984). That is, they are simultaneously changing-yet-stable. At first, a system can be said to be structurally constant but open with regard to the flow of feedback of some type. Such feedback loops are a key characteristic of non-linear systems in general. In the case of simple thermodynamic systems it is energy that flows back through the system. In the case of human beings and social systems, it is information (Capra 2002). If the flow of feedback continues to increase past a certain critical point, however, the system can't accommodate the stress in its present state, and one of two things must happen. The system either breaks down into chaos or spontaneously transforms into a more complex ordered state that is qualitatively different to its predecessor. Importantly, it is impossible to predict in advance what form such transformations might take (Capra 1997). Accordingly, creative individuals need to occasionally 'stand back' and observe what's developing before them in order to facilitate such feedback of information into consciousness. The process is necessarily iterative: the artist responds, observes again, responds once more and so on. Only after considering what is gradually coming together can the artist know how to respond in a way that honours the integrity of the emerging work. Csikszentmihalyi expands:

> Whereas a conventional artist starts painting a canvas knowing what she [*sic*] wants to paint, and holds to her original intention until the work is finished, an original artist with equal technical training commences with a deeply felt but undefined goal in mind, keeps modifying the picture in response to the unexpected colors and shapes emerging on the canvas, and ends up with a

finished work that probably will not resemble anything she started out with. If the artist is responsive to her inner feelings, knows what she likes and does not like, and pays attention to what is happening on the canvas, a good painting is bound to emerge. On the other hand, if she holds on to a preconceived notion of what the painting should look like, without responding to the possibilities suggested by the forms developing before her, the painting is likely to be trite. (1990: 208)

The Beatles producer George Martin used the analogy of a painter looking at their canvas to explain the Beatles' creative process on their *Sgt. Pepper* album:

> [it] grew of its own accord. I don't think they really knew what they were doing on it, and I didn't have a great deal of an idea either. . . . They would come in and say, 'We've got an idea for a bit here, but we're not quite sure how it's going to develop. So, let's put it down and we'll go away and think about it'. . . . In many incidences this just grew. . . . It was rather like painting an enormous canvas in a way, and putting a bit of extra colour on it every day and standing back and looking at it, saying, 'Yes, I think we'll do a bit more here'. (Badman 2000: 258)

While a psychological application of Prigogine's dissipative structures model, as described by Bütz (1997), justifies stress and anxiety as necessary to the creative process, there is only so much an individual might choose to tolerate before giving up. Despite demonstrating the ability to complete many of the actual *SMiLE* modules (in particular, the backing tracks: for which he wasn't dependent upon the Beach Boys' help), Wilson's ability to withstand the emotional and psychic stress necessary to facilitate the metamorphosis of the modules into finished songs, and a pop album of appropriate length, wasn't forthcoming in 1967.

Indeed, Wilson wasn't an island, accountable as he was to the larger network of Capitol Records and the Beach Boys as the commercial vehicle for his artistry. By January of 1967, the label was anxious to further exploit the recent success of the single 'Good Vibrations' (1966a) before it faded from the public's memory. They even went to the extent of printing up 400,000 record covers, complete with full-colour photographic booklet inserts (a lavish package for the time) and taking out trade advertisements heralding the imminent arrival of the album (Priore 2011). Wilson was therefore increasingly under pressure to finish the project quickly, and to do so in a manner that didn't adversely affect the Beach Boys' innocuous public personae by being too 'far out'.

The process of trialling tape edits with razors was a much more time-consuming and potentially destructive practice than today's high-speed computer-editing process, as was the need to cut trial acetate discs to play outside the studio. Wilson was also concurrently juggling the multiple roles of composer, arranger, performer, musical director, producer and mixdown co-engineer. It's not surprising that he simply scrapped the project in May 1967, unable to bridge the gap between his artistic vision and the confines of 1960s pop formulae. Perhaps it wasn't so much Wilson who couldn't withstand the mental and emotional chaos of the creative journey any longer but those around him. He later claimed he felt *SMiLE* was too self-indulgent, fearing he was letting the Beach Boys down, 'It was too fancy for the public. I was getting too fancy and arty and doing things that were just not Beach Boys, at all. They were made for me' (Badman 2004: 163). Thirty-seven years later, in 2003, within the context of a new supportive environment, Wilson was finally able to stand back and look at *SMiLE* for what it was, or might be.

Whereas the affect of *Brian Wilson Presents SMiLE* (2004a) is that of a well-integrated symphonic whole, it was nonetheless, famously, an afterthought. Thirty-seven years of cognitive incubation preceded the process, a period of time that allowed recording technology to catch up with Wilson's artistic vision. While the primary process of creating the modules themselves – as separate texts – was one of combinatorial play, the task of fashioning these resultant texts into larger structures was a similar, but secondary, compositional process of combinations and associations, albeit on a larger scale. This ongoing activity of, and, cognitive playfulness rather than abstract logic, provided the opportunity for vital clues to emerge. As *SMiLE* lyricist Van Dyke Parks states: 'Brian's music had an . . . audio novelty to it. The invention was Edisonian, empirical – it had to be toughed out by this process of trial and error' (Priore 2005: 80). Once again, the process was a heuristic one rather than algorithmic. When a high degree of fit is evident, however, analysts can mistake it as the product of conscious adherence to deterministic principles.

A key example of such a successful join, one that gives the impression of real premeditated compositional intention, is the 2nd movement segue from the 'Child Is Father of the Man' (2004b) into the 'Surf's Up' (2004c) section. This is achieved by the inclusion of a thirty-six-second-long module best described as containing a 'wandering/searching' piano figure. In this context, the fragment functions as a bridge between the two sections. In one 2011 boxset sequence, however (CD 1: Track 11), the module is featured earlier on in the piece resulting in a less convincing sense of integration. In this way, even though the modules featured are the same, simply rearranging their order can make an easily discernable, qualitative difference to the whole. This asymmetrical phenomenon has its counterpoint in language. Robert and Chapouthier use the term 'anchoring' to explain how 'the development of the meaning of an utterance emerges from a series of connections between the different component parts' (2006: 162). The initial polysemy of any given term is reduced by its linear context; and so too, it can be argued that the musical function of any given motif can, likewise, be transformed by its placing. Robert and Chapouthier go on to say that 'language is nothing more than relationships' (2006: 162).

The term 'compositional morphology' can be used to denote how a new emergent whole displays characteristics not reducible to the 'sum of its parts', while the parts themselves retain their own individual characteristics (2006: 161). Though this concept has been described in terms of linear organization, it can also occur within a musical context in a concurrent fashion. Brian Wilson discusses how by studying the work of Phil Spector he learnt to produce new emergent sounds: 'achieving one sound out of two, mixing two things to become one. Making a guitar and a piano sound like a third thing. Rather than, 'Hey! I hear that as a guitar and piano.' They say, 'Hey! Dig that sound!'' ('Brian Wilson Interview 2' 1997).

Part 2: *SMiLE*, humour, play and creativity

Humour

Humour was a core element of *SMiLE*: a 'vital ingredient' (Doggett 2003: 66). In 1967, with the sessions still in progress, Wilson confidently declared, 'the album will include lots of humour – some musical and some spoken' (Priore 2005: 105). He even proclaimed, albeit prematurely, that the forthcoming single ('Heroes and Villains') would constitute a surprising new sound for rock music, calling it 'a three-minute musical comedy' (Priore 2005: 104). Listening to a 'Alternate Version' of the song (1990) – which leaves out the 'Bicycle Rider' theme featured so prominently in the 'homespun' post-*SMiLE* single version (1967a), in favour of the musical-comedy inspired 'Cantina' section – it is clear that Wilson wasn't making an empty claim, even if he didn't fully achieve his goal at the time. Decades later, after re-recording and assembling key *SMiLE* modules into a forty-eight-minute album in 2004, Wilson could finally lay claim to producing 'a very uplifting, jovial album' (Priore 2005: 9). David Anderle recalls: 'The key word for Brian was humour. If he could get humour into the world, into any situation he wouldn't have problems. . . . He felt that the moment somebody laughed, that while they're laughing all control is gone. They cannot control themselves and at that moment they can have a spiritual experience' (*Beautiful Dreamer* 2004).

Fragments of *SMiLE* released over the years bring a sense of humour and child-like spirit of playfulness to the listener. The process of writing and recording the project was intentionally infused with the same spirit. Wilson stated in a 1977 radio interview that just before starting work on 'Heroes and Villains' he 'was just in a playful mood. I get that way. Just before I go in and do something great' (Badman 2004: 153). It is noteworthy that by the time work began on *SMiLE*, Wilson was aware of the creative benefits of humour postulated by Koestler in his *The Act of Creation* (1964). When asked in a 2005 interview what sort of literature affected him when he was growing up in Hawthorne, Wilson answered: '*The Act of Creation* . . . Koestler's book really was the big one for me' (Brown 2005).

As well as producing music during the *SMiLE* sessions, Wilson recorded several improvised and humorous spoken-word scenarios, role-playing games and child-like chants with his friends. Although he'd originally envisaged releasing a number of albums from the *SMiLE* sessions including humour, sound effects and, even, a health-food themed LP, Capitol Records vetoed the idea (Badman 2004). It wasn't the first time he had recorded spoken-word or comedic musical numbers for inclusion on Beach Boys records, but only ever as 'filler' material. Even an interview and audio 'blooper-reel' were used to make up for shortfall on previous albums. Efforts such as '"Cassius" Love vs. "Sonny" Wilson' (1964), and 'I'm Bugged at My Ol' Man' (1965) were light-hearted ways of letting off steam, dealing as they did with Beach Boy taboos like the rivalry between cousins Wilson and Mike Love, and Wilson's ongoing problems with his abusive father and former manager Murry. In light of the fact that he had previously used humour to relieve some of the anxiety caused by intergroup politics on previous albums, it is reasonable to assume that Wilson saw humour as a means of attenuating any anxiety that a departure from familiar Beach Boys territory might cause (for both fans and the band alike). As it happened, Love and the rest of the Beach Boys appreciated jovial songs like 'Heroes and Villains' and 'Vega-Tables' much more than the esoterica of 'Surf's Up' (Badman 2004).

Playfulness

Martin states that the 'social context of humor is one of play. Indeed, humor is essentially a way for people to interact in a playful manner' (2007: 5). Nowhere is the inventive use of humour and spirit of playfulness more evident than on the collection of *SMiLE* recordings compiled under the title 'Psycodelic Sounds'. These recordings feature Wilson and his close friends and colleagues, including Michael Vosse, David Anderle, Danny Hutton and Van Dyke Parks, clowning around and playing out various silly scenarios. Reum (2011) refers to the group as 'The Vosse Posse'. Notably, the Beach Boys are conspicuous in their absence from the fun. Though available as bootlegs in their entirety, a portion of the 'Psycodelic Sounds' tapes is included – some eight minutes out of approximately two hours of material – in the 2011 boxset. Badman (2004) states that the tapes aren't particularly funny. And he's right. Rather, it is the child-like, improvised associations and hopped-up sense of joyful camaraderie that impresses. There's an unselfconscious sense of energy present in the recordings, as well as a disregard for the sacred cows of the adult world.

Ludicrous scenarios are played out with real conviction in many of the 'Psycodelic Sounds' tracks. In one case, Wilson supposedly falls into a microphone, causing it to short circuit (2011 boxset CD 2: Track 37). Other sections sound manic with, more often than not, thoughts leading effortlessly and mercurially to others. In one example, Wilson plays a melody in the upper register of the piano. Somebody asks where the sound's coming from, and various word associations start flowing. Wilson interjects with the bridge *ostinato* from 'Good Vibrations' (still in a high register of the piano), the tinkling of which reminds one of the participants of an ice-cream van. The rest of the Vosse Posse start play-ordering various ice confections, with Van Dyke Parks commenting (satirically) that he wants white ice cream, since they're eating in such a 'nice white' neighbourhood.

The playful use of association, so evident in the 'Psycodelic Sounds' tapes, is also adopted in the *SMiLE* songs and their arrangements. It is as if they document an ongoing stream of consciousness. A lyrical pun by Van Dykes Parks featured in the song 'Surf's Up' illustrates the point, bringing together Edgar Allen Poe's locus of torture and the classical concert hall using the word 'pit' (i.e. pit and pendulum/orchestra pit) in a manner that Koestler would describe as 'appropriately inappropriate' (1964: 92). Composer Wilson also found creative potential in seemingly innocuous points of 'bisociation' but in a multi-modal manner. A lyrical reference to a diamond necklace in the same track inspired him to ask a session percussionist to play the shaker so it should sound like rattled jewellery (2011 boxset CD 3: Track 18). While it is unlikely that Wilson expected the sound to connote 'jewellery' to the listener

– the shaker part is too subtle and ongoing to warrant attention – nonetheless, such unself-conscious, even corny, use of simile is a good example of playful, associative thinking.

Elsewhere in the 'Psycodelic Sounds' tapes, there's an abundance of chants. For example, there are several 'vegetable' chants, 'underwater' chants and 'swimming' chants, as well as sound effects including breathing sounds followed by moaning and laughter. In what starts out as a particularly mundane *audio verité* recording titled 'Bob Gordon's Real Trip', a chatty Chicago taxicab driver who seems to take himself, and his job, too seriously is suddenly and inexplicably zoned out: his voice drenched in spring reverb. It is as if the bored passenger has started tripping on acid. Some of the relatively subtler features in the musical *SMiLE* modules share the same uninhibited inventiveness. For example: the childish 'Doing, doing' backing vocals evoking banjos in the 'Home on the Range' section of 'Cabin Essence'; the laughing French horns that surface momentarily in 'Surf's Up' (first movement); and the sound of crunching celery in time to the music of 'Vega-Tables'.

Playfulness and concentration

To describe a situation as playful doesn't mean it should be lacking a sense of challenge, effort or focus. According to Amabile (1996), intellectual playfulness experienced during creative action involves high levels of concentration: an overwhelming sense of involvement in the task at hand. Csikszentmihalyi, similarly, states 'activities that for adults correspond to play show increased concentrations' (1979: 259), so that the pleasurable nature of task engagement is a result of 'the ability [of individuals] to screen out stimulation and to focus only on what they decide is relevant for the moment' (Csikszentmihalyi 1990: 87). When attention is channelled, the resulting experience of heightened awareness, and the sense of self it reinforces, brings rewards in-the-moment. According to Csikszentmihalyi, disordered thought simply isn't enjoyable.

Despite *SMiLE* being a project that embodied the spirit of playfulness, it was every bit as much a labour of love. The session tapes reveal Wilson shaping the musician's interpretations of his arrangements, as might any experienced orchestral conductor. His interactions are rapid and focused – as one might expect for a record producer working under union-imposed time constraints – displaying a level of concentration that is consistently high. Nonetheless, his tone with the musicians remains always assertive but polite. The tapes give the impression that he is acutely aware of subtle nuances of performance, honing in on specifically what needs to be altered where, and how.

When it came to working with the Beach Boys during vocal sessions, Wilson was just as demanding. Member Bruce Johnston likened Wilson's resolve during the *SMiLE* sessions to General Patton ('Behind Studio Doors' 2011). Mike Love has often recounted just how challenging it was recording vocals for the project: 'On one passage of "Good Vibrations" we did it over and over again. . . . It was so exhausting! I can remember doing 25 to 30 vocal overdubs of the same part, and when I say part, I mean the same section of the record, maybe no more than two, three, four, five seconds long!' (Badman 2004: 145). Van Dyke Parks states that during the *SMiLE* sessions, he and Wilson remained productive despite being surrounded by great pressure. 'I was dazzled by his talent. In spite of all the social pressures around us. . . . I was swept up by the prodigiousness of his activity. He did a lot of stuff' (Priore 2005: 81). Wilson explains that he tried to make *SMiLE*'s challenging process of writing and recording as much fun as possible, to keep himself and Parks focused on the task (Wilson 2011). This is in keeping with Apter's observation that play forms an 'enchanted' zone that keeps the rest of the world at bay for a time: 'play . . . is a state of mind, a way of seeing and being, a special mental "set" towards the world and one's actions in it' (1991: 13). In this way, the protective bubble of the playful frame of mind banishes from consciousness the fear of harm, since clearly 'this is not real'.

Playframes

The *SMiLE* modules exemplify the limiting aspect of playframing. By restricting the recording and arrangement task to short, singular structures, Wilson's attention was limited, for the moment, to that zone alone. Moreover, each module constitutes a discreet entity with rules of its own. Once it has been recorded, that particular game is over. A new module can be then approached afresh as a completely new 'field of play' with different rules. As a result, there is a tendency towards great divergence with regard to timbre, instrumental combinations and mood: even between modules intended for the same song. There is also a playful toying with each module's various components that leans as much towards Lieberman's (1977) figurative kaleidoscope of combinatorial play as it does the more functional backing arrangements of Wilson's pre-*Pet Sounds*, Phil Spector-influenced efforts. This is possible since there is no obvious, immediate debt to a larger linear string of events. The minute-long track 'Mama Says' (1967b) – a later remake of the *SMiLE* 'Sleep a Lot' module – illustrates how when Wilson focused on a strictly limited musical field (the track contains only two lines of lyric sung over repeatedly, retaining the same group of notes), without the need to consider extrinsic concerns such as functionality, then more of his attention was freed to toy with the 'givens' within that field (which, in this case, included the rhythm and phrasing of the words/notes). If the 2004 production of 'Vega-Tables' (2004d) is an oil painting, then 'Mama Says' is a page ripped from a notepad full of doodles, sketches and studies.

In addition to using modules as frames, Wilson used the concept of physical zones to inspire a playful frame of mind during the *SMiLE* sessions. These 'fun zones' are a common point of discussion for chroniclers of the *SMiLE* story, and include such things as: the piano in a sandpit; an indoor Arabian tent fitted out with hookahs and cushions; a gymnasium in the living room; and business meetings in the swimming pool. Costumes and props were also used to signify a playful mood was appropriate. Perhaps most famously, fire helmets were worn by session musicians during the session for 'The Elements: Fire', with a fire lit in a waist-paper basket that released smoke into the recording studio (Badman 2004). Wilson's friend Danny Hutton adds:

> He's saying things that he was gonna do, and I'd look at him. 'Is he testing me', you know? 'Yeah, I'm gonna get a sandbox in the living room with a piano.' And it just seemed so bizarre when he talked about it. But then when you saw it, and he'd be sitting there in bare feet playing with his feet in the sand . . . Why not? Shut your eyes and you're feeling the sand. Then it made sense. (Anderle, Hutton and Vosse 2011)

If Wilson's use of fun zones, costumes and props seems eccentric, then consider that institutionalized forms of play rely on the same types of framing. Take, for instance, the proscenium arch and costumes used in theatre or the boundary lines on a sports field and uniforms worn by players (Apter 1991). Given that Wilson, at the time, approached his compositions first by creating 'feels', then the need to use such props seems logical, if not just plain necessary.

Cognitive incubation

When asked how he might define his artistic approach with *SMiLE*, Wilson answered, 'To take my time. I wanted to take a little longer when recording' (Myers 2011). Looking at the chronological progress of the sessions, it is noteworthy that

Wilson paced himself at first, allowing adequate time to gain some distance from the emerging artefacts and make use of cognitive incubation. In August 1966, only three sessions were conducted, spaced evenly apart, with slightly more occurring in September (six). By October, however, Wilson was recording every other day. But instead of working on one song at a time, he would record a few modules – potentially for use in one particular song – and then leave them for an extended period while he worked on other tracks. In this manner, when the song was picked up again he would approach subsequent modules in quite a different way, producing a number of divergent modules, any of which could be used alternatively within the song's basic pattern or, in some cases, as part of other songs.

To illustrate, the very first *SMiLE* session was conducted on 3 August 1966, with Wilson recording three modules for the song 'Windchimes' (2011 boxset CD 4: Track 4). The track was then put aside for two months, as work commenced on another six songs. Vocal overdubs for the track (unused) were recorded on October 3. Two days later, Wilson re-recorded two of the previous 'Windchimes' modules using very different instrumental timbres and arrangements, this time featuring multitracked marimbas and densely multitracked tack pianos to replace the original harpsichord and rhythm section configuration (2011 boxset CD 4: Tracks 5 and 6). Lead and group vocals were overdubbed onto both modules from the 3 August and 3 October sessions, some five days later.

Most of the *SMiLE* material recorded up until late November 1966 followed a similarly fruitful pattern of activity interrupted by periods of inactivity, while other songs were attended to. The results have an effortless, inspired quality. Beatles recording engineer Geoff Emerick asserts that this method was also used to good effect on the Beatles' *Sgt. Pepper's Lonely Hearts Club Band* (1967a) album (Stewart 2011). However, as the original Christmas deadline for the album's release edged closer, Wilson began to work almost exclusively on the next single ('Heroes and Villains') for two months without pause. While the results are still admirable, if taken as discreet entities, the modules lean further towards divergence than was previously the case. It is as if Lieberman's (1977) kaleidoscope of play wouldn't stop spinning long enough for Wilson to orientate himself. The December 1966 'Heroes and Villains' scenario demonstrates that external pressure to produce a radio-friendly successor to 'Good Vibrations' (which took seven months, on and off, to perfect) within a mere few weeks was untenable. The modular approach, a method that had thus far consistently proved beneficial, was now just another formula or pacifying algorithm rather than an appropriate heuristic response to the extrinsic pressures and constraints facing Wilson at the time. The demands were too great and the time frame too small. What Wilson lacked in this case was the sense of perspective that cognitive incubation, or a trusted second opinion, could best provide.

The many small 'Heroes and Villains' modules recorded between 19 December 1966 and 2 March 1967 (2011 boxset CD 2: Tracks 7–30) represent a premature, germinal process of exploration, rather than the 'conceptual reorganization and consolidation' of play that builds upon such activity (Hutt 1979: 192). Judging by a work-in-progress edit made almost two weeks after he'd missed the second deadline of 15 January 1967, the song was clearly still in its early stages of development (2011 boxset CD 2: Track 18). Wilson later confessed, 'I couldn't do it. I went on a . . . two month bummer over that record' (Badman 2004: 173). The delicate balance between unity and variation maintained throughout previous *SMiLE* tracks such as 'Child Is Father of the Man', 'Wind Chimes' or 'Cabin Essence' – wasn't forthcoming in any productions of the song 'Heroes and Villains' until Wilson finally completed his 'symphonic' *SMiLE* remake in 2004. To revisit Chapouthier's (2009) terminology, until that time, the modules were merely 'juxtaposed' rather than fully 'integrated'. Most of the 'Heroes and Villains' vocal arrangements to feature on subsequent releases were recorded much later in mid-June 1967, one month after the *SMiLE* project had been publicly announced as having been scrapped. These benefit from a sense of perspective. The following song to be worked on (i.e. 'Vega-Tables') saw a return to sessions that produced inspired and appropriate material with a good balance of both divergent and convergent traits. Not surprisingly, the sessions were preceded by a month-long break during March 1967, where Wilson recorded no *SMiLE* material at all.

Being 'in-the-moment'

Wilson once explained how much of his initial work with the Beach Boys resulted from a preoccupation with the consequences of his actions:

> There was a lot of ambition around and a lot of pressure too. . . . Like when Mike would say, 'You gotta write a number one record!' I would get like (whistles) that feeling and I'd go do it, 'cause it was contagious . . . C'mon guys lets get a touch down!' And the company said, 'Look . . . we have a schedule to meet here. We have to have a Beach Boys record in ten days.' You don't want to be scared all the time. There are other emotions besides fear. (McCulley 2003: 198)

With *SMiLE*, however, Wilson attempted to follow his own intrinsic motivation rather than be swayed by external pressures, setting out to seek the joy of creativity in-the-moment as his reward. As Csikszentmihalyi states, 'The most important step in emancipating oneself from social controls is the ability to find rewards in the events of each moment' (1990: 19). For a time, at least, Wilson succeeded in following his creative bent, managing to keep both the Beach Boys and Capitol Records at bay long enough to allow his work to emerge as a by-product of play.

The 2011 boxset features not only music but also excerpts in between takes where Wilson can be heard interacting with the session musicians. Tape collator Mark Linett comments that the most remarkable things he gleaned from the recordings were the rapid pace in which musical arrangements evolved in the studio and the symbiotic nature of Wilson and his session musicians' interaction. The team moved ahead rapidly and with a minimum of fuss, so as not to ruin the mood or lose a fleeting idea ('#118 – Mark Linett 2011'). Similarly, TV producer David Oppenheim recalls how he spent time with Wilson in late 1966, observing a process of incredible creative flow, with the many modules changing shape, context and musical function on a daily basis. The down side of all this flow, however, was Wilson's compulsive desire to have his every whim fulfilled, even outside of the studio, regardless of the time of day or the impracticality of his ideas (Badman 2004).

Lieberman (1977) states that it is important to make the distinction between spontaneous and impulsive behaviour. Whereas the former term indicates the ability to play with objects or ideas in unusual or transformative ways, the latter simply denotes a tendency to act before sufficient thought or consideration has occurred. Whereas the modules produced during the early *SMiLE* sessions display ample evidence of cognitive spontaneity and combinatorial play, the 'Heroes and Villains' modules from early 1967 seem to be representative of a more impulsive approach. While there's no lack of interesting ideas in evidence, they don't seem to have been developed as well as material recorded before December 1966. Each module seems like a rough sketch, having little in common with other modules intended for the same song. For Koestler's (1964) 'bisociation' to occur, there must be a point of connection, despite how obscure it might be. Wilson is described at the time as having had many 'spur of the moment' ideas (both in and outside of the studio) but lacked the desire to see them through if they couldn't be implemented immediately (Badman 2004). A little like Lennon without his McCartney.

Another indication that Wilson was becoming increasingly unfocused and unable (or unwilling) to see ideas through to full realization of their potential was his increasingly erratic tape management regime. While the studio sessions, at least during 1966, were disciplined and well documented, Badman (2004) describes the black-acetate trial discs Wilson often took home at the end of each day – used to reflect upon and share with friends over dinner – were mostly unlabelled and piled up on the floor. The session logs likewise show that as of early 1967, studio tapes increasingly seemed to get lost. Co-producers of the 2011 boxset, Mark Linett and Alan Boyd, note that most acetates are now also lost ('#130 – Mark Linett 2011), which is most regrettable, since the many divergent trial sequences of modules they held would speak volumes about Wilson's creative process at the time.

Conflict in group creativity

The *SMiLE* sessions make for a formidable record-production case study because they include both examples of harmonious, if not symbiotic, group creative flow, as well as periods of considerable group conflict. According to Badman, the early stages of the sessions saw all parties involved ('friends, bandmates, press agents, Capitol personnel') as having great faith in the project (2004: 147). Such optimism, though, he qualifies, was based on the assumption that the project would be conducted in a similar fashion to previous albums. The differences in each party's expectations only became apparent several months into proceedings. An indication of the growing atmosphere of dissent is evident in Mike Love's admission that by October 1966 he couldn't relate to the material at all (2004: 149). By November, he was strongly opposed to singing Van Dyke Parks's lyrics (2004: 163).

There were multiple sources of conflict between Wilson, the Beach Boys and Capitol Records. These included:

1. Wilson's autocratic production style;
2. the appearance on the scene of 'The Vosse Posse';
3. the unprecedented, extended timeframe required to complete the sessions;
4. Wilson's attempts to abandon the Beach Boys' hit-making 'formula' and experiment with different production approaches;
5. the potential difficulty of performing *SMiLE* live at the time;

6. the negative sides of Wilson's whimsy and impulsiveness;
7. Wilson's increasingly high profile in the musical press of the time as the genius 'puppet-master' behind the Beach Boys (Priore 2005).

Wilson admits that prior to the *SMiLE* sessions he was used to 'working on my own in the Studio. I was used to everybody doing exactly what I told them to do' (Wilson 2011). After enjoying more than three years of unchallenged control, he was ill-prepared to deal with the resistance generated by his bandmates' growing realization that there was simply no precedent for the new music he was making. This sense of uncertainty was further exacerbated by the fact that 'Good Vibrations' lyricist and co-lead singer Mike Love was effectively demoted to the role of backing vocalist for much of the project. Wilson's new lyrical collaborator Van Dykes Parks, on the other hand – also a talented multi-instrumentalist – was now acting as his 'right-hand man' in the studio as well.

Wilson's growing sense of camaraderie with the Vosse Posse further alienated the Beach Boys when they returned home after a successful tour of England and America in late November 1966 (Anderle, Hutton and Vosse 2011). Capitol Records, on the other hand – while not overly enthused about the new material – just wanted releasable Beach Boys product delivered as soon as possible. To make matters worse, advertisements promising *SMiLE*'s imminent release were published in *Billboard* and *Teen Set* magazines in December 1966, despite Wilson being far from finished (Priore 2011) and yet to produce a single with which to promote album sales. In retrospect, it's easy to see how *SMiLE* was a record-production disaster waiting to happen.

Prince (1975) explains that wherever group creativity is concerned, there's always the question of power to consider. McIntyre concurs, stating that this is as true for record production as any other field: 'it is in the interplay between . . . and the power that each enacts, that creativity in the studio is produced' (2008: 8). Prince's thesis states that many of our habitual ways of relating to others are based on bolstering a sense of self-worth by attaining (and maintaining) power. Accordingly, self-esteem is potentially damaged in collaborative efforts where one is simply carrying out another's ideas. The more control-orientated the situation, the more negative the effects are for both controller and 'lackey'. In win-lose situations such as these, the victor's success may be short-lived if the loser(s) subsequently attempt to undermine the former's authority in a passive-aggressive fashion (consciously or otherwise). Such retaliations can range from subtle undermining to outright confrontation. A feeling of co-authorship in group-creativity situations can lessen the negative effects on one's self-concept, however. This explains, perhaps, Mike Love's need to begin his liner notes in the 2011 boxset (Love 2011) with an assertion of his own lyrical contribution to 'Good Vibrations'. Only much later in the article does he, in passing, dismiss Van Dyke Parks's words as 'acid alliteration'. Love's ongoing hostility towards Van Dyke Parks is clearly evident by the fact he fails to make any reference to him by name in his notes.

Creativity is the most regrettable casualty of situations where such combative and competitive behaviour is the norm. In particular, the ability to think speculatively – a key component of creative thinking – is severely compromised since it leaves one vulnerable to ridicule by peers (Prince 1975). For this reason, Wilson augmented his work with the Beach Boys by adopting outside collaborators more open to new his ideas. With the Vosse Posse's moral support he could unselfconsciously follow 'any idea, any notion that came into his head to see where it took him' (Anderle, Hutton and Vosse 2011). These were people that Wilson didn't see himself in direct competition with. Despite being a talented composer/arranger in his own right, Van Dykes Parks recalls deferring that role entirely to Wilson, instead, sticking to writing lyrics when and where Wilson required them (Priore 2005). Unlike the very real power struggle going on within the Beach Boys, Wilson's new entourage had less history with him, and much less to lose.

The early sessions for *SMiLE* focused on recording backing tracks using session musicians, the 'Heroes and Villains' sessions however, required Wilson to collaborate more consistently with the Beach Boys on vocal parts. Wilson's colleague David Anderle recalls:

> The Beach Boys . . . were generally very aware of the commercial market when Brian really wanted to space out and take off. . . . He'd have to go through a tremendous paranoia before he would go into the studio, knowing he was going to have to face an argument. He would come into the studio uptight, he would give a part to one of the fellas or to a group of the fellas, say 'This is what I would like to have done' and there would be instant resistance . . . there'd be endless takes and then he would just junk it . . . after they left to go on tour, he would come back in and do it himself. All their parts . . . it was very taxing and it was extremely painful to watch. Because it was . . . a great wall had been put down in front of creativity. (Priore 1997: 266)

Getzels and Jackson have the following to say regarding creative autonomy and the possible benefits of voluntary isolation: 'It is certain that some kinds of creative performance require permitting the person to set his [sic] own problem, to proceed at his own pace, to cogitate on the issues in his own way, to play with his own ideas in his own fashion ... even if it means working alone' (1962: 126). Far from being supported in his vision, Wilson was being pressured into going back to his old production-line ways, even if they didn't inspire him anymore. He'd come too far.

Mike Love's recollections of SMiLE in more recent times centre around his concern that Beach Boys fans 'in Omaha' might not be able to relate to its fanciful lyrics ('Inventing Language' 2011). This statement implies that he saw the success of 'Good Vibrations' (1966a) as being in no small way dependent on his own lyrical contribution: one that grounded the song in familiar boy-meets-girl territory. It is certainly true that his rewriting of the song's chorus lyric was a marked improvement on Wilson's original 'Good, Good, Good, Vibrations' version (2011 boxset CD 5: Track 23) and may have, indeed, contributed considerably to the song's chart success. Being unable to influence the rest of the album in any similar fashion, Love felt too much was at stake to just follow blindly. He had the following to say when interviewed in June 1993:

> [Wilson] became an egomaniac, taking too much acid, smoking so much grass that he just couldn't focus any more.... He went from being the most influential musician of his generation to being a paranoid wreck.... Am I supposed to be evil because I wanted to salvage my career and Al and Carl and Bruce's livelihoods? Am I unreasonable to try to make Brian act responsibly? He was a grown man who had been indulged, acting like an idiot kid and our reputations were all going down with him. (Jones 1995)

Wilson might have had more success getting both Love and the rest of the Beach Boys onside if they hadn't felt so much like redundant players left on the sidelines watching Wilson risk their career. Perhaps if they'd felt more like active participants, truly part of the game (like the Vosse Posse), their frame of mind might also have been more often playful (paratelic) than reward-orientated (telic).

The 2011 boxset reveals Wilson as having quite a different manner of relating to his session musicians (including co-writer Van Dykes Parks) than with the Beach Boys. Whereas his tone with the paid musicians (the Wrecking Crew) is straightforward, even urgent, when dealing with his own band he tries to keep things light and silly. Listening to the tapes, it is obvious he shared a good working rapport and sense of mutual respect with the Wrecking Crew. Rather than gently coaxing the best out of the session players, he gives feedback in plain but diplomatic (if unflattering) terms. Wilson also sounds well aware of the need to wrap up the sessions before the limiting frame of the union-specified time limit runs out. A clear hierarchy is evident, with the musicians clearly satisfied to follow Wilson's musical whims. After all, they're getting paid to do a job.

With the Beach Boys on the other hand, Wilson tends to goof off with the guys, partaking in occasional, innocuous word association and using more conciliatory language and tone of voice. The atmosphere is comparatively more jovial than with the backing-track sessions with the Wrecking Crew but nothing like the wild reverie of many of the Vosse Posse recordings. Wilson is clearly trying to come across as 'one of the boys' with his own band. Despite not wanting to appear like he's in control, he most certainly is. Wilson urges the Beach Boys on to manifest his arrangement ideas, playing up the positives of the group's efforts and making his commands seem almost incidental, as if he is well aware of the need to placate his peers and avoid causing offence. In this way, humour was used to avoid potential conflict with a group who are clearly unafraid to voice their differences of opinion. The band, too, used humour as a means of playfully keeping Wilson on their level.

What was lacking between the Beach Boys and Wilson during the *SMiLE* project was an explicit agreement on how they could proceed together, at least temporarily, with power being distributed according to negotiated (Sutton-Smith 1979), rather than imposed, rules. Prince states that the degree to which 'one is able to create a climate that makes stimulating demands without threat, and explicitly appreciates process . . . those in the climate including oneself will flourish and grow as problem-solvers, learners and accomplishers' (1975: 265). Unfortunately, this is something Wilson was unable to achieve with the Beach Boys. While members of the Vosse Posse recall some of Wilson's sillier games – such as taking on the identities of various animals or vegetables – with delight (*Beautiful Dreamer* 2004), Beach Boy Bruce Johnston interpreted Wilson's more unorthodox methods as the actions of a *schadenfreude*: 'Brian degraded us, made us lay down for hours and make barnyard noises, demoralised us, freaked out. I can't tell you a lot of it, it's really fucked up. He thought it was hilarious' (Jones 1995). Fellow Beach Boy Al Jardine – while insisting he liked the *SMiLE* material – similarly remembers the particular 'Heroes and Villains' session in question, likening it to being trapped inside an insane asylum (Sharp 2000).

Power relations – a factor that McIntyre (2008) states is central to creative enterprise in a recording-studio environment – can be temporarily suspended, or even reversed, if mutual agreement is forthcoming. In this way, new 'rules of the game' can be established for a temporary field of play. A musical 'serf' can become a 'king for a day' or, even, musical roles can be overturned so that band members might swap instruments from song to song. The Beatles were able to free themselves from the usual Beatles-as-system phenomenon somewhat by temporarily assuming playful new identities as Sgt. Pepper's Lonely Hearts Club Band. The power relation being overturned in this case, however, was the weight of responsibility every recording artist feels towards their fans' expectations with regard to new products: the '"elephant in the room" at every recording session' (McIntyre 2008: 3). Paul McCartney explains that in 1966 after hearing the Beach Boys' *Pet Sounds* (1966b) album, he failed to see how, given the restrictions of the Beatles' style and line-up at the time, they could possibly compete with Wilson's lush orchestrations and sense of musical invention: 'Sgt. Pepper eventually came out from the idea that I had about this band. It was going to be an album of another band that wasn't us. We were going to call ourselves something else, and just imagine all the time that it wasn't us playing this album' (Badman 2000: 256). Using this simple device, the Beatles could make an album that didn't have to sound like 'the Beatles' at all. The key to such a playful approach, however, was that the (Sgt. Pepper) masks were temporary and could be easily discarded before starting the next project which, as it turned out, was simply named *The Beatles* (1968b), as if to allude to the fact that they were still there.

    History shows that the Beach Boys – still fitted out in their candy stripe stage outfits as the music scene was becoming increasingly psychedelic in late 1966 – were the ones who misjudged the rising influence of the 'underground' music scene in 1967. While they may have been aware of what formerly constituted popular taste, they were dismissive of a new cultural movement in a rapid state of becoming, one that Wilson was acutely aware of and eager to respond to. In part, this 'sea change' was facilitated by the rise of FM radio, a new format that enabled bands such as Led Zeppelin to break through to the mainstream without the aid of seven-inch vinyl singles and their limited play capacity. Although the overall sequencing of *SMiLE* was a problematic affair, the session chronology clearly shows that it was the 'Heroes and Villains' modules that most strongly resisted Wilson's attempts at organization. The modules recorded prior to January 1967 had already been compiled into linear 'master edits' ready for the Beach Boys to record their vocal overdubs onto. It was this highly anticipated single that needed to be fit and proper for both AM radio airplay and live performance. Wilson simply couldn't reconcile his new creative bent with the then limitations of pop-music formats that would, ironically, soon be redundant as the FM radio and rock-album era emerged.

Pathology of play

While a belief in the power of humour and a playful frame of mind were no doubt beneficial during the early stages of the *SMiLE* project, these same approaches had an increasingly negative impact as time went on, upon both the project itself and Wilson's relationship with the Beach Boys and Capitol Records. Implicit in play is a kind of rebelliousness, where an individual rejects the ways and means of the real world in favour of their own self-imposed norms. While this negativism is a necessary aspect of play, in cases where rebellion or negativism become habitual reactions to life, rather than temporary and discerningly implemented, they can lead to a 'pathological form of play with dysfunctional consequences' (McDermott 1991: 98). Wilson's belief that humour was the unqualified answer to every question led him to act in ways that were often impulsive, counter-productive and alienating. According to the Beach Boys' then publicist Derek Taylor, Wilson's unpredictable whims were most unsettling for some, and would often 'wreak havoc over everything'. He goes on to say: 'Well, personally I was frightened of him. He made me nervous and uncomfortable. God, he was so temporary, it was awful – and I'd dread the phone call at 4 a.m. demanding that I come over . . . [a] man of whims, surges, arrogance. . . . Always demanding too much' (Priore 1997: 262).

Wilson's playfulness and drugtaking (another activity conducive to the paratelic state) facilitated a creative surge at the beginning of the *SMiLE* project. However, this same frame of mind became so habitual, and inappropriate at times, that he became increasingly disorganized and unable to cope with the serious business of meeting deadlines. By June 1967, Wilson stepped down as the Beach Boys producer altogether. *Smiley Smile* (1967c), the next album to be released, and subsequent albums, contained some contributions by Wilson but were instead produced by the Beach Boys, with less and less input by Wilson as time went on (Sharp 2000).

This state of affairs may not have been entirely due to a pathological predilection towards fantasy and escapism, however. Wilson has since admitted he felt guilty about stealing the limelight from the Beach Boys during the *SMiLE* period (McCulley 2003) and may have acquiesced his role as producer in order to share power more equally with the band. There is evidence to support this.

In March 1967, Wilson stopped work on his own *SMiLE* material for an entire month in order to co-produce (non-modular) songs written by his Beach Boy siblings Carl and Dennis Wilson.

Summary and conclusion

This case study examined Brian Wilson and the Beach Boys' abandoned, but well documented, 1966–7 *SMiLE* project. Designed to use playful humour as a means to facilitate creative flow, *SMiLE* employed non-linear working methods that predate, by decades, the now ubiquitous 'cut and paste' approach to music production. The project is also notable for being fraught with factionalism and power struggles. By addressing these various issues, there is much to be learnt about contemporary DAW-based record production.

Analysis of the *SMiLE* sessions clearly illustrates how adopting a playful attitude promotes ways of thinking beneficial to creative action, including cognitive spontaneity, associative thought and high levels of concentration. However, since play in adults is best defined as a frame of mind – a way of experiencing one's actions in a world without consequences – it is important for practitioners not to remain stuck in that state irrespective of the needs of the moment. Doing so can lead to significant (inter)personal problems and a lack of broader focus that impedes rather than facilitates progress. Indeed, adopting a serious frame of mind is necessary for stages of creative process where critical thinking is required.

Sequencing of the *SMiLE* modules, while a difficult and time-consuming task using tape-splicing methods, was impeded moreso by a lack of clarity regarding clear points of convergence. Despite employing themes such as Americana, the elements and, even, the Zodiac to provide a general sense of structure, Wilson lacked a pop-music equivalent of, say, sonata form or the character arc of a specific hero[ine] to pin the many divergent modules upon. Although he was used to working within the confines of the three-minute radio-friendly song format, *SMiLE* started to come unstuck precisely when Wilson was unable to finish a 'pocket' musical comedy ('Heroes and Villains') that could be a worthy successor to 'Good Vibrations' (1966a), his 'pocket symphony'. Compressing manifold ideas into a very limited space is always a challenging enterprise. When one's career and reputation – as well as that of your family and friends – depends on it, it is that much harder. It would be another eight years before bands like Queen and 10cc could produce their own 'pocket' musical comedies-cum-tragedies ('Bohemian Rhapsody' (1975) and *'Une Nuit a Paris'* (1975) respectively), both of which ran considerably longer than three minutes. The Cantina module of 'Heroes and Villains' hints towards the greatness that might have been had Wilson less extrinsic pressures to deal with, not least all, his own expectations and sense of responsibility. If delaying the product by just a few months more seems the obvious fix in hindsight, then one should factor in the rapid pace of pop-music release schedules of the time. Such was the unabashed disposability of pop culture in the 1960s that failure to put out a record every three months guaranteed a band's obsolescence.

The *SMiLE* story provides evidence of the negative impact that systems resistant to new ideas and change can have upon visionary artists. The project was an attempt by Brian Wilson to respond to the changing mood of the times, but in doing so, he pushed the Beach Boys and their relationship with Capitol Records to the point of collapse (Priore 2005). Unable to convince his bandmates to let go of their old ways of reasoning – ways of thinking that couldn't possibly conceive how such 'airy-fairy' counterculture ideas could ever be integrated successfully into their tried-and-tested hit-making system – Wilson and the Beach Boys reached a stalemate by December 1966. Furthermore, the band felt well and truly out of the *SMiLE* loop, and so much so, that any chance of becoming a new band for a new era was negligible. The Beach Boys, an organization centred around AM radio hits and live touring, was no longer a system able to handle Wilson's new creative vision, and the *SMiLE* project finally ground to a halt some five months later. But if it sounds like too big an ask for any music-making team to change course so radically, so quickly, in order to change with the times, then consider that that is precisely what the Beatles did when they released *Sgt. Pepper's Lonely Hearts Club Band* in mid-1967. And they did so, largely, by pretending to be someone else: by acting 'as if'.

Last thoughts

Miles Davis once commented that if Charlie Parker had started out in the 1980s, rather than the 1930s, he would have been involved in hip hop rather than jazz. This observation acknowledges the fact that music makers are embedded in a social, cultural and historical matrix that both informs and receives their efforts. All genres owe their existence to particular times and places and are shaped by movements, technologies, economic realities and traditions (if only as something for emerging artists to react against).

Herein lies the danger of having heroes. Without an intimate knowledge of their life conditions – something that may or may not have been adequately examined by historians – it can be difficult to separate which aspects of their legacy resulted from their own individual talents and which were gifts the wider creative matrix presented to them. Case in point: it is hard to imagine what the Beatles might have sounded like without the many early influences they absorbed like blotting paper: rock 'n' roll; Motown; Brill Building songs; Broadway showtunes; pop 'standards'; skiffle (i.e. folk and country); and blues music. Just as important in shaping artists' styles, however, can be their misfortunes. Without having been struck down by polio (leaving the dexterity of her left hand compromised) one can only wonder if Joni Mitchell would have developed her unique approach to harmony using simpler-to-play open guitar tunings, not to mention how overcoming such a trauma might have strengthened her to face other (career and creative) obstacles with similar resolve.

While it may be tempting to erect mental statues in honour of our musical heroes, doing so only projects our power outward and leaves us thinking that if only we had been born in their time and their place, and had their toys, that things might have been better or easier. All artists, regardless of their chosen discipline, are obliged to work within the confines of their own era. The answers to our present-day creative problems cannot be found following the same – once unbeaten – paths our heroes cleared for us. Author Herman Hesse understood the danger of romanticizing the past (and the future for that matter), noting in his book *Steppenwolf* that humour and play direct us to the ever-present moment:

> You should not take old people who are already dead seriously. It does them injustice. We immortals do not like things to be taken seriously. We like joking. Seriousness, young man, is an accident of time. It consists, I don't mind telling you in confidence, in putting too high a value on time. I, too, once put too high a value on time. For that reason I wished to be a hundred years old. In eternity, however, there is no time, you see. Eternity is a mere moment, just long enough for a joke. ([1927] 2015: 173)

So, how is it that rare individuals can exhibit the resilience and determination necessary to do what most adults (who having successfully adapted to their environment, don't desire change) dare not. Being marginalized (socially, ethnically, economically and/or religiously) is a great place to start, since one is not personally invested in maintaining the status quo (Csilszentmihalyi 1999). We have seen that naivety and playfulness can bring about a similar, albeit temporary, sense of detachment. Even then, however, the odds are seldom in favour of would-be innovators and iconoclasts. As Sutton-Smith said, 'Play is the fool that might become King' (1979: 320). That is, play and playfulness only potentialize one's chances of success. The real world still needs to play along before any young hopeful's dreams can be realized.

That there is something of the perennial child at work in the artist (or scientist) is hardly a new observation. However, this should not be seen as neuroses (although play and neuroses share certain similarities). For some, the vague promise of a better, more prosperous and pleasurable life (seemingly always a hair's breadth out of reach and keeping so much of humanity hooked as if to some cliffhanger in an otherwise dreary soap opera) just doesn't ring the same Pavlovian bell once real fulfilment in the form of creative flow has been experienced. Such a realization must surely be a sign of healthy openness to life. For those who can reconcile their place in the world with their inner child and find a way to experience flow in their working life (i.e. to frame instrumental activities playfully), not only will their life be richer but society benefits as well.

Hopefully, by mapping out areas of creativity that even musicians so often ignore (such as the role of frame of mind), the resulting discussion will inspire greater confidence in practitioners of playfulness everywhere and, with it, facilitate more effective self-advocacy. Although being in a band might look like a lot of fun (and it can be), it is still really hard work. That is why it is young people most often who try to make a go of making original music: naivety, boundless energy and optimism are essential job requirements (as is the ability to sleep on other people's floors and couches at times). And it is so often the songwriters who, if successful, are the most celebrated and, if not, are the most maligned. Once again, this is since writing doesn't look the same as most other productive activities. Dedication to one's craft, as a writer, can easily be mistaken for malingering (but then again, so can malingering), with days or weeks spent seemingly aimlessly, perhaps all-the-while being vague and moody (wishing not to be disturbed for hours-on-end) as one ruminates, letting ideas form and then rewriting over and over and over again until finally a hazy feeling gives rise to something concrete. Conversely, compositions can come suddenly, almost flippantly, as things are thrown together. Make no mistake, however, just as bourgeois society needed Steppenwolves, our current-day bastions of fiscal responsibility and STEM need the A of both ('useful') artisans and ('useless') fine artists. That motivation (both extrinsic and intrinsic) is essentially about directing attention may seem benign enough. It is, however, anything but. Without artists to playfully challenge common perceptions and provoke (as well as delight and inspire), only Orwell's 'rod' and Huxley's 'carrot' remain.

Societies and cultures are developed by humans in order to provide structure where otherwise there would be chaos. The trouble starts when those same structures become so restrictive (or, conversely, so open) that an optimal flow of new ideas and contributions necessary to keep the system thriving (just as nutrients are necessary for biological systems) is no longer forthcoming. There will, however, always be those stronger individuals defiant and creative enough to both assert their autonomy and use their powers of discernment. And, even when creative systems enter periods of decline – or are abruptly abandoned by major players in favour of new frontiers – artists will be there to fashion something new out of what has been cast aside. So too, small like-minded groups of practitioners will continue to self-organize and, for a time, flourish with the invaluable support of mediators. When they too are gone, their artefacts may well live on. As Tom Waits once reflected, pointing to a jukebox: 'The studio is torn down, all the people who played on it are dead, the instruments have been sold off. But you are listening to a moment that happened in time 60 years ago and you are hearing it just as sharp as when it was made. That remains an amazing thing to me' (Adams 2011).

That society still has a long way to go before it adequately acknowledges (in word and in deed) the valuable contribution that the arts in general make, let alone that of individual artists, is powerfully illustrated by the following anecdote. Fran Lebowitz recalls that when a Picasso painting was displayed at Christie's in New York recently, there was little commotion. Only when the auctioneer's hammer came down and the unprecedented sale price was proclaimed did the room erupt: 'We live in a world where they applaud the price [$179.4 million], not the Picasso!' ('Cultural Affairs' 2021). For this reason I do not refer to the work by name, only by price.

The painting in question owed its existence to crucial years Pablo Picasso spent developing his work and ideas far from home, living in the squalor of a converted piano factory (Le Bateau Lavoir) in a derelict area of Montmartre on Paris' outskirts. This 'rabbit warren' of makeshift studios-cum-living-spaces was home to many other artists – Juan Gris and Modigliani included – and despite the privations they experienced there, the mood was jovial and playful. Their sense of camaraderie, combined with cheap rent, cheap wine and colourful fringe-dwelling neighbours (who often featured as subjects in their work), generally resulted in good times, freethinking and artistic experimentation.

Even if the Bateau Lavoir had not burnt down in 1970 (leaving only a street-level facade for tourists to come and pay homage), it would have long since succumbed to gentrification, just as CBGBs has recently. Creative people need time (lots of it), tools and materials, a place to work, intellectual stimulation and freedom from extrinsic pressures. Without cheap, draughty lofts and old factories where artists and musicians can work and play uninterrupted, practitioners must today look to universities (if they have the money), parents' garages or the bedroom project studio (i.e. the virtual world) for asylum. Just as important, however, is relative proximity to patrons. For Picasso et al. that meant Gertrude and Leo Stein, both of whom understood and appreciated the intrinsic value of the work they collected: as did Alfred Stieglitz in New York. For Talking Heads, it was Seymour Stein (no relation), every bit as much the enthusiastic fan as an investor.

Incoming news

As I write, five days ago, digital artist Beeple's (Mike Winklemann) online collage '*Everydays: The First 5000 Days*' (2007–21) was auctioned in the form of a non-fungible token (NFT) at Christie's New York for a sale price of $69,346,250. The sale has set a record not only for being the first of its kind at a major auction house but also for the (optional) acceptance by Christie's of cryptocurrency (i.e. Ether) as payment. And then, of course, there is the price. It would appear that digital art has been welcomed in by the establishment. Creative artefacts that have until now been problematic in terms of assigning ownership can now be bought and sold readily. That is, anyone, regardless of their powers of discernment, can now take the work seriously.

The introduction of NFTs as proof of authorship and ownership for digital artefacts effectively means that the concept of supply and demand can now be introduced into the online world (although the tokens can be tied to items in the real world also). These details are authenticated and tracked via a 'blockchain' (i.e. 'a distributed ledger technology (DLT) that allows data to be stored globally on thousands of servers – while letting anyone on the network see everyone else's entries in near real-time' (Mearian 2019). That is, the token certifies a (artificial) limited supply just as a physical painting would (i.e. an authenticated one-off). However, limited runs can also be certified (similar to prints made by an artist or baseball trading cards).

Apart from the obvious implications for digital artists (and that includes music makers!) as a means of connecting with collectors and remunerating them for their work, there are other implications worth considering. The first is that NFTs do not restrict the public from having access to the file, so private ownership does not equate to locking the work away from public view and enjoyment. There are, however, concerns that have been raised regarding the fact that anyone can potentially attach an NFT certificate to any file accessible via the internet, resulting in an increasing number of digital artists who have discovered their own content has been sold off as 'authentic' without their knowledge or consent. There is also the matter of adverse environmental impact, since the NFT system is highly inefficient in terms of the energy required to keep the blockchain's network running (n.b. Beeple has stated that he will be buying carbon offset to address the concern (Kastrenakes 2021)). Then there is the hype factor. With so many would-be vendors and collectors eager to get in on a nascent scene and make some easy money, the question of a digital work of art's intrinsic versus extrinsic value (as seen with the physical Picasso example earlier) becomes a point of contention.

If you are wondering what George Maciunas or Marcel Duchamp might have made of all this then read on. On the 26th of February this year (2021) the conceptual artist Max Haarich uploaded a work of art (authenticated by the NFT exchange openseas.io) as a comment on the 'hysteric'/'historic' nature of the NFT boom. The item in question – a single transparent pixel (as close as you can get to a visual digital 'nothing') only three kilobytes in size – has a starting price of one Etherium coin, which Haarich estimates has a current value of about

$1,400. The point of the exercise reiterates some of the concerns already noted earlier, as he states:

1. This barely perceptible pixel is a comment on the current **divergence between financial and fundamental valuations**. For a good year now, the prices for shares and cryptocoins have been exploding, without any corresponding fundamental increase in the value of the companies or currencies.
2. The practical immateriality of the pixel is in absolute contrast to its heavy **ecological footprint**. According to Memo Akten's online calculator the release of the 'Single Pixel' collection caused an emission of 125 Kg carbon.
3. This sweet little nothing is to take the new promise of **digital authorship** ad absurdum. After all, how does one want to be the creator or owner of something that has virtually no perceptible properties? (Haarich 2021, bold emphasis in original)

The end

One of my regrets during the writing of this book was that I didn't have the opportunity to discuss the work of jazz pianist and composer Thelonious Monk. I say this because discovering his music was one of those rare moments when everything seems transformed. Monk's approach to music was playfulness par excellence. Hearing him perform is like being granted a private audience to listen in on the act of composition in real time. He seems to always be playing on a knife's edge: in the best possible way. Listen to anything by Monk (I mean *anything*) and this book becomes, in many ways, redundant. That being said, he used the recording studio in a fashion that doesn't speak to contemporary creative-practice issues to the same degree that, say, Miles Davis' post-1969 work does. Hence, his absence.

So why discuss Bob Dylan then, you may well ask? Partly because I wanted to highlight the crucial role played by mentor-mediators like John Hammond Sr (it is a miracle that Dylan ever became a recording artist at all, let alone a successful one: the same applies to Elvis and the Beatles) and partly because Dylan was such a public figure: iconic even. A generation idolized him and hung off his every word. As a result, Dylan's influence on songwriting has been of such magnitude that it is impossible to imagine what contemporary music might sound like otherwise. And yet, Dylan's innovations were made possible by his flagrant disregard for the trappings and machinations of stardom. He didn't covet it the way that so many have and so many still do. He played with it. And yet, Dylan's playfulness has been largely overlooked in critiques of his work for some strange reason. To this day, I'm unable to fathom why people take Dylan and his work so seriously. He is culturally significant, yes. His songs and records have been immensely influential, true. But while he might have much to say that is profound, just as often, he might be singing a news bulletin or reciting his shopping list. Song forms are just frames. You can fill them with anything (thanks Jim).

And so, that brings us to the end. If you wonder why so much emphasis has been placed upon art rather than entertainment, then consider it a sign of the times as much as anything else. The post-war period saw the line between the two blur such that the Beatles could progress from the *faux* innocence of 'I Want to Hold Your Hand' (1963) to the *musique concrète* of 'Tomorrow Never Knows' (1966c) in less than three short years. This monograph is, however, no attempt to canonize the work of mighty heroes of yesteryear. It is as much an invitation to reject as it is to preserve. Adequate hindsight simply draws a bigger picture, so that a different class of patterns might emerge. What the good reader chooses to do with this information is, of course, an extrinsic and external matter.

Appendix

Interview with Bill Bruford

Drummer and author Dr Bill Bruford has had a distinguished career as a recording artist and performer spanning some forty or so years. During that time, he witnessed a sea change in both recording-studio practice norms and the structure of the music industry: from the tape-edit tapestry of *Close to the Edge* (1972) to the advent of the DAW, project studio and 'artist-as-retailer' paradigms. Inducted into the Rock and Roll Hall of Fame in 2017 as a founder member of Yes, Bill has performed with many other progressive bands over the years including Genesis, Gong and UK, as well as collaborating with Swiss keyboardist Patrick Moraz (Moraz Bruford) and with Ralph Towner and Eddie Gomez. He has also led his own outfits Bruford (featuring Alan Holdsworth) and the jazz ensemble Earthworks. He is, arguably, most famous for his creative contributions with the band King Crimson. In 2015, Bill was awarded his PhD by the University of Surrey and has since published the book *Uncharted: Creativity and the Expert Drummer* (2018). In this interview – conducted via email during July 2018 – he has kindly agreed to share some of his personal (and, as he emphasizes, somewhat fluid) perceptions and memories regarding what it is like to be a professional recording artist, performer and musical collaborator.

Marshall Heiser: The traditional recording studio layout made a clear demarcation between the creative 'lightning' within the studio space and the 'bottle' of the control room. When you recorded at Peter Gabriel's Real World studios in the mid-1990s that model gave way to a more unified open space arrangement. How did that layout influence your mood as a performer? Did it have any bearing upon the quality of the performances or recordings themselves?

Bill Bruford: The relative power and importance of the artist/performer/conductor on one side of the glass and scientist/producer on the other had, since the advent of recording, been reflected in the respective physical spaces allotted to both: initially, the more spacious, better-lit room for the former, the dingy cubby-hole/electronics workshop for the latter. By the 1990s the design of Real World foregrounded and enabled both the rise of the scientist/auteur in its grand 'control' room (and note the language here) but also the notion of solo 'overdubbed' performances by at most one or two performers simultaneously. Such overdubs would likely be rendered in the spacious control room, overseen by the producer. Large-scale simultaneous collective performance of six or more was backgrounded and not anticipated. Being somewhat old-fashioned, however, King Crimson clung to the idea that something special happens when musicians play together, and sought to reshape the several small dingy performance spaces such that sight-lines might be reinstated and/or video screens installed – critical, certainly, for the two drummers to cue each other with body language. Furthermore, the monitoring system had also to be laboriously reconfigured so all participants could hear as much or as little of their colleagues as might be necessary for an organic performance. So all in all it was something of a technological nightmare getting the studio to do something it wasn't really designed to do. We would have been better, probably, at Abbey Road.

MH: You once described the process of making a King Crimson record (in the 1980s) as 'agonizing... quite slow.... We have no method and we can never seem to find one... or perhaps we're not looking for one' (Tamm 1990: 115). In retrospect, would an autocratic record producer have been a beneficial addition here? Or was the band attempting to let something surprising emerge out of the chaos?

Bruford: A producer would have produced something different, not necessarily better. An autocratic producer wouldn't have got a record at all. We had, perhaps, a benevolent dictator, Captain Robert Fripp, who was not unreasonably frustrated on occasion by the more-strong minded crew members' apparent disinclination to provide what the captain required, even though what was required was nebulous, little spoken. I think the well-meaning crew generally wanted what the captain wanted – a smooth passage to some undefined artistic excellence – but collaborative creation is ever full of misunderstandings, communication breakdowns and methodological pitfalls. I've seldom worked with producers and when I did it wasn't helpful.

MH: The issue of power (and pecking orders) arguably influences a musician's ability to negotiate creative constraints when collaborating. Can power sharing make for better musical outcomes or are imposed constraints (paradoxically) liberating?

Bruford: I'm not sure this is an either/or issue. Yes, power sharing (although I'm not quite sure how you are envisioning that in the context of a music group) can make for better outcomes, and yes, I find constraints liberating, be they imposed by self or other. The two are not mutually exclusive. Crimson's modus operandi for music creation was more flexible and looser than many imagine. Broadly, an idea would emerge from somewhere; a partial or fully completed composition, an instrumental timbre or combination of instrumental timbres, half of a song lyric, a mood abstracted from an improvisation ('Sheltering Sky' (1981)), a thematic umbrella (the Beat poets) or industrial wastelands (tracks like 'Industry' (1984a), 'No Warning' (1984b)). Individuals then devised or completed their own parts to further the idea with minimal instruction or input from others. Approval of one's contribution was signalled by people remaining in the room to continue the process: disapproval by people fragmenting and wandering off, listless and bored. There was little overt discussion about a co-performer's individual contribution. Benefit of the doubt was given. If the drummer had thought it was the right thing to play, then it probably was, until or unless it was superseded by further incoming information necessitating subtle adjustment or a wholesale rethink. This could be slow, laborious and hence expensive.

MH: You've said that when you toured with Genesis in 1976 you'd previously been more accustomed to 'making it up as you went along' whereas the band expected a more functional approach. Recordings of the gigs seem to indicate you found a workable balance between an acceptance of rote parts and unknown outcomes. Do you think you were able to push the boundaries somewhat because of your own fame/power or did a sense of camaraderie foster tolerance?

Bruford: Although I didn't know it at the time, the band (Genesis) broadly saw me as a 'star' player on the back of Yes/KC success: they'd caught themselves a top fish. So, yes, I got away with murder and a fair bit of sloppiness (I wasn't familiar with their songs when I started with them). They afforded me a degree of tolerance that I would not be afforded today were I playing with say, Steely Dan, or Journey, or similar. Precise reproduction of the record is absolutely required now that the ticket price might be north of 200 USD. Genesis, in my time, was interested only in outcomes of the known variety!

MH: When you reformed King Crimson in early 1981 it seems that the consensual deliberation between yourself and Robert Fripp regarding how to approach your role as drummer – within a band that reframed the role of guitars in a radical new manner – was ongoing and very deliberate. Was this process stressful? Did the resulting negotiated constraints pay off creatively?

Bruford: Yes, the role of the drummer seemed to be a key focus of Robert's approach. The guitars were settled (no chords, just single-note heterophonic weavings) and Robert never seemed to say anything to Tony Levin, whose perfectly-measured contributions appeared to defy discussion. That left the drummer, who clearly needed baby-sitting. Indeed, change is not always easy, and change was fast. I had an unlikely combination of instruments to play in a hybrid electro-acoustic drum kit of my own design, and a short list of instructions as to what not to play and when not to play it. Broadly I could do anything I wanted so long as Robert had not heard it before. If I thought that a tall order, I also thought it entirely possible to fulfil. It seemed to me he had not heard much drumming. I do think the resultant 'negotiated' restraints paid off creatively, and on reflection I'm pleased with my contribution to the 1980s band's body of work.

MH: In the studio, when the red light goes on any sound you produce is no longer transitory but documented to be reproduced at will, manipulated and stored for posterity. Do you find that your frame of mind suddenly changes depending on whether the record button is engaged (or not), or does the overall studio environment have greater influence over your mood?

Bruford: My frame of mind was, or would have been, affected by so many variables of which the recording process – capturing the performance for posterity – would have been but one, and not necessarily the most important. Some react better than others when asked to produce a note-perfect performance *right now*, in the company or presence of others whose performance may be overdubbed later. Am I keeping others waiting? Have I read this right, considering I'm largely guessing what might be coming on top of my performance? Consider also the temporal aspect to this. Technology has changed radically over my time. At the beginning, the drummer's performance was more or less fixed from the start, and became a playground upon which others might frolic. At the end, all aspects of a drummer's performance were entirely manipulable in computer-based post-production. I suppose, broadly, I found recording more difficult than all other aspects of practice. But over-arching that, when I was young I found everything easy. Forty years later, it was all difficult. An illustration of the latter can be found in my book *Bill Bruford: The Autobiography* (2009: 187–93).

MH: Is 'frame of mind' something that you, or your collaborators, spent much time thinking or talking about?

Bruford: No, but no time like the present to start thinking about it. We might take the phrase to mean 'mood' or temporary mental disposition. My mood is, for me, an emotional variable among many more influential environmental variables (room acoustics, physical and emotional health my co-performers, audience disposition, lighting, instrument quality, sound monitoring and so forth) that mediate not only the performance itself, but its effective communication. Everything changes how I play. These variables conjoin to make Monday's performance different from Tuesday's. I don't feel particularly moody as an individual and don't assign my frame of mind much importance, although I've worked with many who seem to be very changeable with their moods, allowing them greater play in the proceedings.

MH: Do you think the project-studio revolution has made it easier or harder for musicians to realise their potential of making great recordings (given there are now so many more roles to juggle individually)?

Bruford: Probably harder. Doubtless the music inventor is now at liberty to produce any sonic confection that he or she wants, but if the confection is to be attributed greatness it implies that it must be heard and assessed by others. And getting your music to those pairs of receptive ears whose owners might confer greatness is now the last and hardest of the creativity roles.

MH: Judging by looking at film footage of your performances over the years, you seem to relish playing live. It certainly looks like you're having fun. Did you ever enjoy recording in the studio as much as playing live?

Bruford: I'm not sure I was ever very good at 'fun'. Most of the fun, for me, was in the looking back, in the remembering. There are recorded passages ranging from the very short in length (a phrase or measure here, an idea there) to the quite substantial (a sustained lunacy here, a great feel there) that I am really happy were captured. They seem evidence of a sort that it wasn't all a waste of time; that there was, on occasion, solid invention. But mostly these passages twinkled out like little diamonds from a more prosaic moonscape of good ideas not very well executed. I thought the arrival of our American players Levin and Belew in 1980-ish raised the bar on execution. Of course, between 'recording in the studio' and 'playing live' lies the twilight world of live recording. As the decades rolled past, that process became increasingly painless and relatively inexpensive. It was quite hit or miss, and contrary to some assumptions Crimson had a culture of 'don't waste money fixing and re-mixing if it's really a turkey, in which case why are we trying to breathe life into this turkey anyway?' Some of us had a harder time than others with the 'warts and all' presentation of our work and saw a potential lowering of standards. It seemed on occasion that what would have in earlier times been left as rubbish on the studio floor was now cobbled together in something of a rush, time being money. There is no rubbish outtake any more, only archival documentation with pecuniary value.

MH: Is it important to have fun when making music?

Bruford: Certainly if one wishes to communicate something to an audience, an appearance of, at minimum, committed engagement will go a long way. Whether the performer is actually committed and engaged may be another matter. The appearance of having fun I found easy; the having fun I found harder. Sometimes I couldn't tell the difference, even if I was thinking about it.

MH: Paul McCartney once said that he doesn't work for a living, he gets paid to play. Creativity scholar J. Nina Lieberman (1977) calls artists the Practitioners of Playfulness. Is that a job description you can relate to?

Bruford: Certainly, yes. One way of re-framing McCartney's view is that the performance is free – it is everything else before and after it that you get paid for (travel, practice, rehearsal, composition etc.). Educationalists now suggest we teach playfulness and creativity out of our children at school. The creative engagement of children at play is something to behold, and the interesting (adult) artists manifest that in their work. Again, that's what you're paying us/them to do.

MH: Is it important to have such people in society whose main function is to have fun and take creative risks?

Bruford: Yes, certainly. Those people, Lieberman's Practitioners of Playfulness, are perhaps more usually called artists. The work of a work of art is to communicate experience, as John Dewey has pointed out (1934).

MH: When is adopting a playful frame of mind appropriate in creative practice? When is it not appropriate?

Bruford: Interestingly, drummers perceive of themselves as having the most powerful instrument on stage with which to make the music 'work', or to fail to make it work. This, they attest, is their primary function. After that, they may see ways to be creative, but only once the music is 'working' functionally, that is: 'swingin', 'groovin', 'happenin'. According to drummers, if these things are not happening, it would be inappropriate to get playful.

MH: You make a distinction in your doctoral dissertation between two poles of a continuum of control in musical performance: the Functional/Compositional Continuum (FCC). As the name indicates, there's the 'functional' approach (playing as directed by others) at one end and the 'compositional' (self-created parts) at the other, with most players operating somewhere in between most of the time (Bruford 2015: 45). Is the playful frame of mind a luxury only a performer closer to the 'compositional' end can afford to adopt?

Bruford: The playful attitude is more likely to find fertile ground and induce playfulness in others in compositional performance rather than functional, because the former admits both greater interaction and greater intent to surprise. This in no way necessarily excludes playfulness from functional performance; it's just harder to bring it about. In fact, I'm having trouble thinking of an example. But my research people found little 'creative corners' in all genres and styles of music (Bruford 2018: 65).

MH: Is it important to share a similar sense of humour with your musical collaborators? Why?

Bruford: It is important. It helps as both ice-breaker and social adhesive; it reinforces the 'us-against-them' culture that bonds a group of outsiders catapulted into (frequently) an alien culture. Performance seems only millimetres away from catastrophic absurdity, and colleagues unable to recognise that tend to be viewed with suspicion. How did Kraftwerk keep a straight face?! Along with many in the pre-rock first half of the twentieth century, my father viewed performance as an over-paid form of showing off, and thus a sort of indictable crime.

MH: How important is it to be curious as a creative practitioner?

Bruford: Curiosity is surely an essential component of creativity; it sparks the sort of thinking and then action, which may result in creative outcomes. The curious person or organisation asks questions, and creativity may be involved in finding the answers. In King Crimson, one good question was 'How can we go further?'

MH: Do you derive joy from taking creative risks?

Bruford: Undertaking creative risks is a core job-description for the instrumentalist who wants to push things forward. In a band like King Crimson, pushing ideas about, and maybe in a forward direction, is meat and drink.

MH: The King Crimson of 1981–4 was originally proposed to you explicitly by Robert Fripp in proscriptive terms. It was to be a band that wouldn't do this, wouldn't do that and so on. You've said that this approach really excited you. Why?

Bruford: Limitations and constraints are the bread and butter of the creative thinker or inventor. They force you to dig deeper in the hunt for solutions. 'If I can't play time on a ride cymbal, what can I play it on? Should I play it at all?'

MH: Did this negative approach to collaboration always bring out the best in you or your band mates? Was there ever any resentment as a result of the approach?

Bruford: Creative collaborations can require high levels of emotional fitness. Creative friction produces combustion whose unpredictability may leave participants feeling diminished or belittled even as the project seems to be yielding interesting results. But that's the job. I developed a thick fire-proof hide.

MH: How did it feel to consciously have to avoid former musical habits? Was it a fun challenge? Did it cause anxiety at times?

Bruford: Being in a band like this could be both anxiety-making and fun, sometimes almost simultaneously. I'm perhaps more interested in Csikszentmihalyi's idea of 'flow' (1990). In positive psychology, flow or 'being in the zone', is the mental state of operation in which a person performing an activity is fully immersed in a feeling of energised focus and full involvement in the process of the activity. The concept is widely referenced across a variety of fields including music, as I'm sure you know, and that was my idea of fun, I think, being 'in the moment'. I like to be stretched, certainly, and can't quite see how else I'm going to provide anything that interests me and/or possibly others until or unless I am stretched. I get queasy when I feel I know what's going on. I bore easily.

MH: You have mentioned in the past that King Crimson involved some 'ground rules'. Does this relate to Fripp's analogy of the band as a sports field where players have freedom within its limited boundaries?

Bruford: Certainly, yes. Here is the perimeter of the ball park. We're going to play with these balls: we want to avoid this, and we won't be doing that. Now let's play. Robert also was good at proposing a strategy with no accompanying demand that it be acted upon. He described it as throwing some balls in the air. If we, King Crimson, caught some of them and ran with them, great: if they dropped to the ground that was fine too. We ran with the idea of a double trio in the mid-1990s, but I thought that had less bang for the buck than one might have expected.

MH: Play scholar Brian Sutton-Smith states that to '"play with something" means conceptually to frame it in another way' (1979: 306). He uses the term 'playframing' to explain how in play participants must negotiate (and continually renegotiate) binding rules of engagement that temporarily suspend the normal ways of framing classes-relations and reverse 'the usual contingencies of power' (1979: 308). It appears that the design of King Crimson (then known as

Discipline) in early 1981 could be described as a band-as-playframe. How much input did other members of the band have with regard to this 'negotiation' of terms (either explicitly or tacitly) in the early days? Was power shared equally?

Bruford: I think Sutton-Smith has it about right, based on your two sentences above. There are two questions here: one about negotiating terms and the other about sharing power. I think we negotiated terms in the same way as unsupervised children in a sandpit (negotiations can be successful and unsuccessful, of course). We threw some sand about and built castles. Occasionally sand went in someone's face and there were tears, there was heated discussion as to who had the best castle, but there was no identifiable sandpit bully. It seemed that all members had equal input in the negotiations, but they exercised this at different times, in different ways and to different extents. With regard to power sharing, RF was beyond doubt the most powerful individual, in the sense in which he selected the musicians, arranged when, where and how the organisation might work (or play) together, and issued some restraints or rules. After that though, he was in the sandpit pretty much with everyone else. He vehemently denied he was any sort of bandleader, a function he was more likely to offload to 'King Crimson' or the band ghost or the third in a perfect pair.

MH: Was this combination of ground rules and creative restraints applied on a song-by-song basis, as an aid to arrangement or composition (i.e. songs as unique sets of rules and restrictions)?

Bruford: On reflection, a tune that had its genesis in Robert's head would be readily amenable to any of his strategies, rules, or restraints. One that emerged from Adrian's guitar as 'his' composition seemed to be less easy to 'Crimsonify', the process of stamping some sort of collective identity on it. Adrian's songs were always highly personal, despite (or because of) the fact that he often had to write under a great degree of pressure. The instrumental components of the piece might not have settled till almost the end of the session, leaving Adrian to finish melody and lyrics at the eleventh hour.

MH: Do you think the rules and restraints approach to collaborative music making necessarily requires great confidence and mastery of one's instrument?

Bruford: Yes, both would be helpful. An ability to play things a different way, to offer an alternative on the turn of a dime, while accommodating and balancing the demands of the other participants, demands a degree of confidence. One of the endearing faults of popular-music small groups is that all the musicians tend to play all the time, for understandable reasons. It's hard to stand around under a blaze of super-trouper spotlights and do nothing, trust me. 'Laying out', though, is a particularly effective music strategy with lots of consequences, generally welcomed by co-performers.

MH: Do you think the rules and restraints approach could be used as a way of 'lowering the bar' (i.e. matching skill level to challenge) so that novices can make music together effectively?

Bruford: An excellent idea that I think that would be entirely fruitful. One might say that one current rule in rap or hip hop might be to avoid (or at least background) music harmony. The removal of such a foundational and advanced component of traditional Western music making throws light on those remaining, in particular, rhythm and timbre.

References

Print

Abbott, K. (2001), *The Beach Boys' Pet Sounds: The Greatest Album of the Twentieth Century*, London: Helter Skelter Publishing.

Adams, T. (2011), 'Tom Waits: "I Look Like Hell But I'm Going to See Where It Gets Me"', *The Guardian*, 23 October. Available online: https://www.theguardian.com/music/2011/oct/23/tom-waits-interview-bad-as-me (accessed 24 March 2021).

Akrich, M. and B. Latour (1992), 'A Summary of a Convenient Vocabulary for the Semiotics of Human and Nonhuman Assemblies', in W. E. Bijker and J. Law (eds), *Shaping Technology, Building Society: Studies in Sociotechnical Change*, 259–64, Cambridge, MA: MIT Press.

Alcock, S. (2006), 'A Socio-Cultural Interpretation of Young Children's Playful and Humorous Communication', PhD diss., Massey University, Palmerston North.

Alcock, S. (2009), 'Dressing Up Play: Rethinking Play and Playfulness from Socio-Cultural Perspectives', *He Kupu: The Word*, 2 (2): 19–30. Available online: https://www.hekupu.ac.nz/article/dressing-play-rethinking-play-and-playfulness-socio-cultural-perspectives (accessed 10 August 2019).

Aldridge, A. (2009), 'Beatles Not All That Turned On', in M. Evans (ed.), *The Beatles: Paperback Writer: 40 Years of Classic Writing*, 164–9, London: Plexus.

Amabile, T. (1983), 'The Social Psychology of Creativity: A Componential Conceptualization', *Journal of Personality and Social Psychology*, 45 (2): 357–76.

Amabile, T. (1987), 'The Motivation to be Creative', in S. G. Isaksen (ed.), *Frontiers of Creativity Research: Beyond the Basics*, 223–54, Buffalo: Bearly Ltd.

Amabile, T. (1996), *Creativity in Context*, Boulder: Westview Press.

Amabile, T. and M. Pratt (2016), 'The Dynamic Componential Model of Creativity and Innovation in Organizations: Making Progress, Making Meaning', *Research in Organizational Behaviour*, 36: 157–83. Available online: http://dx.doi.org/10.1016/j.riob.2016.10.001 (accessed 17 July 2019).

Anderle, D., D. Hutton and M. Vosse (2011), 'Anecdotes', *The Beach Boys: The Smile Sessions*, [CD and vinyl boxset booklet] New York: Capitol Records.

Apter, M. J. (1982), *The Experience of Motivation: The Theory of Psychological Reversals*, New York: Academic Press.

Apter, M. J. (1991), 'A Structural Phenomenology of Play', in J. H. Kerr and M. J. Apter (eds), *Adult Play: A Reversal Theory Approach*, 13–29, Amsterdam: Swets & Zeitlinger.

Apter, M. J. (2003), 'On a Certain Blindness in Modern Psychology', *The Psychologist*, 16 (9): 474–5.

Apter, M. J. (2018), *Zigzag: Reversal and Paradox in Human Personality*, Leicestershire: Matador. Kindle Edition.

Archer, M. S. (1995), *Realist Social Theory: The Morphogenetic Approach*, New York: Cambridge University Press.

Awbi, A. (2016), 'Tim Gane: Cavern of Anti-Matter and Stereolab Lynchpin Tim Gane on His New LP, The Art of Musical Futurism and His Problem with Band Reunions...', *M Magazine*, 4 March. Available online: https://www.prsformusic.com/m-magazine/features/interview-tim-gane/ (accessed 9 May 2019).

Badman, K. (2000), *The Beatles Off the Record*, London: Omnibus.

Badman, K. (2001), *The Beatles – The Dream Is Over: Off the Record 2*, London: Omnibus Press.

Badman, K. (2004), *The Beach Boys: The Definitive Diary of America's Greatest Band, on Stage and in the Studio*, San Francisco: Backbeat Books.

Banks, M. and K. Oakley (2016), 'The Dance Goes on Forever? Art Schools, Class and UK Higher Education', *International Journal of Cultural Policy*, 22 (1). Available online: https://eprints.whiterose.ac.uk/84297/3/publications.leeds.ac.uk.pdf (accessed 23 March 2021).

Barrett, M. S. (2011), 'Towards a Cultural Psychology of Music Education', in M. S. Barrett (ed.), *A Cultural Psychology of Music Education*, 1–16, Oxford: Oxford University Press.

Barron, F. (1968), *Creativity and Personal Freedom*, Princeton: Van Nostrand.

Barron, F. (1969), *Creative Person and Creative Process*, New York: Holt.

Bateson, G. (1972), *Steps to an Ecology of Mind*, New York: Chandler Publishing Company.

Beck, J. and M. Cornford (2012), 'The Art School in Ruins', *Journal of Visual Culture*, 11 (1): 58–82.

Beecher, M. (1981), 'Kraftwerk Revealed!: An Interview with Ralph Hutter', *Electronics & Music Maker*, September: 62–7. Available online: http://www.keepwerking.co.uk/kraftwerkrevealed/ (accessed 13 September 2019).

Bell, M. (2004), 'The Resurrection Of Brian Wilson's SMiLE', *Sound On Sound*, October. Available online: https://www.soundonsound.com/people/resurrection-brian-wilsons-smile (accessed 5 January 2012).

Benji, B. (2014), 'Tom Tom Club', *Red Bull Music Academy*. Available online: https://www.redbullmusicacademy.com/lectures/tom-tom-club (accessed 20 February 2019).

Bessemer, S. P. and D. J. Treffinger (1981), 'Analysis of Creative Products: Review and Synthesis', *The Journal of Creative Behavior*, 15: 159–79.

Blake, M. (2005), *Dylan: Visions, Portraits & Back Pages*, New York: DK.

Blau, M. (2012), '33 Musicians On What John Cage Communicates', *npr music*, 5 September. Available online: https://www.npr.org/2012/08/30/160327305/33-musicians-on-what-john-cage-communicates (accessed 9 May 2019).

Boden, M. A. (1992), *The Creative Mind: Myths and Mechanisms*, London: Abacus.

Boden, M. A. (1994), *Dimensions of Creativity*, Cambridge, MA: MIT Press.

Bollinger, N. (2016), 'Music: "and the Anonymous Nobody" by De La Soul', *The Sampler*, 6 September. Available online: https://www.rnz.co.nz/national/programmes/thesampler/audio/201814640/and-the-anonymous-nobody-by-de-la-soul (accessed 2 February 2019).

Boyd, A. (2011), 'Producer's Notes', in *The Beach Boys: The Smile Sessions*, [CD Booklet] New York: Capitol Records.

Brogden, H. E. and T. B. Sprecher (1964), 'Criteria of Creativity', in C. W. Taylor (ed.), *Creativity: Progress and Potential*, New York: McGraw-Hill.

Brown, E. (2005), 'Influences: Brian Wilson', New York, 4 August. Available online: https://nymag.com/nymetro/arts/music/pop/12377/ (accessed 5 January 2012).

Bruford, B. (2009), *Bill Bruford: The Autobiography*. London: Jawbone Press.

Bruford, B. (2015), 'Making it Work: Creative Music Performance and the Western Kit Drummer', PhD diss., University of Surrey.

Bruford, B. (2018), *Uncharted: Creativity and the Expert Drummer*, Ann Arbor: University of Michigan Press.

Burns, T. R., N. Machado and U. Corte (2015), 'The Sociology of Creativity: Part I: Theory: The Social Mechanisms of Innovation and Creative Developments in Selectivity Environments', *Human Systems Management*, 34 (3): 179–99. Available online: https://content.iospress.com/articles/human-systems-management/hsm0839 (accessed 9 September 2019).

Bütz, M. R. (1997), *Chaos and Complexity: Implications for Psychological Theory and Practice*, Washington, DC: Taylor & Francis.

Byrne, D. (2012), *How Music Works*, San Francisco: McSweeney's.

Cage, J. (1952), '4'33"', [Sheet music] Glendale: Edition Peters.

Cage, J. (1961), *Silence: Lectures and Writings*, Middletown: Wesleyan University Press.

Cajiao, T. (1991). '"We Were the Only Band Directed by an Ass!": An Interview with Scotty Moore', *Elvis: The Man and His Music*, 10: 17–28.

Capra, F. (1997), *The Web of Life*, London: Flamingo.

Capra, F. (2002), *The Hidden Connections: Integrating the Biological, Cognitive, and Social Dimensions of Life into a Science of Sustainability*, New York: Doubleday.

Cavanagh, J. E. (2003), *The Piper at the Gates of Dawn*, New York: Continuum.

Chan, J. (2011), 'Towards a Sociology of Creativity', in L. Mann and J. Chan (eds), *Creativity and Innovation in Business and Beyond: Social Science Perspectives and Policy Implications*, 135–53, New York: Routledge.

Chan, J. (2013), 'Researching Creativity and Creativity Research', in K. Thomas and J. Chan (eds), *Handbook of Research on Creativity*, 21–32, Northampton: Edward Elgar Publishing.

Chapman, R. (2010), *Syd Barrett: A Very Irregular Head*, London: Faber and Faber.

Chapouthier, G. (2009), 'Mosaic Structures – A Working Hypothesis for the Complexity of Living Organisms', *E-Logos (Electronic Journal for Philosophy)*, 17. Available online: https://www.researchgate.net/publication/242475275_Mosaic_structures_-_a_working_hypothesis_for_the_complexity_of_living_organisms (accessed 7 December 2011).

Claxton, G. (1997), *Hare Brain Tortoise Mind: Why Intelligence Increases When You Think Less*. London: Fourth Estate.

Cohen, F. (2016), 'De La Soul's Legacy Is Trapped in Digital Limbo', *The New York Times*, 9 August. Available online: https://www.nytimes.com/2016/08/14/arts/music/de-la-soul-digital-albums.html (accessed 12 May 2019).

Cook, N. (2018), *Music as Creative Practice*, Oxford: Oxford University Press.

Copeland, S. (2009), *Strange Things Happen: A Life with The Police, Polo, and Pygmies*, New York: HarperStudio.

Corsaro, W. A. (1997), *The Sociology of Childhood*, Thousand Oaks: Pine Forge Press.

Corsaro, W. A. (2012), 'Interpretive Reproduction', *American Journal of Play*, 4 (4): 488–504.

Corsaro, W. A. and D. Eder (1990), 'Children's Peer Cultures', *Annual Review of Sociology*, 16: 197–220.

Cott, J. (2009), 'Interview with John Lennon', in M. Evans (ed.), *The Beatles: Paperback Writer: 40 years of Classic Writing*, 218–26. London: Plexus.

Crutchfield, R. (1962), 'Conformity and Creative Thinking', in H. Gruber, G. Terrell and M. Wertheimer (eds), *Contemporary Approaches to Creative Thinking*, 120–43, New York: Atherton Press.

Csikszentmihalyi, M. (1975), *Beyond Boredom and Anxiety: The Experience of Play in Work and Games*, San Francisco: Jossey-Bass.

Csikszentmihalyi, M. (1979), 'The Concept of Flow', in B. Sutton-Smith (ed.), *Play and Learning*, 257–74, New York: Gardner Press.

Csikszentmihalyi, M. (1990), *Flow: The Psychology of Optimal Experience*, New York: Harper & Row.

Csikszentmihalyi, M. (1999), 'Implications of a Systems Perspective for the Study of Creativity', in R. J. Sternberg (ed.), *Handbook of Creativity*, 313–35, New York: Cambridge University Press.

Csikszentmihalyi, M. (2014), 'Creativity and Genius: A Systems Perspective', in M. Csikszentmihalyi (ed.), *The Systems Model of Creativity*, 99–125, New York: Springer.

Currin, G. (2018), 'Angélique Kidjo on the Myth of Cultural Appropriation and Covering Remain in Light', *Pitchfork*, 7 June. Available online: https://pitchfork.com

/thepitch/angelique-kidjo-interview-myth-of-cultural-appropriation-covering-remain-in-light/ (accessed 20 February 2019).

daphneoram.org (n.d.), *The Oramics Machine*. [Webpage] Available online: https://www.daphneoram.org/oramicsmachine/ (accessed 11 May 2020).

David Byrne Interview – Library of Congress (2017), 23 May. Available online: https://www.loc.gov/static/programs/national-recording-preservation-board/documents/DavidByrneInterview.pdf (accessed 18 March 2021).

Dayal, G. (2009), *Brian Eno's Another Green World*, New York: Continuum.

DeRogatis, J. (2003), *Turn on Your Mind: Four Decades of Great Psychedelic Rock*, Milwaukee: Hal Leonard.

Detel, W. (2001), 'Social Constructivism', in N. Smelser and P. Baltes (eds), *International Encyclopedia of Social & Behavioral Sciences*, 14264–7, Oxford: Pergamon Press. Available online: https://www.sciencedirect.com/topics/computer-science/actor-network-theory (accessed 15 February 2020).

Dewey, J. (1934), *Art as Experience*, New York: Penguin Books.

Doggett, P. (2003), 'Smile: The Great Lost Album', in K. Abbott (ed.), *Back to the Beach: A Brian Wilson and The Beach Boys Reader*, 65–74, London: Helter Skelter Publishing.

Doggett, P. (2011), *The Man Who Sold the World: David Bowie and the 1970s*, New York: Random House.

Doherty, H. (1977), 'The Things We Do For Art', *Melody Maker*, 24 September: 10–45.

Du Noyer, P. (1995), 'The Beatles Interview', *Q*, December: 118–28.

Dylan, B. (2004), *Chronicles: Volume One*, New York: Simon & Schuster.

'Editorial: YOU' (1966), *International Times*, 1 (1): 1–8. Available online: http://www.internationaltimes.it/archive/index.php?year=1966&volume=IT-Volume-1&issue=1&item=IT_1966-10-14_B-IT-Volume-1_Iss-1_001 (accessed 6 April 2018).

Eliot, A. (1972), 'Encounters with Artists', *Atlantic Monthly*, 230 (4): 99–104.

Elitzur, A. C. (1990a), 'Humour, Play, and Neurosis: The Paradoxical Power of Confinement', *Humor*, 3 (1): 17–35.

Elitzur, A. C. (1990b), 'Biomimesis: Humour, Play and Neurosis as Life Mimicries', *Humor*, 3 (2): 159–75.

Elliot, P. (2001), 'Hey Hey We're the Monkeys!', *Q Magazine*, August. Available online: https://gorillaz-news.livejournal.com/11140.html (accessed 19 March 2020).

Emerick, G. and H. Massey (2006), *Here, There, and Everywhere: My Life Recording the Music of the Beatles*, New York: Gotham Books.

Epstein, R. (1996), *Cognition, Creativity, and Behavior: Selected Essays*, Westport: Praeger.

Epstein, R. and G. Laptosky (1999), 'Behavioral Approaches to Creativity', in M. A. Runco and S. R. Pritzker (eds), *Encyclopedia of Creativity*, Vol. 1, 175–83, Cambridge: Academic Press.

Evans, M., ed. (2009), *The Beatles: Paperback Writer: 40 Years of Classic Writing*, London: Plexus.

Eysenck, H. J. (1990), 'Creativity and Personality: A Theoretical Perspective', *Psychological Inquiry*, 4: 147–78.

Fear, D. (2019), '"I'm Just Sick of Zombies, Man": Jim Jarmusch on "The Dead Don't Die"', *Rolling Stone*. Available online: https://www.rollingstone.com/movies/movie-features/jim-jarmusch-the-dead-dont-die-interview-847447/ (accessed 16 June 2020).

Feldman, D. H. (1999), 'The Development of Creativity', in R. J. Sternberg (ed.), *Handbook of Creativity*, 169–86, New York: Cambridge University Press.

Feynman, R. P., R. Leighton and E. Hutchings (1985), *"Surely You're Joking, Mr. Feynman!": Adventures of a Curious Character*, New York: W.W. Norton.

Fielder, H. and P. Sutcliffe (1984), *The Book of Genesis*, London: St. Martin's Press.

Finke, R. A., T. B. Ward and S. M. Smith (1992), *Creative Cognition: Theory, Research, and Applications*, Cambridge, MA: MIT Press.

Forte, D. (1987), 'The Jungle Music & Posh Skiffle of George Harrison', *Guitar Player*, November: 83–97.

Fox, K. (2016), 'Me and the Muse: DJ Shadow on His Sources of Inspiration', *The Guardian*. Available online: https://www.theguardian.com/music/2016/jun/26/me-and-the-muse-dj-shadow-inspirations-mountain-will-fall (accessed 26 January 2021).

Freud, S. ([1908] 1990), 'The Relation of the Poet to Daydreaming', in J. M. Thompson (ed.), *20th Century Theories of Art*, 124–31, Ottawa: Carleton University Press.

Fricke, D. (1982), 'Old Cult Groups Never Die (They Just Become More Popular): King Crimson Hits the Road', Trouser Press, March.

Fricke, D. (2006), 'Exclusive Q&A: The Final Word From Patti Smith on CBGB', *Rolling Stone*, 17 October. Available online: https://www.rollingstone.com/music/music-news/exclusive-qa-the-final-word-from-patti-smith-on-cbgb-93787/ (accessed 1 February 2020).

Frissen, V. (2015), 'Playing with Bits and Bytes: The Savage Mind in the Digital Age', in V. Frissen, S. Lammes, M. De Lange, J. De Mul and J. Raessens (eds), *Playful Identities: The Ludification of Digital Media Cultures*, 149–64, Amsterdam: Amsterdam University Press.

Frith, S. and H. Horne (1987), *Art Into Pop*, London: Methuen.

Frith, S. and S. Zagorski-Thomas, eds (2012), *The Art of Record Production: An Introductory Reader for a New Academic Field*, London: Ashgate.

Fromm, E. (1959), 'The Creative Attitude', in H. H. Anderson (ed.), *Creativity and its Cultivation, Addresses Presented at the Interdisciplinary Symposia on Creativity, Michigan State University, East Lansing, Michigan*, 1st edn, New York: Harper.

Fulgosi, A. and J. P. Guilford (1968), 'Short Term Incubation in Divergent Production', *American Journal of Psychology*, 81: 241–6.

Gabriel, P. (2010), Liner Notes, *Scratch My Back*, [CD booklet] Box: Real World/Virgin Records.

Gaiman, N. (2005), 'Keeping It (Un)real', *Wired*. Available online: https://www.wired.com/2005/07/gorillaz-2/ (accessed 16 June 2019).

Galton, F. (1869), *Hereditary Genius: An Inquiry into Its Laws and Consequences*, London: Macmillan and Co.

Garbarini, V. (1988a), 'Keith Richards: The Heart of the Stones', in *The Best of Musician: The Beatles and the Stones*, Gloucester: Amordian Press.

Garbarini, V. (1988b), 'Paul McCartney: Lifting the Veil on the Beatles', in *The Best of Musician: The Beatles and The Stones*, 9–79, Gloucester: Amordian Press.

Garbarini, V. (1988c), 'Ringo', in *The Best of Musician: The Beatles and The Stones*, 38–47, Gloucester: Amordian Press.

Gardner, H. (1994), 'The Creator's Patterns', in M. Boden (ed.), *Dimensions of Creativity*, 143–58, Boston: The MIT Press.

Gelder, K. (2007), *Subcultures: Cultural Histories and Social Practice*, New York: Routledge.

Gert, V. (1931), *Mein Weg*, Leipzig.

Getzels, J. W. (1975), 'Creativity: Prospects and Issues', in I. A. Taylor and J. W. Getzels (eds), *Perspectives in Creativity*, 326–44, Chicago: Aldine.

Getzels, J. W. and M. Csikszentmihalyi (1976), *The Creative Vision: A Longitudinal Study of Problem Finding in Art*, New York: Wiley.

Getzels, J. W. and P. W. Jackson (1962), *Creativity and Intelligence: Explorations with Gifted Students*, New York: Wiley.

Giddins, G. (1981), *Riding on a Blue Note: Jazz and American Pop*, New York: Da Capo Press.

Gillett, C. (2009), 'The Sound of the City', in M. Evans (ed.), *The Beatles: Paperback Writer: 40 Years of Classic Writing*, London: Plexus.

Gilmore, M. (2013), 'Dylan's Lost Years', *Rolling Stone* (Australia), November: 70–77.

Gittins, I. (2004), *Talking Heads: Once in a Lifetime: The Stories Behind Every Song*, London: Carlton Books.

Godley, K. (2015), *Spacecake*, Hand Held Company Ltd. iBooks.

Goetz, E. M. (1989), 'The Teaching of Creativity to Preschool Children: The Behavior Analysis Approach', in J. A. Glover, R. R. Ronning and C. R. Reynolds (eds) *Handbook of Creativity*, 411–28, New York: Plenum Press.

Goffman, E. (1956), *The Presentation of Self in Everyday Life*, Edinburgh: University of Edinburgh, Social Sciences Research Centre.

Goffman, E. ([1974] 1986), *Frame Analysis: An Essay on the Organization of Experience*. Boston: Northeastern University Press.

Goldwyn, M. (2011), *During the Pause*, [Web-log post] 7 March. Available online: https://www.artslant.com/ny/articles/show/22078-during-the-pause (accessed 1 December 2019).

Gollner, A. (2015), 'Classic Dionysian Shit: An Interview with Richard Hell', *The Paris Review*, 8 December. Available online: https://www.theparisreview.org/blog/2015/12

/08/classic-dionysian-shit-an-interview-with-richard-hell/ (accessed 11 November 2018).

Graustark, B. and V. Garbarini (1988), 'John Lennon', in *The Best of Musician: The Beatles and The Stones*, 18–79, Gloucester: Amordian Press.

Groos, K. (1898), *The Play of Animals*, trans. E. Baldwin, New York: D. Appleton and Company.

Gruber, H. E. and S. N. Davis (1988), 'Inching Our Way Up Mount Olympus: The Evolving-Systems Approach to Creative Thinking', in R. J. Sternberg (ed.), *The Nature of Creativity: Contemporary Psychological Perspectives*, 243–70, New York: Cambridge University Press.

Guilford, J. P. (1950), 'Creativity', *American Psychologist*, 5: 444–54.

Guilford, J. P. (1959), 'Three Faces of Intellect', *American Psychologist*, 14 (8): 469–79.

Guilford, J. P. (1975), 'Creativity: A Quarter Century of Progress', in I. A. Taylor and J. W. Getzels (eds), *Perspectives in Creativity*, 37–59, Chicago: Aldine.

Guitard, P., F. Ferland and E. Dutil (2005), 'Toward a Better Understanding of Playfulness in Adults', *OTJR Occupation, Participation and Health*, 25 (1): 9–22.

Guralnick, P. (1994), *Last Train to Memphis: The Rise of Elvis Presley*, Boston: Little, Brown, and Co.

Haarich, M. (2021), *NFT Art – Historic or Hysteric?: Making a Point About the Latest Crypto Hype That Might End With Three Guinness World Records*, 28 February. Available online: https://max-haarich.medium.com/nft-art-historic-or-hysteric-e8edc30f4098 (accessed 16 March 2021).

Hadamard, J. (1945), *An Essay on the Psychology of Invention in the Mathematical Field*, Princeton: Princeton University Press.

Harris, J. (2005), 'Into the Woods: The Making of "The Basement Tapes"', in M. Blake (ed.), *Dylan: Visions, Portraits & Back Pages*, 118–31, New York: DK.

Harrison, J. (n.d.), *Random Oblique Strategies Online*. Available online: http://www.joshharrison.net/oblique-strategies/ (accessed 1 December 2020).

Hasted, N. (2005), 'Punk's Founding Father, Richard Hell', *The Independent*, 19 August. Available online: https://www.independent.co.uk/arts-entertainment/music/features/punks-founding-father-richard-hell-306738.html (accessed 11 November 2018).

Heiser, M. (2012), 'SMiLE: Brian Wilson's Musical Mosaic', *Journal on the Art of Record Production*, 7. Available online: /http://www.arpjournal.com/asarpwp/smile-brian-wilson's-musical-mosaic (accessed 9 April 2021).

Hennessy, B. A. and T. Amabile (2010), 'Creativity', *Annual Review of Psychology*, 61: 569–98.

Henricks, T. (2008), 'The Nature of Play', *American Journal of Play*, 1 (2): 157–80.

Henriksen, D. and M. Hoelting (2016), 'A Systems View of Creativity in a YouTube World', *TechTrends*, 60 (2): 102–6. Available online: https://www.researchgate.net/publication/297612072_A_Systems_View:of_Creativity_in_a_YouTube_World (accessed 17 June 2019).

Hepworth-Sawyer, R. and C. Golding (2010), *What Is Music Production?: Professional Techniques to Make a Good Recording Great*, Waltham: Focal Press.

Herrmann, M. E., G. Goldschmidt and E. Miron-Spektor (2018), 'The Ins and Outs of the Constraint-Creativity Relationship', *Proceedings of The Fifth International Conference on Design Creativity*, 160–7. Available online: https://www.designsociety.org/publication/40712/THE+INS+AND+OUTS+OF+THE+CONSTRAINT-+CREATIVITY+RELATIONSHIP (accessed 10 May 2019).

Hesse, H. ([1927] 2015), *Steppenwolf*, trans. B. Creighton, J. Mileck and H. Frenz, New York: Picador Modern Classics.

Holmberg, A. (1996), *The Theatre of Robert Wilson*, New York: Cambridge University Press.

Homer (1990), *The Odyssey*, trans. R. Fitzgerald, London: Vintage Classics.

Howlett, K. (2018), 'On the Road to "The White Album"', in *The Beatles and Esher Demos*, [CD booklet] London: Calderstone Productions Ltd./Apple Corps Ltd.

Huizinga, J. (1949), *Homo Ludens: A Study of the Play-Element in Culture*, London: Routledge & Kegan Paul.

Hutcheon, D. (2011), 'You Can't Do That...', *Mojo*, August: 74–87.

Hutt, C. (1971), 'Exploration and Play in Children', in R. E. Herron and B. Sutton-Smith (eds), *Child's Play*, 231–60, New York: Wiley.

Hutt, C. (1979), 'Exploration and Play (#2)', in B. Sutton-Smith (ed.), *Play and Learning*, 175–94, New York: Gardner Press.

Ivie, D. (2020), 'Jerry Harrison on the Virtuosic Legacy of Talking Heads' "Remain in Light", 40 Years Later', *Vulture*, 15 October. Available online: https://www.vulture.com/article/jerry-harrison-interview-talking-heads-remain-in-light-anniversary.html (accessed 20 March 2021).

Jackson, P. W. and S. Messick (1965), 'The Person, the Product and the Response: Conceptual Problems in the Assessment of Creativity', *Journal of Personality*, 33: 309–29.

Johnson, K. (2011), 'Liberating Viewers, and the World, With Silliness', *The New York Times*, 23 September. Available online: http://fluxusfoundation.com/reviews/the-new-york-times-fluxus-and-the-essential-questions-of-life/ (accessed 22 October 2020).

Johnson-Laird, P. N. (1988), 'Freedom and Constraint in Creativity', in R. J. Sternberg (ed.), *The Nature of Creativity: Contemporary Psychological Perspectives*, 202–19, New York: Cambridge University Press.

Jones, A. and D. Love (2014), 'Saved?', *Uncut*, July: 50–60.

Jones, C. (1995), 'The Thirty Year Face Off: Brian: Hero, the Rest: Villains. Can It Really Be That Simple?', *Mojo*, August. Available online: http://brianwilsonfans.com/page10.php (accessed 21 January 2012).

Jones, C. (1996), 'Wish You Were Here', *Mojo*, September. Available online: http://sydbarrett.net/syd-barrett-articles/wish-you-were-here-mojo-1996/ (accessed 12 July 2011).

Joyce, J. (1922), *Ulysses*, Paris: Shakespeare and Company.
Kastrenakes, J. (2021), 'Beeple Sold an NFT for $69 Million: Through a First-of-its-Kind Auction at Christie's', *The Verge*, 11 March. Available online: https://www.theverge.com/2021/3/11/22325054/beeple-christies-nft-sale-cost-everydays-69-million (accessed 16 March 2021).
Kelly, M., T. Foster and P. Kelly (2010), *The Golden Age of Fender*, London: Cassell Illustrated.
Kitching, S. (2018), 'The Idea Vs. The Real: Devo Discuss Their New Book', *The Quietus*, 5 August. Available online: https://thequietus.com/articles/25078-devo-book-the-brand-unmasked-interview-mark-mothersbaugh-gerald-casale (accessed 21 April 2020).
Koestler, A. (1964), *The Act of Creation*, New York: Macmillan.
Kostelanetz, R. (2000), *John Cage, Writer: Selected Texts*. Lanham: Cooper Square Press.
Kris, E. (1952), *Psychoanalytic Explorations in Art*, New York: International Universities Press.
Kubie, L. S. (1958), *Neurotic Distortion of the Creative Process*, Lawrence: University of Kansas Press.
Larry the O. (2009), 'To Sir with Love', *Electronic Musician*. Available online: http://www.emusician.com/gear/1332/to-sir-with-love/40689 (accessed 17 February 2010).
Latour, B. (1996), 'On Actor-Network Theory: A Few Clarifications Plus More Than a Few Complications', *Soziale Welt*, 47: 369–81.
Leaf, D. (1990), Liner Notes, *The Beach Boys: Pet Sounds*, [CD booklet] Los Angeles: Capitol Records.
Leaf, D. (1993), Liner Notes, *Good Vibrations: Thirty Years of The Beach Boys*, [CD boxset booklet] Los Angeles: Capitol Records.
Leary, T., R. Metzner and R. Alpert (1964), *The Psychedelic Experience*. New York: University Books.
Lennon, J. (1964), *In His Own Write*, London: J. Cape.
Levy, J. (1998), 'The Beastie Boys Are Back in Town', *Rolling Stone*, August. Available online: https://www.rollingstone.com/feature/the-beastie-boys-are-back-in-town-2-190310/ (accessed 4 November 2020).
Lewis, J. (2010), 'Album by Album: Frank Zappa', *Uncut*, November: 168–70.
Lewisohn, M. (1988), *The Complete Beatles Recording Sessions: The Official Story of the Abbey Road Years*. London: Hamlyn.
Leyshon, A. (2009), 'The Software Slump?: Digital Music, the Democratisation of Technology, and the Decline of the Recording Studio Sector within the Musical Economy', *Environment & Planning A*, 41 (6): 1309–31.
Lieberman, J. N. (1965), 'Playfulness and Divergent Thinking: An Investigation of their Relationship at the Kindegarten Level', *Journal of Genetic Psychology*, 107: 219–24.
Lieberman, J. N. (1977), *Playfulness: Its Relationship to Imagination and Creativity*, New York: Academic Press.

Lombroso, C. (1891), *The Man of Genius*, London: Walter Scott.
Love, M. (2011), Liner Notes, *The Beach Boys: The Smile Sessions*, [CD and vinyl boxset booklet] New York: Capitol Records.
Lowe, S. (2005), 'The Fab Five: Dylan and The Beatles', in M. Blake (ed.), *Dylan: Visions, Portraits & Back Pages*, 44–51, New York: DK.
Luria, A. R. (1928), 'The Problem of the Cultural Development of the Child', *Journal of Genetic Psychology*, 35: 493–506.
Mao, J. (2011), 'Frankie Knuckles', *Red Bull Music Academy*. Available online: https://www.redbullmusicacademy.com/lectures/frankie-knuckles-lecture (accessed 5 January 2020).
Marshall, S. (2008), 'The Story of the Radiophonic Workshop', *Sound On Sound*, April. Available online: https://www.soundonsound.com/people/story-bbc-radiophonic-workshop (accessed 14 September 2020).
Martin, G. and J. Hornsby (1994), *All You Need Is Ears*, New York: St. Martin's Press.
Martin, R. A. (2007), *The Psychology of Humor: An Integrative Approach*, Boston: Elsevier Academic Press.
Maslow, A. H. (1954), *Motivation and Personality*, New York: Harper.
Maslow, A. H. (1959), 'Creativity in Self-actualizing People', in H. H. Anderson (ed.), *Creativity and Its Cultivation, Addresses Presented at the Interdisciplinary Symposia on Creativity, Michigan State University, East Lansing, Michigan*, New York: Harper.
Maslow, A. H. (1964), *Religions, Values, and Peak Experiences*, Columbus: Ohio State University Press.
Massey, H. (2000), *Behind the Glass: Top Producers Tell How They Craft the Hits*, San Francisco: Miller Freeman Books.
Massey, H. (2009), *Behind the Glass. Volume II: Top Producers Tell How They Craft the Hits*, Milwaukee: Backbeat Books.
McCulley, J. (2003), 'Trouble in Mind: A Revealing Interview with Brian Wilson', in K. Abbott (ed.), *Back to the Beach: A Brian Wilson and The Beach Boys Reader*, 187–204, London: Helter Skelter Publishing.
McDermott, M. (1991), 'Negativism as Play: Proactive Rebellion in Young Adult Life', in J. H. Kerr and M. J. Apter (eds), *Adult Play: A Reversal Theory Approach*, 87–99, Amsterdam: Swets & Zeitlinger.
McDermott, P. D. (2018), 'Your Best American Mitski Interview: For the Release of "Be The Cowboy", Mitski Goes Deep on Her Life as an Artist', *Fader*, 10 August. Available online: https://www.thefader.com/2018/08/10/mitski-interview-be-the-cowboy (accessed 16 March 2021).
McGhee, P. E. (1979), *Humor, Its Origin and Development*, San Francisco: W. H. Freeman.
McIntyre, P. (2007), *Rethinking Creative Practice in the Light of Mihalyi Csikszentmihalyi's Systems Model of Creativity*. Available online: https://www.researchgate.net/publication/238725021_Rethinking_Creative_Practice_in_the_Light_of_Mihaly_Csikszentmihalyi%27s_Systems_Model_of_Creativity (accessed 12 May 2018).

McIntyre, P. (2008), 'The Systems Model of Creativity: Analyzing the Distribution of Power in the Studio', *Journal on the Art of Record Production*, 3. Available online: https://www.arpjournal.com/asarpwp/the-systems-model-of-creativity-analyzing-the-distribution-of-power-in-the-studio/ (accessed 22 September 2009).

McIntyre, P. (2013), 'Creativity as a System in Action', in K. Thomas and J. Chan (eds), *Handbook of Research on Creativity*, 84–97, Northampton: Edward Elgar Publishing.

McKee, J. (2012), 'Ann Arbor Film Festival: A 50-Year Timeline', *The Ann Arbor News*, 24 March. Available online: http://www.annarbor.com/entertainment/ann-arbor-film-festival-a-50-year-timeline/ (accessed 21 April 2020).

Meares, R. (2005), *The Metaphor of Play: Origin and Breakdown of Personal Being*, New York: Routledge.

Mearian, L. (2019), 'What Is Blockchain?: The Complete Guide', *Computer World*, 30 January. Available online: https://www.computerworld.com/article/3191077/what-is-blockchain-the-complete-guide.html (accessed 16 March 2021).

Mednick, S. A. (1962), 'The Associative Basis of the Creative Process', *Psychological Review*, 69: 220–32.

Mertens, W. ([1983] 2007), *American Minimal Music: La Monte Young, Terry Riley, Steve Reich, Philip Glass*, London: Kahn and Averill.

Miles, B. (1998), *Paul McCartney: Many Years From Now*, London: Vintage.

Miles, B. (2006), *Pink Floyd: The Early Years*, London: Omnibus Press.

Montuori, A. and R. E. Purser (1995), 'Deconstructing the Lone Genius Myth: Toward a Contextual View of Creativity', *Journal of Humanistic Psychology*, 35: 69–111.

Mulhern, T. (1986), 'On the Discipline of Craft & Art: An Interview with Robert Fripp', *Guitar Player*, January. Available online: http://www0.mulhern.com/articles/Fripp.html (accessed 25 August 2020).

Murray, C. S. (2005), 'Talk About the Passion: The Making of "The Freewheelin Bob Dylan"', in M. Blake (ed.), *Dylan: Visions, Portraits & Back Pages*, 20–1, New York: DK.

Myers, M. (2011), 'Still Picking Up Good Vibrations', *The Wall Street Journal*, 7 October. Available online: http://online.wsj.com/article/SB10001424052970204524604576609000066845070 (accessed 15 January 2012).

Newell, A. and H. Simon (1972), *Human Problem Solving*, Englewood Cliffs: Prentice-Hall.

Newman, J. (2019), 'The Last Word: RZA on Wu-Tang's Legacy, Turning 50 and Why He Prays Daily', *Rolling Stone*, 7 May. Available online: https://www.rollingstone.com/music/music-features/rza-wu-tang-clan-interview-last-word-831770/ (accessed 21 February 2020).

Noz (2011), 'Bootsy Collins', *Red Bull Music Academy*. Available online: https://www.redbullmusicacademy.com/lectures/bootsy-collins (accessed 12 April 2020).

Nyman, M. (1999), *Experimental Music: Cage and Beyond*, Cambridge: Cambridge University Press.

Oram, D. (1972), *An Individual Note of Music, Sound and Electronics*, London: Galliard Ltd.

Oring, E. (2003), *Engaging Humor*, Urbana: University of Illinois Press.
Partridge, A. and T. Bernhardt (2016), *Complicated Game*, London: Jawbone Press.
Pearson, T. (2021), *Cindy Wilson for Women of Rock Oral History Project*, 21 March. Available online: https://www.youtube.com/watch?v=nyfB0BTMKlk (accessed 21 March 2021).
Polizzotti, M. (2006), *Highway 61 Revisited*, New York: Continuum.
Prigogine, I. and I. Stengers (1984), *Order Out of Chaos: Man's New Dialogue with Nature*, New York: Bantam Books.
Prince, G. M. (1975), 'Creativity, Self, and Power', in I. A. Taylor and J. W. Getzels (eds), *Perspectives in Creativity*, 249–77, Chicago: Aldine.
Priore, D. (1997), *Look! Listen! Vibrate! Smile!*, San Francisco: Last Gasp.
Priore, D. (2005), *Smile: The Story of Brian Wilson's Lost Masterpiece*, London: Sanctuary.
Priore, D. (2011), 'Smile: A History', in *The Beach Boys: The Smile Sessions*, [CD and vinyl boxset booklet] New York: Capitol Records.
Rennison, J. (2018), 'George Clinton: Characters Evolve But People Are Confined To Their Generation', *Financial Times*, 24 August. Available online: https://www.ft.com/content/17897604-a55f-11e8-926a-7342fe5e173f (accessed 15 May 2019).
Reum, P. (2011), 'Lost and Found: The Significance of Smile', in *The Beach Boys: The Smile Sessions*, [CD Booklet] New York: Capitol Records.
Reyes, J. (2020), 'On Her Latest Project, Meredith Monk Revisits Her Past', *Bandcamp Daily*, 13 April. Available online: https://daily.bandcamp.com/features/meredith-monk-memory-game-interview (accessed 10 May 2020).
Rhodes, M. (1961), 'An Analysis of Creativity', *Phi Delta Kappan*, 42: 305–10.
Ribot, T. (1900a), 'The Nature of Creative Imagination', *The International Quarterly*, 1: 648–75.
Ribot, T. (1900b), 'The Nature of Creative Imagination', *The International Quarterly*, 2: 1–25.
Robert, S. and G. Chapouthier (2006), 'The Mosaic of Language', *Marges Linguistiques*, 11: 160–6.
Rogers, C. R. (1963), 'The Concept of the Fully Functioning Person', *Psychotherapy*, 1: 17–26.
Rosso, B. (2014), 'Creativity and Constraints: Exploring the Role of Constraints in the Creative Processes of Research and Development Teams', *Organization Studies*, 35 (4): 551–85.
San Francisco Museum of Modern Art (2020), *Robert Rauschenberg, White Painting [three panel], 1951: Overview*. Available online: https://www.sfmoma.org/artwork/98.308.a-c/ (accessed 3 February 2020).
Sandlin, J. A. and J. L. Malim, (2008), 'Mixing Pop (Culture) and Politics: Cultural Resistance, Culture Jamming, and Anti-Consumption Activism as Critical Public Pedagogy', *Curriculum Inquiry*, 38 (3): 323–50.

Sawyer, R. K. (2002), 'Unresolved Tensions in Sociocultural Theory: Analogies with Contemporary Sociological Debates', *Culture & Psychology*, 8 (3): 283–305.

Sawyer, R. K. (2003), 'Nonreductive individualism: Part II-Social Causation', *Philosophy of the Social Sciences*, 33 (2): 203–24.

Sawyer, R. K. (2006), 'Educating for Innovation', *Thinking Skills and Creativity*, 1 (1): 41–8.

Sawyer, R. K. (2012), *Explaining Creativity: The Science of Human Innovation*, New York: Oxford University Press.

Sawyer, R. K. and S. DeZutter (2009), 'Distributed Creativity: How Collective Creations Emerge from Collaboration', *Psychology of Aesthetics, Creativity and the Arts*, 3 (2): 81–92.

Schachtel, E. G. (1959), *Metamorphosis: On the Development of Affect, Perception, Attention, and Memory*, New York: Basic Books.

Schnee, S. (2015), 'Guitars, Microphones and Lobsters That Rock: An Exclusive Interview with Kate Pierson', *Amped*, 27 February. Available online: https://www.ampeddistribution.com/2015/02/exclusive-interview-kate-pierson-b-52s-new-album-guitars-microphones (accessed 21 March 2020).

Schnipper, M. (2018), 'Don't Cry for Mitski', *Pitchfork*, 12 July. Available online: https://pitchfork.com/features/profile/dont-cry-for-mitski/ (accessed 16 March 2021).

Scoppa, B. (2010), 'It's a Big Explosion...', *Uncut*, November: 134–8.

Sharp, K. (2000), 'Alan Jardine: A Beach Boy Still Riding the Waves', *Goldmine*, 28 July. Available online: http://brianwilsonfans.com/page11.php (accessed 15 January 2012).

Sheffield, R. (2019), 'Karen O and Danger Mouse on Time Travel, Female Energy, Pink Floyd and Beyoncé', *Rolling Stone*, 18 March. Available online: https://www.rollingstone.com/music/music-features/karen-o-danger-mouse-lux-prima-interview-807198/ (accessed 13 March 2020).

Sheppard, D. (2009), *On Some Faraway Beach: The Life and Times of Brian Eno*, Chicago: Chicago Review Press.

Sherman, L. W. (1975), 'An Ecological Study of Glee in Small Groups of Preschool Children', *Child Development*, 46: 53–61.

Singleton, I. (2016), 'In Their Own Words King Crimson 1995', *DGM Live*, [Webpage] 14 November. Available online: https://www.dgmlive.com/in-depth/in-their-own-words-king-crimson-1995 (accessed 19 February 2020).

Slater, A. (2020), 'Interview: Garbage's Shirley Manson', *Songwriting*, 8 March. Available online: https://www.songwritingmagazine.co.uk/interviews/garbage-shirley-manson (accessed online 16 September 2020).

Slowinski, C. and A. Boyd (2011), 'The Beach Boys Smile – Sessionography', in *The Beach Boys: The Smile Sessions*, [CD and vinyl boxset booklet] New York: Capitol Records.

Southall, B., P. Vince and A. Rouse (2002), *Abbey Road: The Story of the World's Most Famous Recording Studios*, London: Omnibus.

Spariosu, M. (1989), *Dionysus Reborn: Play and the Aesthetic Dimension in Modern Philosophical and Scientific Discourse*, Ithaca: Cornell University Press.

Sternberg, R. J. and T. I. Lubart (1991), 'An Investment Theory of Creativity and Its Development', *Human Development*, 34: 1–32.

Sternberg, R. J. and T. I. Lubart (1992), 'Buy Low and Sell High: An Investment Theory of Creativity and Its Development', *Current Directions in Psychological Science*, 1 (1): 1–5.

Sternberg, R. J. and T. I. Lubart (1995), *Defying the Crowd: Cultivating Creativity in a Culture of Conformity*, New York: Free Press.

Sternberg, R. J. and T. I. Lubart (1996), 'Investing in Creativity', *American Psychologist*, 51: 677–88.

Sternberg, R. J. and T. I. Lubart (1999), 'The Concept of Creativity: Prospects and Paradigms', in R. J. Sternberg (ed.), *Handbook of Creativity*, 3–15, New York: Cambridge University Press.

Stewart, A. (2011), 'A Day in the Life of Geoff Emerick', *Audio Technology*, August: 26–33.

Strachan, R. (2018), *Sonic Technologies: Popular Music, Digital Culture and the Creative Process*, New York: Bloomsbury. Kindle Edition.

Strand, R. (1987), *A Good Deal of Freedom: Art and Design in the Public Sector of Higher Education, 1960–1982*. London: CNAA.

Sutton-Smith, B. (1976), 'Current Research in Play, Games and Sports', in T. T. Craig (ed.), *The Humanistic and Mental Health Aspects of Sports, Exercise and Recreation*, 1–4, Chicago: American Medical Association.

Sutton-Smith, B. (1979), 'Epilogue: Play as Performance', in B. Sutton-Smith (ed.), *Play and Learning*, 295–322, New York: Gardner Press.

Sutton-Smith, B. (1997), *The Ambiguity of Play*, Cambridge, MA: Harvard University Press.

Sutton-Smith, B. (2001), *The Ambiguity of Play*, Cambridge, MA: Harvard University Press.

Tamm, E. (1990), *Robert Fripp: From King Crimson to Guitar Craft*, Boston: Faber and Faber.

Tamm, E. (1995), *Brian Eno: His Music and the Vertical Color of Sound*, New York: Da Capo Press.

Taylor, G. (2003), *The Oblique Strategies*. [Webpage] Available online: http://www.rtqe.net/ObliqueStrategies/ (accessed 2 February 2015).

Taylor, I. A. (1975a), 'A Retrospective View of Creativity Investigation', in I. A. Taylor and J. W. Getzels (eds), *Perspectives in Creativity*, 1–36, Chicago: Aldine.

Taylor, I. A. (1975b), 'An Emerging View of Creative Actions', in I. A. Taylor and J. W. Getzels (eds), *Perspectives in Creativity*, 297–325, Chicago: Aldine.

Taylor, I. A. and B. J. Sandler (1972), 'Use of a Creative Product Inventory for Evaluating Products of Chemists', *Proceedings of the 80th Annual Convention of the American Psychological Association*, 7: 311–12.

Tegano, D. W. (1990), 'Relationship of Tolerance Ambiguity and Playfulness to Creativity', *Psychological Reports*, 66: 1047–56.
'The Billboard Hot 100: 1969' (2007), *Billboard.com*, [Webpage] 11 November. Available online: https://web.archive.org/web/20071111162104/http://www.billboard.com/bbcom/charts/yearend_chart_display.jsp?f=The+Billboard+Hot+100&g=Year-end+Singles&year=1969 (accessed 17 June 2020).
Thompson, P. (2019), *Creativity in the Recording Studio: Alternative Takes*, London: Palgrave MacMillan.
Thomson, G. (2010), 'And the Heat Goes On', *Uncut*, November: 140–4.
Tingen, P. (2005), 'Brian Eno: Recording Another Day On Earth', *Sound On Sound*, October. Available online: https://www.soundonsound.com/people/brian-eno (accessed 23 April 2016).
Torrance, E. P. (1961), 'Priming Creative Thinking in the Primary Grades', *Elementary School Journal*, 62: 139–45.
Torrance, E. P. (1974), *Torrance Tests of Creative Thinking*, Lexington: Personnel Press.
Truhon, S. A. (1983), 'Playfulness, Play, and Creativity: A Path Analytic Model', *Journal of Genetic Psychology*, 143: 19–28.
Wallach, M. and N. Kogan (1965), *Modes of Thinking in Young Children*, New York: Holt, Rinehart & Winston.
Warmuth, S. (2010), 'Bob Charlatan: Deconstructing Dylan's "Chronicles: Volume One"', *New Haven Review*, 6. Available online: http://www.newhavenreview.com/issue-006 (accessed 11 April 2011)
Warren, E. (2013), 'Brian Eno', *Red Bull Music Academy*. Available online: https://www.redbullmusicacademy.com/lectures/brian-eno (accessed 1 March 2020).
Wehner, L., M. Csikszentmihalyi and I. Magyari-Beck (1991), 'Current Approaches used in Studying Creativity: An Exploratory Investigation', *Creativity Research Journal*, 4 (3): 261–71.
Weisberg, R. W. (1986), *Creativity: Genius and Other Myths*, New York: W. H. Freeman.
Weiss, D. (2018), '"Synchronicity" by The Police Turns 35: How Producer Hugh Padgham Survived the Experience', *SonicScoop*, 18 June. Available online: https://sonicscoop.com/2018/06/18/synchronicity-police-turns-35-producer-hugh-padgham-survived-experience/2/ (accessed 11 January 2021).
Wells, D. H. (1986), 'Behavioral Dimensions of Creative Responses', *The Journal of Creative Behavior*, 20 (1): 61–5.
Wertsch, J. V. (1998), *Mind as Action*, Oxford: Oxford University Press.
Williams, R. (2009), 'George Harrison 1943–2001', in M. Evans (ed.), *The Beatles: Paperback Writer: 40 Years of Classic Writing*, 331–5, London: Plexus.
Wilson, B. (2011), 'Music Is God's Voice', in *The Beach Boys: The Smile Sessions*, [CD and vinyl boxset booklet] New York: Capitol Records.
Wilson, E. (1994), *Shostakovich: A Life Remembered*, Princeton: Princeton University Press.

Winston, A. S. and J. E. Baker (1985), 'Behavior Analytic Studies of Creativity: A Critical Review', *The Behavior Analyst*, 8 (2): 191–205.

Wolfe, D. (2011), 'Producer Notes', in *The Beach Boys: The Smile Sessions*, [CD and vinyl boxset booklet] New York: Capitol Records.

Zagorski-Thomas, S. (2014), *The Musicology of Record Production*, Cambridge: Cambridge University Press. Kindle Edition.

Zagorski-Thomas, S., K. Isakoff, S. Lacasse and S. Stévance (2019), *The Art of Record Production: Creative Practice in the Studio*, London: Ashgate.

Zak, A. J. (2007), 'Recording Studio as Space/Place', *Journal on the Art of Record Production*, 1. Available online: https://www.arpjournal.com/asarpwp/recording-studio-as-spaceplace/ (accessed 30 September 2019).

Zak, A. J. (2010a), *I Don't Sound Like Nobody: Remaking Music in 1950s America*, Ann Arbor: University of Michigan Press.

Zak, A. (2010b), 'Painting the Sonic Canvas: Electronic Mediation as Musical Style', in A. Bayley (ed.), *Recorded Music: Performance, Culture and Technology*, 307–21. New York: Cambridge University Press.

Zappa, F. (1997), 'All About Music', in F. Barron, A. Montuori and A. Barron (eds), *Creators on Creating: Awakening and Cultivating the Imaginative Mind*, 195–7, New York: Putnam.

Ziv, A. (1984), *Personality and Sense of Humor*, New York: Springer Pub. Co.

Ziv, A. (1989), 'Using Humor to Develop Creative Thinking', *Journal of Children in Contemporary Society*, 20 (1–2): 99–116.

Zollo, P. (1997), *Songwriters on Songwriting*, New York: Da Capo Press.

Zwerin, M. (1983), 'Brian Eno: Music Existing in Space', *International Herald Tribune*, 14 September: 7.

Audio

10cc (1975), 'Une Nuit a Paris', on *The Original Soundtrack*, [Vinyl album] London: Phonogram Ltd.

'#118 – Mark Linett Beach Boys SMiLE Part One' (2011), [Podcast radio programme] *Icon Fetch*, 11 October. Available online: https://iconfetch.com/shows/mark-linett-beach-boys-smile-interview (accessed 30 January 2012).

'#130 – Mark Linett & Alan Boyd – SMiLE Followup Part Two' (2011), [Podcast radio programme] *Icon Fetch*, 4 December. Available online: https://iconfetch.com/shows/smile-followup-part-two-mark-linett-a-alan-boyd (accessed 30 January 2012).

1910 Fruitgum Company (1967), 'Simon Says', [Vinyl 7" single] New York: Buddah Records.

1910 Fruitgum Company (1968), '1, 2, 3, Red Light', [Vinyl 7" single] New York: Buddah Records.

1910 Fruitgum Company (1969), 'Indian Giver', [Vinyl 7" single] New York: Buddah Records.
Arnold, K. (1934), 'Milk Cow Blues', [Shellac 10" single] New York: Decca Records.
Barrett, S. (1969), 'Octopus', [Vinyl 7" single] London: Harvest Records.
Barrett, S. (1970a), *Barrett*, [Vinyl album] London: Harvest Records.
Barrett, S. (1970b), 'No Good Trying', on *The Madcap Laughs*, [Vinyl album] London: Harvest Records.
Barrett, S. (1970c), *The Madcap Laughs*, [Vinyl album] London: Harvest Records.
Beyond the Fringe (1961), *Beyond the Fringe*, [Vinyl album] London: Parlophone Records.
Bowie, D. (1969), 'Space Oddity', [Vinyl 7" single] Richmond: Mercury Records.
Bowie, D. (1971), *Hunky Dory*, [Vinyl album] New York: RCA Records.
Bowie, D. (1972), *The Rise and Fall of Ziggy Stardust and the Spiders from Mars*, [Vinyl album] New York: RCA Records.
Bowie, D. (1977), *Heroes*, [Vinyl album] New York: RCA Records.
Bowie, D. (1979a), 'Boys Keep Swinging', on *Lodger*, [Vinyl album] New York: RCA Records.
Bowie, D. (1979b), *Lodger*, [Vinyl album] New York: RCA Records.
'Brian Wilson Interview 2' (1997), [CD] *Mojo*, August: 45.
Coleman, O. (1961), *Free Jazz: A Collective Improvisation*, [Vinyl album] New York: Atlantic Records.
Crazy Elephant (1969), 'Gimme Gimme Good Lovin', [Vinyl 7" single] New York: Bell Records.
Crosby, B. (1950), 'Habor Lights', [Vinyl 7" single] New York: Decca Records.
Crudup, A. (1947), 'That's Alright', [Shellac 10" single] New York: RCA Records.
De La Soul (1989), *3 Feet High and Rising*, [Vinyl album] New York: Tommy Boy Records.
De La Soul (2016), *and the Anonymous Nobody*, [CD album] New York: AOI Records.
Dylan, B. (1963a), 'A Hard Rain's A-Gonna Fall', on *The Freewheelin' Bob Dylan*, [Vinyl album] New York: Columbia Records.
Dylan, B. (1963b), 'Blowin' in the Wind', on *The Freewheelin' Bob Dylan*, [Vinyl album] New York: Columbia Records.
Dylan, B. (1963c), 'Talking World War III Blues', on *The Freewheelin' Bob Dylan*, [Vinyl album] New York: Columbia Records.
Dylan, B. (1963d), *The Freewheelin' Bob Dylan*, [Vinyl album] New York: Columbia Records.
Dylan, B. (1965a), 'Ballad of a Thin Man', on *Highway 61 Revisited*, [Vinyl album] New York: Columbia Records.
Dylan, B. (1965b), 'Desolation Row', on *Highway 61 Revisited*, [Vinyl album] New York: Columbia Records.
Dylan, B. (1965c), *Highway 61 Revisited*, [Vinyl album] New York: Columbia Records.
Dylan, B. (1965d), 'Highway 61 Revisited', on *Highway 61 Revisited*, [Vinyl album] New York: Columbia Records.

Dylan, B. (1965e). 'Tombstone Blues', on *Highway 61 Revisited*, [Vinyl album] New York: Columbia Records.

Dylan, B. (1966), *Blonde on Blonde*, [Vinyl album] New York: Columbia Records.

Dylan, B. (1975), *Blood on the Tracks*, [CD album] New York: Columbia Records.

Dylan, B. (1989), *Oh Mercy!*, [CD album] New York: Columbia Records.

Dylan, B. (1997), *Time Out of Mind*, [CD album] New York: Columbia Records.

Eno, B. and D. Byrne (1981), *My Life in the Bush of Ghosts*, [Vinyl album] London: EG Records.

Fleetwood Mac (1968), 'Albatross', [Vinyl 7" single] London: Blue Horizon Records.

Gabriel, P. (1986), *So*, [Vinyl album] London: Virgin Records.

Genesis (1972), 'Get 'Em Out by Friday', on *Foxtrot*, [Vinyl album] London: Charisma Records.

Genesis (1973), 'The Battle of Epping Forest', on *Selling England By The Pound*, [Vinyl album] London: Charisma Records.

Genesis (1974a), 'Fly on a Windshield', on *The Lamb Lies Down on Broadway*, [Vinyl album] London: Charisma Records.

Genesis (1974b), *The Lamb Lies Down on Broadway*, [Vinyl album] London: Charisma Records.

Gunter, A. (1954), 'Baby, Let's Play House', [Vinyl 7" single] Nashville: Excello Records.

In Living Memory (2011), [Radio programme] *BBC Radio 4*, 24 August.

Kidjo, A. (2018), *Remain in Light*, [Vinyl album] Canada: Kravenworks Records.

King Crimson (1973), *Larks' Tongues In Aspic*, [Vinyl album] London: EG Records.

King Crimson (1981), 'Sheltering Sky', on *Discipline*, [Vinyl album] London: EG Records.

King Crimson (1984a), 'Industry', on *Three of a Perfect Pair*, [Vinyl album] London: EG Records.

King Crimson (1984b), 'No Warning', on *Three of a Perfect Pair*, [Vinyl album] London: EG Records.

Kraftwerk (1974), *Autobahn*, [Vinyl album] Hamburg: Phonogram GmbH.

Monroe, B. and his Bluegrass Boys (1947), 'Blue Moon of Kentucky', [Shellac 10" single] New York: Columbia Records.

Page, P. (1953), 'The Doggy in the Window', [Vinyl 7" single] Chicago: Mercury Records.

Pink Floyd (1967a), 'Arnold Lane', [Vinyl 7" single] London: Columbia Records.

Pink Floyd (1967b), 'Interstellar Overdrive', on *The Piper at the Gates of Dawn*, [Vinyl album] London: Columbia Records.

Pink Floyd (1967c), 'See Emily Play', [Vinyl 7" single] London: Columbia Records.

Presley, E. (1956), 'Heartbreak Hotel', [Vinyl 7" single] New York: RCA Records.

Presley, E., S. Moore and B. Black (1954a), 'Good Rockin' Tonight' b/w 'I Don't Care if the Sun Don't Shine', [Vinyl 7" single] Memphis: Sun Records.

Presley, E., S. Moore and B. Black (1954b), 'Milk Cow Blues Boogie' b/w 'You're a Heartbreaker', [Vinyl 7" single] Memphis: Sun Records.

Presley, E., S. Moore and B. Black (1954c), 'That's All Right' b/w 'Blue Moon of Kentucky', [Vinyl 7" single] Memphis: Sun Records.

Presley, E., S. Moore and B. Black (1955), 'Baby, Let's Play House' b/w 'I'm Left, You're Right, She's Gone', [Vinyl 7" single] Memphis: Sun Records.

Queen (1975), 'Bohemian Rhapsody', on *A Night at the Opera*, [Vinyl album] London: EMI Records.

Talking Heads (1978a), 'Artists Only', on *More Songs About Buildings and Food*, [Vinyl album] New York: Sire Records.

Talking Heads (1978b), 'Found A Job', on *More Songs About Buildings and Food*, [Vinyl album] New York: Sire Records.

Talking Heads (1978c), *More Songs About Buildings and Food*, [Vinyl album] New York: Sire Records.

Talking Heads (1979a), 'Animals', on *Fear of Music*, [Vinyl album] New York: Sire Records.

Talking Heads (1979b), 'Drugs', on *Fear of Music*, [Vinyl album] New York: Sire Records.

Talking Heads (1979c), *Fear of Music*, [Vinyl album] New York: Sire Records.

Talking Heads (1979d), 'I Zimbra', on *Fear of Music*, [Vinyl album] New York: Sire Records.

Talking Heads (1979e), 'Life During Wartime', on *Fear of Music*, [Vinyl album] New York: Sire Records.

Talking Heads (1979f), 'Mind', on *Fear of Music*, [Vinyl album] New York: Sire Records.

Talking Heads (1980a), 'Once in a Lifetime', on *Remain in Light*, [Vinyl album] New York: Sire Records.

Talking Heads (1980b), *Remain in Light*, [Vinyl album] New York: Sire Records.

Talking Heads (1980c), 'The Great Curve', on *Remain in Light*, [Vinyl album] New York: Sire Records.

Talking Heads (1983), *Speaking in Tongues*, [Vinyl album] New York: Sire Records.

The Archies (1969), 'Sugar, Sugar', [Vinyl 7" single] New York: Calender Records.

The Beach Boys (1964), '"Cassius" Love vs. "Sonny" Wilson', on *Shut Down Vol. 2*, [Vinyl album] Los Angeles: Capitol Records.

The Beach Boys (1965), 'I'm Bugged at my Ol' Man', on *Summer Days (And Summer Nights!!)*, [Vinyl album] Los Angeles: Capitol Records.

The Beach Boys (1966a), 'Good Vibrations', [Vinyl 7" single] Los Angeles: Capitol Records.

The Beach Boys (1966b), *Pet Sounds*, [Vinyl album] Los Angeles: Capitol Records.

The Beach Boys (1967a), 'Heroes and Villains', on *Smiley Smile*, [Vinyl album] Los Angeles: Capitol Records.

The Beach Boys (1967b), 'Mama Says', on *Wild Honey*, [Vinyl album] Los Angeles: Capitol Records.

The Beach Boys (1967c), *Smiley Smile*, [Vinyl album] Los Angeles: Capitol Records.

The Beach Boys (1969), 'Cabinessence', on *20/20*, [Vinyl album] Los Angeles: Capitol Records.
The Beach Boys (1990), 'Heroes and Villains (Alternate Version)', on *Smiley Smile/Wild Honey*, [CD album] Los Angeles: Capitol Records.
The Beach Boys (2011), *The Beach Boys: The Smile Sessions*. [CD albums, vinyl singles and albums] New York: Capitol Records.
The Beatles (1963), 'I Want to Hold Your Hand', [Vinyl 7" single] London: Parlophone Records.
The Beatles (1965), *Rubber Soul*, [Vinyl album] London: Parlophone Records.
The Beatles (1966a), 'Eleanor Rigby', on *Revolver*, [Vinyl album] London: Parlophone Records.
The Beatles (1966b), *Revolver*, [Vinyl album] London: Parlophone Records.
The Beatles (1966c), 'Tomorrow Never Knows', on *Revolver*, [Vinyl album] London: Parlophone Records.
The Beatles (1967a), *Sgt. Pepper's Lonely Hearts Club Band*, [Vinyl album] London: Parlophone Records.
The Beatles (1967b), 'The Fool on the Hill', on *Magical Mystery Tour*, [Vinyl album] Los Angeles: Capitol Records.
The Beatles (1968a), Ob-La-Di, Ob-La-Da', on *The Beatles*, [Vinyl album] London: Apple Records.
The Beatles (1968b), *The Beatles*, [Vinyl album] London: Apple Records.
The Beatles (1969a), *Abbey Road*, [Vinyl album] London: Apple Records.
The Beatles (1969b), 'Sun King', on *Abbey Road*, [Vinyl album] London: Apple Records.
The Kingsmen (1963), 'Louie Louie', [Vinyl 7" single] New York: Wand Records.
The Kinks (1967), 'Waterloo Sunset' b/w 'Two Sisters', [Vinyl 7" single] Burbank: Reprise Records.
The Kinks (1969), 'Plastic Man', [Vinyl 7" single] London: Pye Records.
The Ohio Express (1968a), 'Chewy Chewy', [Vinyl 7" single] New York: Buddah Records.
The Ohio Express (1968b), 'Yummy, Yummy, Yummy', [Vinyl 7" single] New York: Buddah Records.
The Ohio Express (1969), 'Sweeter than Sugar', [Vinyl 7" single] New York: Buddah Records.
The Police (1983), Synchronicity, [Vinyl album] Los Angeles: A&M Records.
The Who (1967), *The Who Sell Out*, [Vinyl album] London: Track Records.
The Who (1969), *Tommy*, [Vinyl album] London: Track Records.
The Who (1970), *Live at Leeds*, [Vinyl album] London: Track Records.
These Hopeful Machines (2013), [Radio programme] Radio New Zealand, 6 August. Available online: https://www.rnz.co.nz/audio/player?audio_id=2565758 (accessed 2 August 2020).
Wills, J. L. and his Boys (1941), 'Milk Cow Blues', [Shellac 10" single] New York: Decca Records.

Wilson, B. (2004a), *Brian Wilson Presents SMiLE*, [CD album] New York: Nonesuch Records.
Wilson, B. (2004b), 'Child Is Father of the Man', on *Brian Wilson Presents SMiLE*, [CD album] New York: Nonesuch Records.
Wilson, B. (2004c), 'Surf's Up', on *Brian Wilson Presents SMiLE*, [CD album] New York: Nonesuch Records.
Wilson, B. (2004d), 'Vega-Tables', on *Brian Wilson Presents SMiLE*, [CD album] New York: Nonesuch Records.
Yes (1972), *Close to the Edge*, [Vinyl album] New York: Atlantic Records.

Audiovisual

2001: A Space Odyssey (1968), [Film] Dir. Stanley Kubrick, UK-USA: Metro-Goldwyn-Mayer.
A Hard Day's Night (1964), [Film] Dir. Richard Lester, UK: United Artists.
An All-Star Tribute to Brian Wilson (2001), [TV programme] Dir. B. Gowers, USA: Radio City Entertainment, Turner Network Television & Rachlin-Leaf-Ramone Productions.
An Interview With Robert Wilson on 'Absolute Wilson' (2006), [Video file] October. Available online: https://www.youtube.com/watch?v=AFUeNFFtloo (accessed 8 December 2010).
Anna Meredith: The Shape of Music (2019), [Video file] Prod. Ableton, 19 November. Available online: https://www.youtube.com/watch?v=ME-Uosxgbio (accessed 30 April 2020).
'Beatles Reunion' (2007), [TV programme] *Larry King Live*, CNN.
Beautiful Dreamer: Brian Wilson and the Story of Smile (2004), [TV programme] Dir. David Leaf, USA: LSL Productions.
'Behind Studio Doors' (2011), [Podcast film] *The Beach Boys - SMiLE Sessions*, 8 November. Available online: https://www.youtube.com/watch?v=jf9n39OWKzI (accessed 16 January 2021).
Celebrating a Masterpiece: Kind Of Blue (2008), [Film] Dir. C. Lenz, USA: Sony Legacy.
'Cultural Affairs', *Pretend It's a City* (2021), [TV programme] Dir. Martin Scorsese, USA: Netflix. Available online: https://www.netflix.com/title/81078137 (accessed 10 February 2021).
Dana Carvey: Straight White Male, 60 (2016), [TV programme] Netflix.
Daniel Lanois on 'The Making of' U2's Achtung Baby (2012), [Video file] Prod. CBC Music, 20 March. Available online: https://www.youtube.com/watch?v=Fm4U4Cfx ZgM (accessed 14 March 2016).

David Byrne Q&A: Stop Making Sense (2014), [Video file] 19 August. Available online: https://www.youtube.com/watch?v=VkwgVU3sQtw (accessed 11 October 2019).

Discovering the genius of Bob Dylan, 1978: CBC Archives (1978), [Video File] CBC. Available online: https://www.youtube.com/watch?v=Sv80gzwDtdg (accessed 7 May 2014).

'Drum Dance/Smoke Rings', *Home of the Brave* (1986), [Film] Dir. Laurie Anderson, USA: Cinecom Pictures.

Friends (1994–2004), [TV programme] NBC.

George Martin Interviews (2007), [Video File]. Available online: http://www.youtube.com/watch?v=6Vf7TuCgy_0 (accessed 26 March 2010).

Gimme Danger (2016), [Film] Dir. Jim Jarmusch, USA: Low Mind Films/New Element.

Hugo Largo Profile (n.d.), [Video file]. Available online: https://www.youtube.com/watch?v=VoDjgAXm3T0 (accessed 10 August 2020).

In the Beginning Was the End: The Truth About De-Evolution (1976), [Film] Dir. C. Statler, USA: Independent.

'Inventing Language' (2011), [Podcast film] *The Beach Boys – SMiLE Sessions*, 9 November. Available online: https://www.youtube.com/watch?v=MPRIBUSNsrQ (accessed 16 January 2021).

Miles! The Definitive Miles Davis at Montreux DVD Collection 1973–1991 (2011), [DVD] Dir. H. Rossacher and R. Dolezal, USA: Eagle Vision.

Neil Young Reveals the Secrets to Hit Records (2019), [Video file] Prod. Musicians Hall of Fame & Museum, 29 December. Available online: https://www.youtube.com/watch?v=CC2jq6gbUR8&t=313 (accessed 22 March 2020).

No Direction Home: Bob Dylan, Part 2 (2005), [Film] Dir. Martin Scorsese, USA: Paramount Pictures.

Press Conference: Bob Dylan (1965), [TV programme] KQED, 3 December. Available online: https://www.youtube.com/watch?v=wPIS257tvoA (accessed 15 June 2017).

'Robert Fripp – The COMPLETE Boffomundo Interview 1979' (1979), *The Boffomundo Show*, [Video file]. Available online: https://www.youtube.com/watch?v=k96zkPrXQh4 (accessed 17 November 2019).

Scared Stiff (1953), [Film] Dir. G. Marshall, USA: Paramount Pictures.

Sesame Street (1969–present), [TV programme] PBS, HBO, HBO Max..

Shot! The Psycho-Spiritual Mantra of Rock (2016), [Film] Dir. B. Clay, USA: Magnolia Pictures.

'Sugar, Sugar', *The Archie Show* (1969), [TV programme] CBS.

The Atlantic Records Story: Hip to the Tip (1994), [TV programme] Dir. J. Davis and U. Fruchtmann, USA, 12 May.

The Beatles Anthology (1995), [TV programme] Dir. B. Smeaton and G. Wonfor, UK: EMI Distribution.

The Milton Berle Show (1956), [TV programme] NBC, 3 April. Available online: https://www.youtube.com/watch?v=x5x3KiNFfkE (accessed 18 January 2020).

'Turtle Dreams' (1983), [TV programme] Dir. Ping Chong, 2 September. Available online: https://www.youtube.com/watch?v=FBlnrRUVfo0 (accessed 21 March 2016).

Artwork

Beeple. (2007–2021), 'Everydays: The First 5000 Days', [Non-Fungible Token (jpg)] In the collection of Metakovan.
Brecht, G. (*c.* 1968), 'Games and Puzzles (Bead and Swim Puzzles)', in G. Maciunas (designer/assembler), *Flux Year Box 2*, [Plastic box with offset label containing four plastic balls and two offset cards] New York: Museum of Modern Art.
Duchamp, M. (1917/1964), 'Fountain', [Ceramic, glaze and paint] San Francisco: San Francisco Museum of Modern Art.
Friedman, K. (*c.* 1968), 'A Flux Corsage', in G. Maciunas (designer/assembler), *Flux Year Box 2*, [Plastic box with offset label containing seeds] New York: Museum of Modern Art.
Kubota, S. (*c.* 1968), 'Flux Medicine', in G. Maciunas (designer/assembler), *Flux Year Box 2*, [Plastic box containing capsules with offset label] New York: Museum of Modern Art.
Lichtenstein, R. (1963), 'Drowning Girl', [Oil and synthetic polymer paint on canvas] New York: Museum of Modern Art.
Rauschenberg, R. (1951), 'White Painting', [One, two, four and seven panel: latex paint on canvases] New York: Robert Rauschenberg Foundation; [Three panel: latex paint on canvas] San Francisco: San Francisco Museum of Modern Art Purchase through a gift of Phyllis Wattis.

Index

10cc 2, 85, 143
   auditioning vocalists 103
   '*Une Nuit a Paris*' 189–90
1910 Fruitgum Company 85

Ableton Live (DAW) 2–3, 125, 168
actor-network theory (ANT) 97
Adé, King Sunny 126, 131
Afrobeat 10, 126, 134–6
Albarn, Damon 82–3
Alcock, Sophie 10, 16, 19, 29–30, 33–4
Allen, Tony 83, 134
Amabile, Teresa 14–15, 54, 56, 74, 99, 141, 152–3
   on challenge 75
   on competition 33
   components of creativity 60–1
   on creative process, five stages of 90–2, 100, 146
   on creative risks 75
   on creativity 70–1
   on intrinsic motivation and innovation 144
   on playfulness and concentration 176
   social psychology of creativity 11, 59–63, 90–2
Anderson, Laurie 80, 86–7
Apter, Michael J. 18–20, 99, 141, 148, 154, 178
   on creative-risk taking 75
   on extrinsic motivation 71–2
   paratelic/telic distinction 19, 75, 91, 146
   paratelic *vs.* autotelic experience 94
   pathologies of play 95, 150–1
   playfulness as present-moment orientated 15, 19, 157, 168
   on playfulness as 'protective frame' 67, 177
   on 'psychodiversity' 146
   reversal theory 19, 146
Aquabats, the 86
Archies, the 84

art and design schools (UK) 144–5
artefact mediation 34
artefacts of play 155–8
The Art of Record Production (Volumes 1 & 2) 5

B-52's, the 114, 157
Barrett, Syd 26–7, 147–9
Bateson, Gregory 67
BBC Radiophonic Workshop 119
Beach Boys, the 3, 7–9, 12, 47, 49, 159–63, 165–7, 171–2, 174–5, 177, 180–90
Beastie Boys, the 103
Beatles, the 8, 23, 30–2, 45–51, 90, 110, 113, 127, 129, 159, 164, 168, 187, 196–7
   Beatlemania 32
   creative practice in the studio (late 1960s) 152–3, 156–7
   early success and impact 47
   A Hard Day's Night 83
   influence of 8
   influence on Dylan 45
   influences 9, 47, 191
   making music 'as if'... 50
   pan-genre style 48
   resilience 32, 48–9
   sense of humour 32, 46, 49
   Sgt. Pepper's Lonely Hearts Club Band 50, 82, 163, 167, 171, 179, 187, 190
   treating work as play 48
   as 'Trojan Horse' 31
Beat movement 25–6, 30, 44, 200
Beeple (Mike Winklemann) 194–5
Belew, Adrian 130–1, 202, 206
Black, Bill 38–42
Bogart, Neil 84
Bourdieu, Pierre 51
   on cultural power relations 34–5
Bowie, David 113
   on the Oblique Strategies 79

rise of   109
use of characters   82
use of mimicry   109–10
Boyd, Joe   26–7, 147
   on   1960s youth zeitgeist   30–1
Brill Building sound   83–6, 191
Bruford, Bill   12, 88, 198–207
   Bill Bruford: The Autobiography   201
   on separation as control   42
bubblegum music   84–6
Byrne, David   28, 80, 123–31, 134–6, 139, 152
   on constraints   73
   How Music Works   136

Cage, John   67, 104–6, 110–11, 113, 124, 136, 143, 154
   '4'33'"   17–18
Capra, Fritjof
   on 'emergence'   170
Carvey, Dana   51
Casale, Gerald   77–8
CBGBs   28–9, 86, 123, 194
Chapouthier, Georges   180
Clinton, George   82
cognition   6, 12, 15, 29, 57, 59–60, 62, 71, 90, 108, 152, *see also* spontaneity
   distributed   33–4
   flexibility of   11, 17, 31, 91
cognitive incubation   11, 152–3, 172, 178–80
Collins, Bootsy   87
   on musical collaboration   106
Collins, Phil   81
contestation
   social   32, 34–5, 52
contrastive action   14, 80, 87–9, 98
Copeland, Stewart   100
   on creative-risk taking   75
Cramps, the   86
Crazy Elephant   85
creativity
   componential model of   90
   as confluence of factors   10
   and constraints   72–5
   creative-risk taking   11, 62, 75–6, 100, 128, 204

distributed   5, 34
early systematic approaches to   55–6
in groups   33
iterative nature of   146
multidisciplinary research
   parochial isolation of   56
post-war research
   ongoing relevance of   57
proscriptive approach to   20–1
psychological approaches   58–9
sociological enquiry into
   paucity of   56
Creme, Lol   14, 85, 143
Crosby, Bing   39
Csikszentmihalyi, Mihalyi   4, 18–19, 92–5, 120, 137, 142
   on 'being-in-the-moment'   181
   Between Boredom and Anxiety   141
   on constraints   21
   on feedback   170–1
   macro *vs*. micro flow   94
   optimal experience (flow)   92, 205
   person-domain-field   110, 146
   on play and creativity   98
   on playfulness in adults   10, 67, 94
   on popular-music domain   108
   on screening out (task-irrelevant) stimuli   176
   systems model of creativity   5, 11, 52–4, 59–64, 97, 108
cultural-historical activity theory (CHAT)   10
culture jamming   30

Dada   110–11, 114, 128, 136
Danger Mouse (Brian Burton)   80, 83
Davies, Ray   81, 144
Davis, Miles   74, 93, 191, 196
De La Soul   51, 83, 158
   and the Anonymous Nobody   158
   creative process of   158
   sampling and litigation issues   158
Devo   77–8
digital DIY culture   115–16
divergent thinking   15, 71, 102–3, 146, 148
domain-relevant skills   11, 35, 60, 62–3, 90–1, 146

Dowd, Tom   36–7
Duchamp, Marcel   111, 136, 195
  'Fountain'   17
Dylan, Bob   23, 30–2, 42–6, 64, 71, 90, 115, 154, 159, 196–7
  autobiography   45
  as 'Hammond's folly'   31, 43
  influence of   8, 47
  influences   9
  No Direction Home   13
  on Red Grooms' influence   43

Einstein, Albert
  on combinatorial play   15
Elitzur, Avshalom   19, 21, 46, 68–9, 151
Emerick, Geoff   50, 156, 179
Eno, Brian   2, 14, 100, 113, 123–8, 130–1, 134–5, 137–9, 144, 164
  on 'art is safe'   17
  on computers   116
  on creative process   157
  on eliminating options   69–70
  on experimental music   105
  on listening   89
  on the Oblique Strategies   78–9
  on practitioners and technologists   109
  on proscriptive approach to creativity   21
  recording as a plastic art   3
Ertegun, Ahmet   36–7, 51
experience
  autotelic   93–4, 137, 145, 154 (*see also* flow)
  inner   4, 55, 110, 141, 169, 171
  optimal   11, 16, 90, 92–5, 98, 110, 137, 150, 154 (*see also* flow)
    in groups   19, 94, 99
    skill-to-challenge balance   96
    subjective dimensions of   94
  peak   137, 150
experimental music   104–5, 124, 136

Feynman, Richard   15
flow   18, 19, 92–6, 98, 110, 150, 154–5, 205
  in groups   19, 94, 99
Fluxus   105, 110–11

'Fourth World' music   138–9
frame of mind   18
  paratelic/telic distinction   19, 75, 91, 146
    oscillations between   146
  playful   14, 20
Frantz, Chris   126, 130
Fripp, Robert   199–201, 204–6
  on commitment   70
  on creative-risk taking   76
  on 'proscriptive' creativity   21

Gabriel, Peter   138, 155
  character vocalizations   81
  on constraints   73–4
Gane, Tim   69
Genesis   81–2, 198, 200
  The Lamb Lies Down on Broadway   81
Gert, Valeska
  'Pause'   17–18
Getzels, J.W.   146
Getzels and Csikszentmihalyi   14
  on challenge   75
  The Creative Vision: A Longitudinal Study of Problem Finding in Art   15, 55, 92, 149–50
  problem finding   55, 92
Godley, Kevin   14, 85, 103, 143
  on playfulness   22–3
  on playfulness *vs.* serious thought   151
Goese, Mimi   86–7
Goffman, Erving
  'dramaturgy'   16, 97
  on play   102
Gorillaz   82–3
grants
  arts (living maintenance) (UK)   144
group glee   32–3
Guilford, J.P.   18, 59
  on cognitive incubation   153
  as creativity research advocate   56–7
Gypsy Davey   44

Haarich, Max   195–6
Hadamard, Jacques   15, 146, 152, 154
Hammond, John   30–1, 42–4, 51, 196
  track record   9, 42

Harrison, George   50–1
   on resilience through humour   49
Harrison, Jerry   124–5, 127–34
   on 1970s New York music scene   28
Hassell, Jon   139
Hell, Richard   28, 68
   on preference for constraints   73
Helm, Levon   44
Hendryx, Nona   130, 132
Henricks, Thomas   19, 88–9, 142
   on play as 'will to power'   33
Hepworth-Sawyer and Golding
   What Is Music Production?   5
Hesse, Herman
   Steppenwolf   169, 191–2
Hewlett, Jamie   82–3
Hopkins, John ('Hoppy')   25–6
Huizinga, Johan
   Homo Ludens   32, 35
Hutt, Corinne   15, 180
   on play as 'idling'   153
   on play *vs.* exploration   147

imagination   34, 45, 51, 77, 80, 86, 89, 96, 99, 109, 115
   distributed   33
impulsiveness
   SMiLE and   183, 188
   vs. spontaneity   64, 181
interpretive reproduction   29
intersubjectivity   33
IT (*International Times*)   25–6

Jardine, Al   186
Johnston, Bruce   163, 177, 186
Jones, Buster   131
Jones, Quincy   151

Kasenetz and Katz   84–5
Kidjo, Angélique   135, 138
   Remain in Light   10
King Crimson   21, 76, 88, 198–200, 202, 204–6
Kirshner, Don
   Brill Building stable   83
   and the Monkees   83–4
Knuckles, Frankie   68
Koestler, Arthur   15, 58, 175

The Act of Creation   174
   bisociation   77, 181
   influence on Brian Wilson   174
   on pictorial thought   169
Kraftwerk   117–19
   Kling-Klang studios   117–19
Kris, Ernst   58
   regression 'in the service of the ego' 147
Kristal, Hilly   28–9
Kuti, Fela   10, 72, 87, 126, 134–5

Langer, Clive
   on Portsmouth Sinfonia   113
Lanois, Daniel   70, 100, 106–7, 155
Leary, Metzner and Alpert
   The Psychedelic Experience   49
Lebowitz, Fran   193–4
Leiber and Stoller   41–2
Lennon, John   31–2, 48–9, 51, 144, 181
   Dylan's influence   45
   and fringe consciousness   153
   and regression   147
   wit ('weapons-grade')   49
Levin, Tony   201–2
Lewisohn, Mark
   The Complete Beatles Recording Sessions   156
libidinal processes (Freud)   137
Lieberman, Josefa Nina   14, 15, 64, 141, 152, 177, 179, 203
   Playfulness: Its Relationship to Imagination and Creativity   63
   on spontaneity *vs.* impulsiveness 64, 181
'local logic'   14–15, 43, *see also* Ziv, A.
Love, Mike   160, 167, 174, 177, 182–5

McCartney, Paul   25, 48–51, 81, 163, 181, 187, 203
   on 'blunt northern humour'   49
   and fringe consciousness   153–4
   on Hamburg   48
McDonald, Dolette   131
McIntyre, Phillip   52, 56, 60, 151
   on power and record production 34–5, 183, 186–7
Maciunas, George   111, 195

Manson, Shirley 154
Martin, Dean
  influence on Elvis 39
Martin, George 30–1, 47, 50–1, 157, 161, 163, 171
  as comedy record producer 46–7
  on signing the Beatles 31, 46
Maslow, Abraham 58, 137, 142–3, 147
Mason, Nick 149
Massenburg, George
  on 'gatekeepers' 52–3
Matisse, Henri
  on naivete in artists 55
Meares, Russell 167, 170
  The Metaphor of Play 169
Meek, Joe 162
Memphis Horns, the 22
Meredith, Anna
  on computers 116
Mertens, Wim 136–7
  on 'dialectical' music 89
Miles, Barry 25, 26, 32, 48–50, 149, 153–4, 167
Mitchell, Joni 191
Mitski 150
Monk, Meredith 65, 86–7
Monk, Thelonious 196
Monkees, the 83–5
Moore, Scotty 38–42
Mothersbaugh, Mark 77
motivation 6, 15, 19, 29, 59–60, 64, 90, 108, 116, 141–4, 193
  extrinsic forces
    impact of 4, 71
  intrinsic 11, 70–2, 74–5, 93, 99, 181
    benefits of 62, 70–1
  task 12, 61, 63, 91, 98
musique concrète 26, 49, 119–20, 164, 167, 197

National Recording Registry (US), the 138, 158
negativism 94–5, 188
  proactive 20
Nesmith, Mike 83–4
Nietzsche, Friedrich 33
non-fungible tokens (NFTs) 194–5

Nyman, Michael 76, 105, 106
  on experimental music 104
  on Portsmouth Sinfonia 112–13

O, Karen 80, 88
Oblique Strategies, the 78–9, 95
Ohio Express, the 85
Ono, Yoko 25–6, 111
  on the Beatles 49
Oram, Daphne 119–21

Padgham, Hugh 100
Parker, 'Colonel' Thom 37, 41
Parks, Van Dyke 160–1, 164, 166–7, 172, 175, 177, 182–5
Parliament-Funkedelic 82
Partridge, Andy
  on creative-risk taking 76
Pat Mastellotto 88
Peelander-Z 86
peer cultures
  as creative social systems 30
performance art 86–7
personality 6, 12, 19, 56–7, 59, 60–1, 90, 107, 142, 145
  autotelic 93, 154
  dimensions of 62–3, 146
  states *vs.* traits 60, 62, 76
phenomenology 5, 16, 68, 76, 94, 136, 141
  of adult play 10, 18–19
  work/play distinction 145
Phillips, Sam 9, 30–1, 37–42, 51
Picasso, Pablo 193–5
Pierson, Kate 157
Pink Floyd 26–7, 147–9, 159
play
  in adults
    phenomenology of 10, 18–20
  as 'biomimetic' 19
  combinatorial 11, 13, 15, 63, 153, 168, 172, 181
    as figurative kaleidoscope 64, 91, 177, 179
  vs. playfulness 15, 64–5
  as 'will to power' 33
playframing 20–1, 65, 68, 75, 80, 147, 177, 205–6

benefits of   11, 15–16, 20–1, 65, 75, 87, 95, 98, 103–4, 115
    negotiations   11, 21, 79, 98–100, 103
    as power management   20, 98
playfulness
    in adults   95, 145, 151
    components of   34
    concentration and   176–7
    creativity and   7, 11, 60–5, 91, 96
    distributed   19, 34
    as frame of mind   94, 96, 115, 145, 151 (*see also* phenomenology)
        benefits of   15
    as Lieberman's '[PF]'   63
    negativism and   15, 95
    as observable behaviour   15
    pathology and   151
    vs. play   15, 64–5
    'practitioners of'   6, 64, 192, 203 (*see also* Lieberman, J. N.)
    as resistance   16, 29
Pop, Iggy   76, 87
    on economy of expression   73
Portsmouth Sinfonia   111–12, 134–5
post-punk   113–14
Presley, Elvis   30–2, 36–42, 44, 196
    influence of   8, 23, 47
    influences   9
Prigogine, Ilya
    dissipative structures   170–1
Prince, George   153
    on power and group creativity   33, 183–4, 186
project studios   12, 23, 69, 94–5, 99, 139, 194, 198, 202
    inherent challenges   2
proxy agents   30, 51, 54
psychology (individual)
    ongoing relevance of   34
    in creativity studies   4
'Psycodelic Sounds' tapes   175–6, *see also* SMiLE

Ramones, the   28, 86
Rauschenberg, Robert   18, 106
    'White Painting'   17
rebelliousness   20, 44
    creative benefits of   64

playful   23, 30–1, 188
Remain in Light   3, 10, 12, 123–39
Rhodes, Mel   59
    'four Ps of creativity'   57
Richards, Keith   152
Riley, Terry
    on creative-risk taking   76
Robert and Chapouthier   169
    on 'compositional morphology'   173
    on language   173
Rock, Mick   109–10, 149
Rutherford, Mike   81
RZA   151

Sadier, Laetitia   67
Sawyer, R. Keith   4, 34, 52, 57–8, 60
Scales, Steve   131
Schmidt, Peter   78
Shadow, DJ (Joshua Davis)   155
Shapiro, Helen   162
Shostakovich, Dmitri   72
SMiLE   3, 7–8, 22, 159–90
    influence of   8
    ongoing relevance   12
Smith, Norman   27, 147, 149
Smith, Patti   28, 68, 86
social construction of technology (SCOT)   97
social psychology of creativity   11, 59–63, 90–2, *see also* Amabile, T.
Sonic Youth   104
Spariosu, Mihai   33
Spector, Phil   47, 162–3, 166, 173, 177
speculation   99, 103, 153
    influence of peers upon   33, 153, 184
spontaneity
    cognitive   15, 64, 181, 189
        as taboo for adults   63
    physical
        as taboo for adults   63
Starr, Ringo
    on cognitive incubation   152
    on Hamburg   48
Stein, Gertrude and Leo   194
Stein, Seymour   28, 51, 194
STEM   144, 193
Stieglitz, Alfred   17, 194
Sting   100

Strachan, Robert
   on 'major' music labels   35
   Popular Music, Digital Culture and the Creative Process   5
Strawberry Studios   85
Super K productions   84–5
Sutton-Smith, Brian   20, 72, 97, 141, 199–202
   The Ambiguity of Play   32
   on constraints   21
   on drama as dialectical   89
   on play   14, 32
      as 'adaptive potentiality'   36, 192
      and boredom   154
      as frame breaking   17, 29, 205
      as frame making   14, 16
      play-as-performance theory   10, 14, 80, 98
      as role reversal   79
   playfaming   10, 15, 205–6
      negotiations   75, 111, 147, 186
   on playfulness   64
systems model of creativity   5, 11, 52–4, 59–64, 97, 108, *see also* Csikszentmihalyi, M.
   application of   5

Talking Heads   9–10, 12, 28, 123–39, 194
   swapping instrumental roles   79–80
tape recording
   advent of   2, 35, 167
Taylor, Derek   8, 160, 188
Taylor, Irving   57–9
   on transactualization   108
technology   20, 115–21
   democratization of   1, 139
   disruption/misuse of   14, 109, 117
   influence of   3–4, 11, 53, 117
   and options   69
   playing with   115
Thompson, Paul
   Creativity in the Recording Studio   5
transactualization   108, 138
   (popular-music) examples of   3

UFO (Club)   26

Verlaine, Tom   68
Vosse Posse, the   175, 182–6

Waits, Tom   80, 108, 193
   on musical 'moments'   108
Wallas, Graham
   fringe consciousness   153
Waters, Roger   149
Weymouth, Tina   125, 127, 130
Wilson, Brian   3, 7–8, 12, 49, 147, 159–64, 166–9, 171–90
Wilson, Cindy   157
Wilson, Murry   160, 174
Wilson, Robert   80–1
workflows   94–5
Worrell, Bernie   131
Wrecking Crew, the   162, 185–6

Xenakis, Iannis
   stochastic processes   22

Young, Neil   1
   on the Memphis Horns   22
   on working with Daniel Lanois   107

Zagorski-Thomas, Simon   89, 97, 99, 102, 115
   on 'anti-program'   117
   on configuration   101
   on Goffman's 'dramaturgy'   16, 97–8
   The Musicology of Record Production   5, 16, 97
Zak, Albin   2, 16
   I Don't Sound Like Nobody   2, 90
   on (post-war) radio   35–6
Zappa, Frank   22
   on frames   16
Zen Buddhism   136
Ziv, Avner
   on 'fun mood'   103
   on laughter   103
   on 'local logic'   14–15
   on social anxiety   103

www.ingramcontent.com/pod-product-compliance
Lightning Source LLC
Chambersburg PA
CBHW062139300426
44115CB00012BA/1986